Public Executions
in Richmond, Virginia

Public Executions in Richmond, Virginia
A History, 1782–1907

HARRY M. WARD

McFarland & Company, Inc., Publishers
Jefferson, North Carolina, and London

ALSO BY HARRY M. WARD

For Virginia and for Independence: Twenty-Eight Revolutionary War Soldiers from the Old Dominion (McFarland, 2011)

Frontispiece: The Virginia Capitol (Dementi Studio, Richmond)

LIBRARY OF CONGRESS CATALOGUING-IN-PUBLICATION DATA

Ward, Harry M.
  Public executions in Richmond, Virginia : a history, 1782–1907 / Harry M. Ward.
     p.   cm.
  Includes bibliographical references and index.

  ISBN 978-0-7864-7083-9
  softcover : acid free paper ∞

  1. Public executions — Virginia — Richmond — History.
I. Title.
HV8699.U6R538 2012
364.6609755'45109034 — dc23   2012026540

BRITISH LIBRARY CATALOGUING DATA ARE AVAILABLE

© 2012 Harry M. Ward. All rights reserved

No part of this book may be reproduced or transmitted in any form or by any means, electronic or mechanical, including photocopying or recording, or by any information storage and retrieval system, without permission in writing from the publisher.

On the cover: Castle Thunder, a Confederate Prison (Library of Virginia); noose © 2012 Shutterstock

Manufactured in the United States of America

McFarland & Company, Inc., Publishers
  Box 611, Jefferson, North Carolina 28640
  www.mcfarlandpub.com

Acknowledgments

Advantages toward research always occur when an author chooses a topic close at hand. One does not have to scrape about a region, nation, or even worldwide to gather information. The convenience is extended when the subject involves a capital city (of the state and the Confederacy) and is a commercial, cultural, and geographical center. Also importantly the area under review is a large urban one. The early Richmond newspapers, highly competitive with each other, brought to life the daily activity of a multiethnic society. The Library of Virginia in Richmond holds as complete a collection as possible of the city's early newspapers, easily accessed through microfilm. The library also has a comprehensive archive of other print media relating to the city's history. I thank members of the reference staff of the Library of Virginia, particularly Ginny Dunn, Sarah J. Huggins, William Luebke, Edwin Ray, and Lisa Wehrman. Although this project did not require the primary use of the splendid Virginia Historical Society, this institution served as a backup facility. The author also made use of the small, limited library collections and photographic services of the Valentine Richmond History Center. The Boatwright Library of the University of Richmond was a valuable basic resource, and I thank James Gwin, the head of Special Collections, reference librarians Rochelle Colestock, Susan Opdycke, and Marcia Whitehead, and especially the two facilitators for securing interlibrary loans, Betty Tobias and Amita Mongia. Helpful assistance was also given by Darlene Slater Herod and Michael Whitt of the Virginia Baptist Historical Society.

I am grateful to Professor John Oritz Smykla of the School of Justice Studies and Social Work at the University of West Florida for information on Virginia executions. The author has been aided by the M. Watt Espy, Jr., file at the Death Penalty Information Center in Washington, D.C., which purports to list all persons executed in the continental United States

Acknowledgments

from 1608 to 2002 (although there are important omissions). The major problem with this file is that it did not provide the locale of executions (e.g., counties or urban sites), other than the states where they occurred. Other locator help comes from the *Daily Dispatch*, post–Civil War, listing on New Year's Day the important events of the previous year, which includes executions. I thank reader-commentators of the book: Stephen A. Northrup, executive director of Virginians for Alternatives to the Death Penalty; William M. Welsch, president of the American Revolution Roundtable — Richmond; William W. Childs, Jr., deputy chief, Parole and Probation (Virginia District 27); and Dr. Lynn Sims, U.S. Army historian (ret.). Deborah S. Govoruhk transformed typewriter print into computer copy and also applied her superb editorial skills. Lissa Searfoss restored illustrations.

TABLE OF CONTENTS

Acknowledgments   v
Preface   1

1. "Usual Place of Execution"   7
2. "A Flood of Tears"   1782–1799   14
3. "Liberty of My Countrymen"   1800–1802   21
4. "Between the Heavens and the Earth"   1801–1826   29
5. "Sleep in Alien Dust"   1827   33
6. "Hideous Curiosity"   1828–1851   41
7. "In Cold Blood"   1852   49
8. "The Mob Is Coming"   1853–1860   57
9. "To Be Shot to Death by Musketry"   1861–1865   67
10. "Farewell, Brave Spirit"   1861–1865   79
11. "Certainly Horrible to Look At"   1861–1865   90
12. "The Last Carnival of Death"   1865–1869   102
13. "You're Gwyne to Hell"   1870–1882   110
14. "Wait, I'm Not Done Yet"   1883   122
15. "Cluverius's Day"   1884–1887   131
16. "Good-Bye, Boys"   1888–1899   141
17. "You Knowed I Won't Crazy"   1900–1907   150

Epilogue   157

Table of Contents

Appendices: 169
  A. Profile of an Executioner — John Caphart 169
  B. The Last Days of Spencer Kellogg Brown in His Own Words,
      September 1865 171
  C. "Sleepless Sentinel at Castle Thunder" 173
  D. Sentencing of James Jeter Phillips by Judge George L.
      Christian of the Henrico Circuit Court, July 10, 1868 176
  E. The Prosecutor, Colonel W.R. Aylett, States the Case Against
      Thomas J. Cluverius, 1885 178
  F. "An act to establish a permanent place in the State penitentiary
      ... [and] to change the mode of execution ... [to] electricity,"
      March 16, 1908 189
  G. Richmond Executions 191

Chapter Notes 195

Bibliography 207

Index 215

Preface

When Americans view their history, they tend to look away from the pervasive violence and injustice of the past and accept it as part of "the good old days." Most historians pass over the horrors and meanness that were so attached to everyday living. One kind of horror that historians have been reluctant to come to grips with is the prevalent legal homicide of the past regularly jutting out from the landscape and touching the very being of most everyone. In Richmond, as elsewhere in the country, citizens turned out by the thousands for a public hanging. In 1818 an estimated 12,000 people witnessed the hanging of Robert Gibson, a curious fact since the 1820 census gave the city a population of 12,046. Indeed the public executions took place in a carnival atmosphere, with crowds following the progress of the condemned person on the route from the jail to the gallows and mixing with the throng of persons from all walks of life, including men, women, and children. Vendors hawked refreshments, the most popular being lemonade and watermelon. Other than gallows humor and shouting, the crowds behaved with reasonable decorum, although on occasion cordons of police officers had to use strong-arm tactics. One important aspect of the public executions, accepted as one of life's necessary rituals, was that they attuned the American psyche, demanding affirmation of divine justice, collective redemption, and vicarious sacrifice.

Public executions, lasting everywhere in America until the mid–nineteenth century and in many locales until well into the twentieth century, validated the ruling elite's insistence that mandated ritual death was a necessary tool for inculcating, in the minds of the more distressed citizens, fear that would act as a deterrent to crime. Common folk went along with their political and spiritual leaders in unquestioning acquiescence to public executions. Only with the passage of time, emerging in the modern era, did enough revulsion surface to compel some reform with an eye towards

Preface

View of the City from Gamble's Hill, April, 1, 1865 (Library of Congress).

humaneness. But even then, an eye-for-an-eye public blood lust has persisted to our own time, with change only in reduction of the number of actual executions and finding supposedly less painful ways of committing legal homicide—but without much success abolishing dubious hidden criteria of race, gender, and status.

"The good old days—were they really good?" asked archival historian Otto Bettmann in 1960. "On the surface they appear to be so," he said. Mainly concerned with the period from the end of the Civil War to the early 1900s, Bettmann concedes that historians have left us a picture of these times that "receded into a benevolent haze ... with the image of an ebullient, carefree America." This "gaiety was only a brittle veneer that covered widespread turmoil and suffering. The good old days were good

Preface

for but the privileged few. For the farmer, the laborer, the average breadwinner, life was an unremitting hardship. This segment of the population was exploited or lived in the shadow of total neglect. And youth had no voice." The "period's dirty business" was "swept under the carpet of oblivion." Americans need to merge their country's ugly past with the present and future; hence a less cataclysmic destiny, contrary to much of the current vision for America, will emerge.[1]

The story of public legal homicide in Richmond embraces a wide span, officially lasting from 1782 to 1869, when jail yards became the gallows site. This latter arrangement endured until 1908, when the penitentiary became the sole location for executions in the state. During the interim period of 1869–1907, only twelve witnesses and a few officials and ticket holders were admitted into a small jail yards to witness an execution. For Richmond executions (not so for Henrico County and penitentiary executions), however, large crowds were still able to view hangings. This was because the Richmond jail, post mid–nineteenth century, was situated at Fifteenth and Marshall streets adjacent to the old "usual place of execution," bordered by the Shockoe Valley hillside; spectators merely had to assemble on the hill to view the gallows inside the walls of the jail yard.

Richmond's public executions seem to have hit full pace during the Civil War. Already the images of death were everywhere. The huge military hospital complex on Chimborazo Hill and lesser army medical-surgical facilities regularly turned out corpses and assorted human limbs. During the war persons went to the gallows for espionage and counterfeiting. The army introduced to the Richmond public military hangings and firing squads, chiefly reserved for deserters, at camps in and around Richmond.

In some ways the Richmond of 1782–1907 was slightly more humane than Virginia's history as a whole. There were none of the burnings at the stake and hangings in irons, infrequently occurring before the American Revolution. Amazingly there were no lynchings in the Richmond vicinity, although there were several close calls. Still, at one time or another persons went to the gallows for murder, accessory to murder, rape, attempted rape, horse stealing, burglary, robbery, arson, espionage, revolt, and counterfeiting. Murder became almost the only capital crime. Almost without exception those who were put to death were drawn from the lower classes of society. Most gallows victims were also black.

What is remarkable is how public executions brought the whole community together as did no other event. Many women and children were spectators. There did seem to be a preponderant number of the very poor

Preface

at the hangings, and blacks usually outnumbered whites, understandable being that most gallows victims were African American.

One might argue that the executions elicited the transforming hand of God. Invariably the condemned criminal bore witness to a born-again experience and on the scaffold declared the anticipation of being "soon with God in Glory." A religious service usually transpired at the gallows, with the chief celebrant being a "minister of the gospel" or a Catholic priest. The proceedings consisted of prayer, preaching, hymn singing, and sometimes a testimonial by the condemned person. Often more than one clergyman participated, and the ceremony took on an ecumenical quality. Baptist African American preachers most frequently participated in the execution ritual.

A marked incongruity that becomes apparent in the study of public executions is that, despite the enormous size of crowds witnessing such events, there is a paucity of recorded impressions. As mentioned already concerning historians, there seems to have been a general reluctance to admit having been attracted to such morbid displays. Almost totally, contemporary diaries and journals omit references to the ritualized mandated deaths. A foreign hanging or guillotining was likely to receive much greater reportage in a Richmond newspaper than a similar local event. As time went on, the local press increasingly amplified coverage of executions as well as that of the relevant court cases. Hence newspaper sources form the spine of this study, and the reportage sheds much light on the character of citizens and the social milieu of the times.

Richmonders hardly blinked an eye over mass executions of poor African Americans, from the death retribution of some two dozen blacks connected with the budding Gabriel revolt of 1800 to the electrocution of the seven alleged Martinsville rapists in 1951. The author, however, has been unsuccessful in tracking down an actual source for a statement in the *Daily Dispatch* for January 9, 1903, referencing an execution about to take place in Manchester (later part of Richmond): "Four negroes were hung just outside of the corporate limits of Manchester about one hundred years ago, for the murder of Mrs. Betty Morrisette." The reporter may have been mistaken; Elizabeth (Betty) Morrisette was still alive in 1809, at which time, incidentally, a mass hanging of four slaves for the murder of an overseer occurred in Mathews County.

The narrative that follows is probably more complete in detailing slave executions than those for whites. For the antebellum period "the Auditor of Public Accounts: Condemned Blacks Executed or Transported,

Preface

1783–1865" at the Library of Virginia affords a comprehensive listing regarding convictions, sentencing, and executions of slaves in the state; the researcher only has to cull out City of Richmond and Henrico County cases from those of the state at large. There are some instances regarding slaves, and elsewhere certainly so concerning whites, where there is no record of follow-up and no mention of actual execution occurring. In such instances, except when the crime was so degrading that execution must have been evitable, the author excludes mention of an execution taking place. While executions from neighboring counties per se do not come under the purview of this study, some of those hangings involving the City of Richmond (such as the condemned person's being lodged in the city or Henrico jail or a sizeable contingent of Richmonders attending the execution) receive coverage in this study. For points of comparison, a few executions elsewhere in Virginia and the United States are mentioned.

The reader will quickly recognize the interlocking areas of the City of Richmond and Henrico County. The situation is much like other situations in the United States, where one leaves one jurisdiction and immediately enters another. Even today Richmond and the county are as one city. For a long time the Henrico County Courthouse was located at Twenty-Second and Main streets, in downtown Richmond. Henrico's executions were held inside what is today's Richmond corporate limits.

1

"Usual Place of Execution"

The macabre drama that played out in Virginia's small capital city may seem inconsequential on the larger stage, but it was replicated in numerous other American communities. The state capital was moved from Williamsburg in 1780, largely to put it further from the reach of any invading British army. In 1782 Richmond was incorporated as a city. By the end of the Revolutionary War the city could boast three hundred houses, many of which had been rebuilt after the city-wide conflagration during the raid of British troops under General Benedict Arnold in January 1781.

Before the Civil War Richmond's population grew slowly, largely due to the western migration of Virginians. Inhabitants numbered four thousand in 1795; 12,000 in 1820; 26,000 in 1840; and 51,000 in 1870. Population spiraled thereafter, hovering around 200,000 (800,000 metro) in modern times.[1]

Despite its small size and retaining some of its frontier character, antebellum Richmond spun out a vibrant economy. Located at the head of navigation of the James River in central Virginia, it became an important entrepôt. Agricultural products came into the city for export. By the time of the Civil War there were forty tobacco factories in the city. Flour milling had a worldwide reach. There was also brick making, and the adjacent counties of Powhatan, Goochland, and Chesterfield comprised the major coal supplying area in the country. Not surprisingly, Richmond, by mid-nineteenth century, had a distinct polyglot population, made up of one-fourth each native whites, slaves, Germans, and Irishmen. Society was sharply divided between retailers, professionals, and industrial managers on the one hand and industrial and service workers on the other, with always a small corps of vagrants.

Indeed the city of Richmond had somewhat of a humorous interplay of petty criminals and alcoholics, not to mention the goings-on of juvenile delinquents and boy gangs. The city magistrates during the nineteenth century frequently assigned culprits to the "cage" (the holding cell at the jail) or to a whipping. Not unlike modern times when youngsters of Oregon Hill (Richmond's preeminent poor section) might expect to wind up in the adjacent state penitentiary, it was as if some residents were bred into crime. Such a propensity did not necessarily produce hardened felons, but it did help to create among attendees at execution sites not only rapport with those condemned but also a lightheartedness, with profuse gallows humor, that exuded a carnival atmosphere.

Various annexations have enlarged the city's bounds. During the Civil War the city contained 2.4 square miles; in 1973, with the last annexation, it covered 62.8 square miles. Some of the sites mentioned in this study were not included within the city during early times but were at a later period, one example being the village of Manchester across from downtown Richmond, incorporated into the city in 1910.

There were enough hangings in Richmond that citizens only had to be informed of the "usual place of execution." Richmond's executions primarily took place at the lower northeastern end of the hill (today's location of the VCU Medical School), in Shockoe Valley, near Shockoe Creek (no longer extant above ground today). The site may be more precisely defined as being on the northwest corner of today's Fifteenth Street and Broad Street. Adjacent to the then Negro Burial Ground, it presently is under an Interstate 95 overpass.[2] Consistently, a Friday was selected as execution day, probably because that day was customarily also reserved for days of publicly proclaimed "humiliation and prayer."[3]

Other sites used by the city for one or several executions were the penitentiary (two executions), the state farm of the penitentiary (one execution), Castle Thunder, Victor's Old Mill (Shockoe Valley), a gulley near the almshouse (Shockoe Valley), and the city jail (when located in Shockoe Valley): at least one execution each was held in a field in Manchester (across the river and now part of the city) and the Manchester Courthouse jail yard. A few of the Gabriel conspirators condemned in 1800 were hanged just outside the city, near Brookfield plantation. Some of the hangings (selectively) held in adjacent counties, a few miles from the city, in which there seemed to be a large number of Richmond attendees are included in this study, along with the hangings of condemned men who had been assigned to Richmond jails for safekeeping.

Henrico County was more flexible in the choice of execution sites.

1. "Usual Place of Execution" 9

In addition to making use of Richmond's "usual place" of execution, the county also executed persons on "the hill near the Penitentiary," the "burying ground below Rocketts" (the site of docks on the James River), and even in the county jail yard[4]; more often than not, the Henrico court simply ordered that "a gallows" be "erected at some fit and suitable place to be selected by the said Sheriff, or one of his deputies."[5]

Doomed federal prisoners met their fate (namely in 1827) in the valley adjacent to the north side of the penitentiary (opened in 1800 at Belvidere Street). Bordering this site was also a black neighborhood known as "Penitentiary Bottom," where the convict chain gang dumped the street refuse.[6] During the Civil War the Confederate army conducted public executions (by hanging or firing squad) at Camp Lee, formerly the Hermitage plantation owned by John Mayo, on the north side of Broad Street at the intersection with Davis Avenue (once the site of Hermitage Fair Grounds, recently the Broad Street Station and now the Virginia Science Museum).[7] Military executions also occurred at an army camp on Williamsburg Road at the city's eastern border and also at an army post at Chaffin's Bluff, ten miles below the city on the James River. Confederate army prisoners awaiting execution were held at the Civil War prison, Castle Thunder.[8]

Civilians condemned to death in Richmond were detained prior to execution in either the city or Henrico County jails. The former was located at Fifteenth and Marshall streets. A report prepared for the city's hustings court in 1823 indicated the dire conditions of this facility: it lacked a fireplace or "any other means of warming" and clean straw and good blankets; 15 to 16 persons slept in each room. Soon, however, a new jail remedied the worst of the conditions.[9] In Henrico County, its jail shared the same site at the courthouse in downtown Richmond at Twenty-second Street until it moved to Seventeenth and Marshall streets and Jail Alley in the 1840s.[10] Interestingly, at no time (at least not until 1908) were prisoners sentenced to death confined in the penitentiary, a state institution. Executions, from the late 1780s to 1908, were held at localities where the convictions had been obtained.[11]

Not surprisingly, crime and vagrancy posed a significant theme as Richmond progressed from its early frontier and rough-and-ready character to an industrial-urban society. A traveler in the 1790s observed that "perhaps in no place of the same size in the world is there more gambling going forward than in Richmond."[12]

During the early period of the city's history, Richmond's newspapers carried almost no local news, only very rarely mentioning notices of meetings and visits of prominent persons, and absolutely nothing about crimes. Not until the near mid–nineteenth century, and particularly with the advent of the daily press, did the newspapers cover, often with wry humor, almost every crime or misadventure. Ethnic derision frequently colored the reports on inebriation and assaults. Favorite items involved the mischief of wayward boys, some as young as five years old; juvenile gangs engaged in pilfering, and fighting over their turfs became common occurrences. For law enforcement the city initially had the "City Watch," created in 1782, which, by the turn of the century employed thirty-two men and a captain. In the nineteenth century, each of the city's three wards had a night-watch and there was also a city-wide Public Guard. By 1877 a police force had emerged, placed under the control of the board of police commissioners (today it falls under the auspices of a director of public safety).[13]

A two-tiered court system assigned convicted felons to the gallows: one set up for whites and free blacks and another for slaves. Trials for capital cases in Virginia as to judicial process did not change from the colonial period to the early years of the Republic. White defendants in death-penalty cases were tried in the general court, which met in the state capital (originally in Williamsburg and then in Richmond). Slaves for all major crimes were tried persistently in specially called courts of oyer and terminer of the municipal hustings courts or county courts. Usually these "slave courts" consisted of five of the city alderman or county justices of the peace. Besides these special courts, the hustings courts and the county courts each had similar powers that included all matters of civil jurisdiction and low-level criminal cases. They also served as examining courts, with authority to send a criminal case involving free persons up to a higher level for trial.[14] The Richmond hustings court did not condemn any slaves to death before 1790.[15] From 1782 to 1820, however, it tried 427 criminal slave cases, excluding misdemeanors.[16] Actually, a slave fared better in a trial before a hustings oyer and terminer court than in a regular court; in the former, justices were more careful as to evidence than a jury and one dissenting vote necessitated acquittal.[17]

In April 1789 the general court was replaced by eighteen district courts, with two judges each. The district court meeting in Richmond served the city and the neighboring counties of Henrico, Hanover, Chesterfield, Goochland, and Powhatan. The district court had full authority to try all cases of treason, murder, felony, and other crimes and mis-

1. "Usual Place of Execution" 11

Ready for the gallows: the execution of Capt. Henry Wirz, November 10, 1865, Washington, D.C. (Library of Congress).

demeanors regarding any person not a slave.[18] The decentralizing trend continued. By a law enacted on February 1, 1808, superior courts replaced district courts. Every county now had a superior court, with powers formerly held by the district courts. Richmond was the only Virginia city to have its own superior court.[19]

A long anticipated revision of the Virginia criminal code was enacted on December 15, 1796. It abolished the death penalty for twenty-seven felonies committed by free persons, except for premeditated murder: specifically, "every person convicted of murder in the first degree, his or her aiders, abettors and counsellors, shall suffer death by hanging by the neck." Imprisonment and labor on public works supplanted the previous capital punishment.[20]

Although the number of executions diminished in Richmond with the opening of the penitentiary, elimination of the many death penalties of the Virginia code of 1796, and the shifting of executions from the capital to various other localities, death sentences for Richmond-area slaves continued at a high rate. But most slave death sentences were remitted by the governor on condition that those condemned be sold and deported outside the state; should any such person return to Virginia he would be put to death. The majority of Richmond slaves were household servants; one-third of them were employed in industry.[21] From 1829 to 1865, fifty-four Richmond-area slaves had their death sentences commuted for transportation out of the state.[22]

Other than for the murder of a white person, only one slave woman was executed in Richmond. Some, however, were under sentence of death, primarily for poisoning, arson, and infanticide, but their sentences were commuted to transportation. Thus, for example, were the cases of Susan (Suckey) and Kesiah, who administered nonfatally to Samuel Cartwright and his wife the poisonous "seed of the James Town weed" in February 1829, and Phillis, who gave morphine with intent to kill Otto Butler in May 1852.[23] Thus also two Richmond women, condemned to death for infanticide, in 1834 and 1852, had their sentences respited in favor of transportation.[24]

Henry Box Brown, an escaped slave, claimed that Richmond whites lived in constant fear of arson.[25] All Richmond-condemned slave arsonists, several of whom were women, had their capital sentences reprieved to transportation, except one who was hanged in 1864.[26] Capital punishment for burglary, frequently applied to slaves before the 1790s, almost entirely gave way to the substitute penalty of transportation.[27] Various assaults by slaves on white persons resulting in the death penalty also were respited.[28] Some reprieved death penalty cases involving slaves mention the crime only as a felony.[29]

Antebellum newspapers regularly published brief obituaries, many of them referring to children and young adults. It was not unusual for an adult to succumb in her 20s or 30s. Sickness and death were almost constant realities, and not infrequently persons were carried off by an epidemical disease such as cholera or typhoid. With death such a constant presence one would expect that public hangings would be met by some degree of indifference. Although this was much the case, increasingly, especially with the coming of sensational media hype by the mid–nineteenth century, executions drew rather emotional crowds, often equaling nearly half to nearly all of an area's population. It is interesting how many of the assemblage, consisting of blacks and whites, men, women, and children, felt a shared identity with the prisoner. The condemned person

1. "Usual Place of Execution"

invariably expressed in his last words an expectation of heavenly redemption. The gallows victim singled out from among the assemblage friends or acquaintances and invited them to join him in the afterlife. Not surprisingly someone would call out, "I'll see you there, but I ain't going with you."

2

"A Flood of Tears"
1782–1799

Richmond, as the new state capital, had its first hanging on January 25, 1782, when James Robinson was executed for burglary and John Chapman for horse thievery. On November 29, 1782, Maurice Wheeler was hanged for murder. Many crimes were still punishable by death, as in colonial times. All death penalty cases involving whites were brought to the capital for trial in the state's general court, and execution took place in Richmond. A Richmond newspaper commented that "we put more people to death by law for trifling offences than all the world besides, except the English."[1]

The year 1782 had begun with the expectation that several dozen Tories convicted of treason would be led to the gallows in Richmond. The final riddance in Virginia of British armies after the battle of Yorktown had emboldened Virginians once and for all to choose the winning side and point fingers at neighbors who gave material aid to the enemy. Of course, a part of the motivation was that the property of traitors would be seized and put up for public sale at low prices. A damper upon condemning traitors to death was the outcome of a case heard before the state's new court of appeals. *Caton v. Commonwealth* upheld the death penalty convictions of James Lamb, Joshua Hopkins, and John Caton. Many persons thought, however, the court of appeals could not review a criminal case or decide on the constitutionality of a law. On petition to the general assembly, Lamb and Hopkins were pardoned on condition of leaving the state. Caton and three other men sentenced to death for treason were pardoned by the general court in its October session on condition that they serve in the Continental army.[2]

Notwithstanding the decisions of the assembly and the general court in the above cases, the state again tried to hang traitors. On November 29,

2. "A Flood of Tears"

1782, seven condemned prisoners—namely two traitors (John Holland and Demsey Butler) and a murderer and two horse thieves—made what would become a familiar trek from the city jail to the gallows erected at the northeastern base of Shockoe Hill. Under the gallows the horse thieves received pardons on condition of joining the army; the murderer was hanged. Butler and Holland, after standing for a while "under the gallows," were informed of their reprieve until the next session of the assembly could redetermine their case. They were eventually pardoned. In December 1782 the general court acquitted two persons of treason. It also failed to convict Isaac Riddle of treason in January 1783, which was the last treason trial of the Revolution in Virginia.[3]

Thus a reign of terror did not succeed, and Virginians could be proud that no one was executed for treason during the war. Thomas Jefferson grasped the significance. In his *Notes on the State of Virginia*, written at the time, he declared, "It may be mentioned as a proof both of the lenity of our government and unanimity of its inhabitants [that] though this war has now raged near seven years, not a single execution for treason has taken place."[4]

Although the Richmond community was spared a wave of executions for treason, the way seemed open to a more egregious implementation of the death penalty. The hangings drew large crowds.[5] On July 18, 1783, James Anderson of Berkeley County, wife murderer, and James Stours, for horse thief, were hanged. Michael Newman of Henrico County, for robbery, and John Raines of Southampton County, for horse stealing, paid with their lives on December 5, 1783. Both men were attended in their cells by a court-appointed Catholic priest and given last rites. Raines freely confessed his crime, but Newman refused to do so until the morning of his execution, when he acknowledged theft of a black mare and also, seven years previously, a sorrel horse and goods from a store.[6]

Continuing through the 1780s, condemned white criminals from throughout the state were brought to Richmond for execution. Starting about 1790 all executions were conducted in the counties or incorporated towns and cities. Slaves all the while were condemned by the special courts of oyer and terminer under auspices of the county courts or municipal hustings courts. Of the twenty slaves (not insurrectionists) ordered to be hanged by the Richmond hustings court from 1782 to 1820,[7] it seems that most of them were reprieved. The first hanging of an African-American, who is identified only as "negro" and probably was a free man, was Thomas Macauly, on August 4, 1786. Macauly, convicted of rape, spent his final days in the crowded Richmond jail, where "distemper" was prevalent and the only sanitation measure was a weekly scrubbing of the floor with vinegar.[8]

Meanwhile, executions of whites occurred. Stephen Yancey of Louisa County went to the Richmond gallows on December 3, 1784, for the murder of his brother. On January 28, 1785, two wife murderers, Matthew Womble and John Tyler, similarly paid with their lives. Womble had also killed his four children.[9] Six months later three burglars—Presley Hunt, John Burton, and one Richards—and a murderer, Reuben Jones, were executed at the lower Shockoe Hill gallows.[10] A single execution was held in late December 1786 or early January 1787, that of James Goss, a horse thief; Goss' defense of insanity did not save him.[11]

Two murderers, Isaac Reade and Elisha Lasseter, were hanged on January 26, 1787.[12] Three persons were executed together on July 27, 1787—two white men, Richard Downs (for burglary), and Joseph Taylor (for horse stealing), and an emancipated slave, Dick (for murder).[13] George Abbott, a murderer, was hanged on June 8, 1787. A double hanging took place at the end of the year, on December 2: James Phillips (for burglary) and William Wilson (for horse stealing).[14] Almost all of the executions of the 1780s were of persons convicted in jurisdictions outside of Richmond.

Almost never in Virginia and American history have any persons of the upper middle class or the aristocracy been executed, especially when a conviction for homicide was not involved. An exception was John Price Posey, a stepbrother of General Thomas Posey of Revolutionary War fame and whose family were close friends of George Washington. The Poseys resided at their homestead, Rover's Delight, on the Potomac River near Mount Vernon. Posey's sister, Amelia "Milly" Posey lived with the Washingtons at Mount Vernon for many years. John Price Posey married Anne Kidley Chamberlayne, daughter of a prominent leader, Colonel William Chamberlayne. Unfortunately, John Price Posey's father, John, fell into debt and lost almost all of his estate and spent time in a debtor's prison in Maryland. George Washington sent John Price Posey with money to bail John Sr. out of jail. Upon his release from prison, John Sr. sold to George Washington the six-acre tract of Rover's Delight, his ferry, and military lands received from service in the French and Indian War. He then lived on charity bestowed by Washington. John Sr. disappears from history about 1774.[15]

Born in 1752, John Price Posey early gave promise. He was well educated. A boyhood playmate of John Parke "Jacky" Custis, Washington's

2. "A Flood of Tears"

stepson, Posey frequently lodged at Mount Vernon. Washington secured for Posey employment in the iron and flour business. Jacky Custis, attaining legal age in 1778, appointed Posey as agent and manager of his plantation in New Kent County. Posey moved to New Kent County, where he became a justice of the peace and from 1780 to 1781 served in the house of delegates. But the death of Jacky Custis in November 1781 marked the beginning of Posey's downfall.[16]

Soon Washington was informed of the "abuse and misapplication" of Jacky Custis' estate. Washington wrote Posey that Posey had "taken advantage of an unsuspecting friend." Washington was especially infuriated that Posey had appropriated to himself profits from the estate and had sold off some of Jacky's slaves for his own benefit. In October 1784 he was brought before the general court for having stolen a cow from the Custis estate and was fined £25. Two weeks later he was back in the same court and fined £200 for mismanagement of the Custis estate. Posey's improprieties came to the attention of the council of state which removed Posey from his post as a justice of the peace.[17]

The contention between Posey and George Washington flared up even more intensely in 1786. Washington was alarmed in September of that year when his former overseer, James Hill, said that he had turned over all moneys and records concerning Washington's farms and also cash obtained from certain of Washington's debtors to John Price Posey. Posey adamantly denied all of Hill's accusations. Meanwhile, Posey had wound up with more trouble. In March 1786 he was convicted in the Northampton County Court of defrauding Bartholomew Dandridge and others concerning debts owed by Posey as administrator of the Custis estate and also destroying "in a passion" an arbitration bond.[18] In June 1787 Posey assaulted Sheriff Robert B. Armistead of New Kent County and was sentenced to one month in jail in lieu of making bail.[19]

On Sunday night, July 12, 1787, John Price Posey, with the help of Thomas Green, escaped from the New Kent County jail. Three days later Posey and Green, accompanied by two slaves, Hercules and Sawney, returned to the jail; inside they placed fence rails and shingles, which they set ablaze using steel, a tinderbox and flint. Going two miles up the main road the arsonists ignited the county clerk's office, which burned to the ground, destroying all the county's records.[20]

Posey did not leave the area, and Green let it be known immediately who the culprits were. Posey was arrested and placed under a strong guard. On August 15 he was brought before eight justices of the New Kent County

Court, acting as an examining court. After deliberations during the whole afternoon, Posey was remanded to stand trial for arson in the general court in Richmond. The next day, in chains, he was sent to the Richmond jail.[21]

At Posey's trial on October 1, 1787, he was found guilty of arson, a capital offense, and sentenced to be hanged.[22] The case then went to the Virginia Court of Appeals in its December term; the verdict was upheld. Two of the state's most prominent trial lawyers, Andrew Ronald, for the defense, and St. George Tucker, for the prosecution, argued the case before the appeals court.[23] The justices were unmoved and sentenced John Price Posey to be hanged on January 18, 1788. The final moments of the court of appeals proceedings were reported in newspaper accounts:

> The Unfortunate John Price Posey was called to the bar on Friday last, to hear the opinion of the Hon. Court of Appeals, which was read by the Clerk, and being asked what he had farther to say for himself why sentence of death should not be pronounced upon him according to law, — a flood of tears choaked the organs of speech, and after some time Judge [Peter] Lyons pronounced the awful sentence, in so affecting manner, as drew tears from the audience and the Court. A solemn silence reigned through the whole, which lasted near half an hour. Mr. Posey's behavior upon the occasion, was decent and firm. He confessed his crime, and said he hoped through the merits of his Saviour, to obtain a pardon for the sins of his past life.[24]

Richmonders viewed with mixed feelings Posey's death sentence. Many persons believed that arson should not be a capital crime, as is evident by the state's repealing that penalty for white persons only eight years after Posey forfeited his life. It is also likely that public opinion associated Posey's destruction of the county buildings in the light of backcountry farmer's insurrectionary activity, versus the alliance between creditors and government, throughout the country and notably Shays's Rebellion in New England. In several Virginia counties, farmers rioted, and in King William County arsonists destroyed court records. As it was, Posey's accomplices were subjects of mercy. Green seems to never have been tried, and the two slaves were pardoned and returned to their owner, William Chamberlayne, Posey's brother-in-law.[25]

On January 9, 1788, Governor Edmund Randolph was handed a request from John Price Posey: "The unfortunate and most unhappy John Price Posey begs that a further indulgence of a few days could be allowed him — Hopeful that it would be attended with giving further relief to the peace of mind that your unfortunate petitioner is now in search of."[26] The

2. "A Flood of Tears"

governor granted a week's stay. On Friday, January 25, 1788, John Price Posey was publicly hanged at Richmond's usual execution site.[27]

In death, Posey had the company of a murderer who was executed at the same time. James M'Connell Fox, who had been delivered to the Richmond jail by the sheriff of Washington County on November 1, 1787, was originally from Pennsylvania and had married a rich young woman. He was twenty-two years old. Fox had been convicted of murdering a youth by knocking him off his horse with a club, cutting the victim's throat from ear to ear, and then riding off on the murdered person's horse. On the way to Richmond, Fox had twice attempted to murder the sheriff who had him in custody.[28]

Posey was buried near his homestead in New Kent County. Unusually, the Virginia legislature restored all his real and personal property, normally confiscated in capital convictions, to his widow.[29] Two children also survived him.

Of eight persons condemned to death in Richmond in May 1788, three were hanged on the Richmond gallows on June 9: John Candy and William Armstrong for burglary and John Coody for the murder of his wife. Candy and Armstrong confessed and received the sacrament before execution, while Coody did neither.[30] On August 3, 1788, navy captain Archibald Carroll, an Irishman, was executed in Richmond for the murder of one of his seamen. It was reported that Carroll had been known to have committed "sundry murders, and was the person who carried the signals of the British fleet to the French whilst off the British channel last war."[31]

The number of executions after 1789 dropped sharply because localities now assumed responsibility for the executions of white felons from their areas; later the 1796 Virginia code revision abolished many capital penalties. There was a three-year hiatus between 1789 and 1792. During the 1790s, of eight slaves condemned to die only three were executed. On January 11, 1793, Harry, a slave convicted by a Henrico County court of oyer and terminer, met his fate on the Richmond gallows for "administering poison."[32]

On August 19, 1796, William "Billy" Harris, a slave, was hanged in Richmond. A former laborer at the Deep Run coal pits in Henrico County, twelve miles northwest of Richmond, Billy was convicted simply for having broken into a store in Richmond, although he was known to have committed "many other villainies." A newcomer to Richmond who had recently arrived in Virginia from England, architect Benjamin Henry Latrobe learned "all the circumstances" of the execution from twenty different people. Latrobe had sympathy for Deputy Sheriff Mosby. Since no one could be found who would act as hangman, Mosby had to perform that duty himself, "with all its circumstances of blindfolding and tying up the criminal, and then driving away the Cart, in which he was mounted along with him."

Because his crime was less than murder, Billy Harris "entertained hope of a reprieve or at least that some Gentleman would buy him, as the phrase is, from under the Gallows, in order to carry him out of the State." As it was, he had to find his redemption in faith in Jesus. The Reverend John Courtney, a Baptist minister of "a large congregation of Negroes" who had a meetinghouse on the north side of Cary Street between Second and Third streets, had frequently visited Billy in jail, and accompanied him to the gallows. Courtney was noted for preaching "the good old doctrine of heaven and hell, the atonement and justification by faith with Stentorian rhetoric." Latrobe observed that Billy Harris was "so perfect a convert" of the Rev. Courtney that he walked from the jail to the gallows "not only with composure but with cheerfulness, declaring his happiness in the prospect of death, and the certainty of *being soon with God in glory*." The condemned man "sung psalms during the intervals of his professions of happiness and comfort. At the gallows he called to his acquaintances whom he saw in the crowd, took leave of them, and told the Sheriff once or twice that he was ready." All the while the Rev. Courtney "attended him with his pious labours."[33]

Benjamin Henry Latrobe (courtesy Library of Virginia).

The last slave execution of the decade occurred on February 9, 1799. The slave, Mayor Bob, went to the gallows for stabbing a white man with intent to kill.[34] Little did Richmonders realize that in little more than a year a great fear would descend upon them that would result in mass hangings of a large number of slaves.

3

"Liberty of My Countrymen"
1800–1802

"Some information has been received of a proposed insurrection of the slaves in this city and its neighborhood of a nature to merit attention," wrote Governor James Monroe in Richmond to the mayor of Petersburg on August 30, 1800. Monroe had just been apprised of a slave uprising scheduled that evening.[1]

One capital crime for slaves acting merely as conspirators was insurrection. Because the horrors of a slave uprising always threatened, a response, in the minds of whites, called for executions en masse. The fact that no major slave insurrection had occurred in Virginia made an eventual outbreak of such an event all the more fearsome. Hence the Gabriel slave conspiracy of 1800 exacted a heavy retribution. The plot, mainly an affair of Henrico County, reached out into adjoining areas; it called for the rebels to secure Richmond, the capital city, and from there to set free slaves throughout the state. If freedom for blacks was not immediately obtained through negotiations, then a bloodbath should ensue. Despite Richmond's being the focus, the actual insurrectionists came from the rural areas; no slaves in the city paid with their lives for a part in the conspiracy.

Slaves in rural Virginia by 1800 had become restless. The harsh treatment by masters and overseers mixed with the vision of liberty thrust upon persons of all races by the late War of Independence had made bondsmen all the more willing to seek out freedom. During the war itself Governor Lord Dunmore, in 1775, had issued an emancipation proclamation to Virginia slaves to flee their masters and join British ranks as free men, and the three large invading British armies during 1781 had gathered in several thousand black refugees.

In the city of Richmond itself there was not much inclination among slaves to start an insurrection. Full employment prevailed among blacks in various retail, shipping, and industrial establishments. Slaves in the city amounted to one-half of the 5,700 population. Yet, even though blacks had a great range of mobility in the city, blacks mixing among themselves and whites, a resentment toward white mastery simmered below the surface. Any insurrection reaching into the city would certainly find recruits. The whipping post in downtown Richmond, used almost exclusively to punish slaves, existed as a visible concrete reminder of oppression by whites.

Into what seemed a placid environment, seeds of rebellion were being nurtured in and around Brookfield, the Thomas Prosser plantation, six miles north of Richmond, in Henrico County. Richmond and the county were meshed together almost as one entity, with the county courthouse in the city. The Prosser plantation had about sixty slaves, among some 4,000 in the county. For a year or so three brothers—Solomon, Martin, and Gabriel—carefully laid the groundwork for rebellion, one they expected to engulf all of central Virginia. Gabriel, born in 1775, the youngest of the brothers, emerged as the leader of the conspiracy, styling himself as "General."

Gabriel cut an imposing figure. Six feet-three inches tall, he had brawn, enhanced by nearly a decade of blacksmith work. His face was scarred, and he had two front teeth missing. Gabriel wore his hair short. Impressively, he had learned how to read and write. Gabriel had charge of the plantation blacksmith shop, and frequently he was hired out in Richmond, where he had leeway to make acquaintances among both freed and enslaved blacks. Hence Gabriel acquired all the credentials to assume leadership of a slave rebellion. He also had motive. Gabriel's world began to darken in 1798. While still a skilled craftsman, with all its privileges and being allowed on occasion to work in the city with minimum restraints, Gabriel found himself more in a confrontational situation with whites. His benign master, Thomas Prosser, died in October 1798, and the master's son, Thomas Henry Prosser, twenty-two years old, soon demonstrated "great barbarity" toward the Brookfield slaves. Actually Thomas Henry Prosser himself spent much of his time in Richmond, where he kept a townhouse and dabbled in the real estate and auction businesses.

In September 1799 Gabriel, his brother Solomon, and another slave were caught stealing hogs from a neighboring farm leased by a former overseer, Absalom Johnson. Gabriel fought with Johnson, biting off "a considerable part" of the latter's left ear. Arraigned before a Henrico County court of oyer and terminer, Gabriel was let go after being permitted to plead benefit of clergy and his master's making bond for Gabriel's future

3. "Liberty of My Countrymen"

good behavior. Prosser, however, on his own, had Gabriel committed for a month in Henrico County's awful jail.

Gabriel was now determined upon a full-scale slave uprising. Along with his brothers he began recruiting other blacks. Gabriel openly ventured among the slaves in the countryside. Using the Prosser plantation as headquarters, the conspirators finalized a plan to be implemented starting at midnight of August 30, 1800.[2]

Like the later John Brown raid of 1859, Gabriel expected that a coup by a limited number of insurgents would inspire a general uprising. After murdering Thomas Henry Prosser and family and Absalom Johnson, the rebels, with their makeshift weapons, would march to Richmond. Once there they would divide into three groups. One section would set fire to the warehouse buildings in the city to draw residents to that area; another led by Gabriel would secure the capitol grounds and capture Governor Monroe; and the third would raid the penitentiary for arms. With success in the city, Gabriel would fly a white flag, which would signal rebellion in the countryside. If negotiations with the whites led to their surrender, Gabriel said he would soon "dine and drink with the merchants of the City." If resistance ensued, then all the whites, except Frenchmen, Methodists, and Quakers would be killed.[3]

Unfortunately for the insurgents, the wiles of nature intervened. On August 30, the appointed day, rain started at noon, and by evening there was a sustained torrential downpour. Flooding wiped out roads and bridges, and all communications broke down among the insurgents. A march to Richmond was impossible. The uprising was rescheduled for the next night, but again participants did not appear.[4]

While the slave conspirators had kept their secret for many months, all of a sudden, in the morning of August 30, slave owners had the plot revealed to them. Tom and Pharao of a neighboring plantation informed their master, Mosby Sheppard, of the conspiracy. Sheppard dispatched a note to Governor Monroe.[5] The governor and Richmonders had reasons to be fearful. Already, successful slave insurrections had occurred in the Western hemisphere, not the least being the triumphant rebellion in Santo Domingo, led by Toussaint L'Ouverture. Gabriel's insurgents in Richmond and various counties could amount to a sizeable force, armed with seized weapons. The governor ordered cannon brought to the capitol grounds and called up 650 militia, who were stationed as guards in Petersburg and in Richmond at the capitol, the magazine, the jail, and the penitentiary. Patrols went through Richmond and its near vicinity.[6]

Public Executions in Richmond, Virginia

By September 15, Governor Monroe considered the insurrection "so completely broken" that he ordered a reduction in the mobilized militia, keeping only 150 men for "protection" of the city, thirty more to guard arms in Manchester, and 25 troops at Prosser's tavern just outside the city. In addition, an artillery company and cavalry were retained on standby status.[7] Further changes were made on October 3 when troops on active duty in Richmond were reduced to seventy-five men to guard the capitol and the jail; militia were also stationed about fifty miles up the James River to guard the arsenal there.[8]

The reason for the lessening of precautions was owing to the quick arrests of slaves thought to be implicated foremost in the plot. Some forty slaves detained for trial for treason (making insurrection) found themselves lodged in the two-story brick building on Fifteenth Street that at the time served as jail for both the city and Henrico County.[9] The accused went on trial in a court of oyer and terminer in the adjoining Henrico County courthouse.

According to Virginia law a slave trial had to be held from five to ten days after the accused had been jailed. In capital cases, the decision of the court had to be unanimous among the five judges. One member of this special court was an esteemed Baptist minister, the Rev. George Williamson, who in one case was the lone dissenter, causing acquittal. For cases involving insurrection a court could order immediate execution. Otherwise a stay of at least thirty days went into effect to allow appeal to the governor.[10]

The trials began Thursday morning, September 11. Justice was swift. The first conspirator found guilty was one of Gabriel's two brothers, Solomon, who was sentenced to be hanged the next morning "at the usual place." Five more slaves were tried on the 12th and sentenced to death. On the morning of September 12, five of the condemned were taken from the jail to the execution site at Fifteenth and Broad streets. Solomon had gained a respite when he informed the authorities that he would tell "numerous and important discoveries" regarding the conspiracy. Refusing to testify against his cohorts, he paid with his life on September 15.[11]

The scene of that fateful morning of September 12 was to be duplicated on the hanging days that followed. As Douglas R. Egerton writes, the whole jail building "exploded into religious chaos." As the jailer, William Rose, rang, as usual, the "daylight Bell," the prisoner slaves, already condemned or soon to be, realized fatal moments had arrived. Hymn-singing reverberated throughout the jail, and slaves prayed for their

3. "Liberty of My Countrymen"

Shockoe Valley at Seventh Street, October 1922 (courtesy of Valentine Richmond History Center).

souls to be set free. A throng of people assembled at the execution site. A tumbril brought the condemned the six blocks to the gallows. Governor Monroe had sent several infantry companies to provide a circle "around the gallows to keep off the crowd." The noise, including derisive shouts, singing of hymns, and moanings of fellow slaves drowned out any audible proceedings. With the mass execution accomplished, families of the executed men took their bodies for burial in the countryside. Three days later (the 15th), five more men met their deaths on the Richmond gallows.[12]

The numerous executions began to trouble Governor Monroe. He wrote Thomas Jefferson on September 15 that "10 have been condemned & executed, and there are at least twenty, perhaps 40 more to be tried, of whose guilt no doubt is entertained." He noted that "when to arrest the hand of the Executioner, is a question of great importance"; it was "difficult to say whether mercy or severity is the better policy in this case," although "when there is cause for doubt it is best to incline to the former council."[13]

Monroe also had in mind the political implications of the executions.

Public Executions in Richmond, Virginia

It just would not do for the party of the Jeffersonian Republicans, as witness to the country and to the world, and especially in the heated election milieu of 1800, to visit excessive bloodletting upon enslaved peoples yearning to be free. The horrors of French Jacobinism were all too fresh. Besides, it was the Federalist Party that was supposed to be anti-liberty, not the Jeffersonian.

On September 18, five more men were hanged. There was a slight change in the hanging ritual because of a complaint of some Richmond ladies who lived near the execution site. Considered most objectionable were the wailings of the children and wives of those executed. The women had presented a petition requesting that the condemned be "hung in some other place."[14] For future hangings of the slave conspirators, the government, for the most part, used alternate sites. Transferring the executions to more secluded locations out of town made for a more terrible death for the condemned. Slaves launched into eternity on the city gallows, a specially constructed edifice, died instantly from broken necks when they fell through the trap door. At the alternate sites, the prisoners, swinging from long ropes fastened to sturdy tree branches, died of slow strangulation.

Two slave conspirators on October 3 were hanged in a clearing near George Watson's tavern on the property of Thomas Henry Prosser. The selection of a hanging site such as this was owing not only to the Richmond ladies' complaint but also to the reality that the death penalty could be made manifest to those rural slaves who had not witnessed the Richmond hangings.[15] Seventeen slaves had now paid with their lives for the intended insurrection. Seven more slaves were executed on October 10. Four were hanged at the tavern site, two others at the crossroads near Four Mile Creek, and the number one prize, the leader of the insurrection, Gabriel, at the Richmond execution site.[16]

Gabriel had eluded captors in Henrico County. On September 14, he had been permitted to board the schooner *Mary* in the James River; the ship's captain, Richardson Taylor, may or may not have immediately known the identity of his new passenger. On board, Billy, a Norfolk slave who had previously hired out in Richmond, recognized Gabriel and told Taylor. Taylor, recently converted to Methodism, decided to let Gabriel stay aboard to Norfolk, and from there to further his escape. At Norfolk Billy passed the word that the fugitive leader was shipboard at the dock. Immediately, local constables seized Gabriel and, tethering him in irons, put him on a vessel bound for Richmond. Debarking at the capital on September 24, the prisoner was taken to the penitentiary.[17]

3. "Liberty of My Countrymen"

View of Shockoe Creek Valley, area of Richmond Gallows, 1866 (courtesy of Valentine Richmond History Center).

Gabriel's trial took place on October 6 at the Henrico County courthouse. Douglas R. Egerton describes the scene outside the courtroom. The "streets were crowded with men and boys." Whites "came to jeer; slaves, free blacks, and the odd white mechanic stood quietly as they awaited word on the man who had tried to make liberty and equality more than slogans."[18]

The two slaves who testified against Gabriel made it clear that the accused actually wanted to avoid a bloodbath and hoped that Richmond would be peaceably surrendered. The trial was quickly concluded and Gabriel was sentenced to hang the next day "at the usual place of execution." Allowed to speak, Gabriel requested only that his execution be postponed three days to coincide with scheduled hangings of other slave conspirators.[19]

In the morning of October 10, three wagons left the Henrico jail in Richmond, together carting seven condemned men. Two prisoners to be hanged went to the crossings near Four Mile Creek; another wagon took four men to die at a clearing near Prosser's tavern, where four ropes were slung over a high, single branch; the sole prisoner on the third wagon,

Public Executions in Richmond, Virginia

Gabriel, headed to Richmond's execution site at 15th and Broad streets. With his hands tied behind him, Gabriel was launched off a cart before a large crowd. He died with "quiet composure." His beloved wife, Nanny, it is thought, was not among the assembled spectators.[20]

Governor Monroe persuaded the legislature to suspend executions until after a legislative investigation into the punishment phase of the Gabriel conspiracy. In the meantime the Henrico court of oyer and terminer, meeting in Richmond, dispatched only one other slave, Peter, to the hangman's noose. Those conspirators remaining to be tried were ordered to be transported out of the state. Thus the executions for the Gabriel conspiracy in Richmond concluded with the twenty-sixth hanging. Besides Monroe's sudden flash of conscience, a major factor in halting the executions was the cost to the government of reimbursing owners of the condemned slaves for their loss.[21]

There were some reverberations from Gabriel's Insurrection. Incipient uprisings were quashed with ten executions, January–May 1802: two in Brunswick County, two in Nottoway County, five in Halifax County, and one in the city of Norfolk. Thus, including the twenty-six persons executed at or in the suburbs of Richmond, a total of thirty-six men paid with their lives in Virginia for the Gabriel conspiracy. Some of the spirit of rebelliousness spilled into North Carolina, where, in 1802, several slaves were executed in Martin and Halifax counties.[22]

As for law and order, one result of the Gabriel conspiracy was the founding of the Public Guard of Richmond. These guardsmen, commanded by a regular army officer, drilled regularly. Their duties consisted of guarding the armory, the capitol, and the penitentiary.[23]

A fitting response uttered in court by one of the Gabriel condemned slaves underscores the hypocrisy of the excessive bloodletting by whites as revenge for the Gabriel conspiracy. As reported by a lawyer, the slave declared that he had done nothing different from what George Washington did. "I have adventured my life in endeavoring to obtain the liberty of my countrymen," said the slave, "and I am a willing sacrifice in their cause.... I know that you have pre-determined to shed my blood, why then all this mockery of a trial?"[24]

4

"Between the Heavens and the Earth"
1801–1826

The noose and the gallows became relatively unfamiliar to Richmonders during the quarter-century after the Gabriel hangings. Richmond was still a small town: a population of 6,000 in 1801 and 13,000 by mid-1820s. With executions now conducted locally, one would not expect many such events as was the case when all hangings of whites and free blacks occurred at the capital. Between 1801 and 1826 only several slaves (other than those convinced of insurrection) were executed under sentence of the Richmond hustings or county courts, and only one white man.

The reforms in the state criminal code (1796, see chapter 2) reduced the number of executions for whites and free blacks. Similarly, the opening of the penitentiary in Richmond provided a punishment option to death. A report on the penitentiary in 1817 revealed that among the 150 prisoners there were those incarcerated for former capital crimes, such as horse stealing and other forms of robbery.[1] The severity in punishment of slaves also ameliorated. As historian Philip Schwarz writes, "improved penal conditions for free people" created "the opportunity for degrees in capital punishment for the unfree."[2] The discontinuance of allowing accused slaves in capital cases to plead benefit of clergy, which removed the death penalty upon submission to branding on the thumb, was offset by selective substitution of transportation out of the state instead of execution. Still, death sentences were meted out as they had been in earlier times, including for all kinds of thievery, for slaves, even though most of the sentences were remitted.[3]

Four slaves went to the gallows in the period under consideration. Stephen, a slave convicted of murder and arson, was hanged on March 7,

Public Executions in Richmond, Virginia

1801.[4] Slaves Billy and Bob were executed in March and May 1805, respectively.[5] Jordan, who murdered William Woodram of Henrico County, died on March 24, 1820, on a gallows erected on "Penitentiary Hill."[6]

An estimated crowd of ten thousand to twelve thousand, equaling the total population of the city of Richmond, turned out for the hanging of a white man, Robert Gibson, on October 27, 1818. Among those assembled were "numerous spectators, from several miles around." As the *Enquirer* reported, "a larger crowd attended" the gallows "that is said to have been witnessed in Richmond." A major factor for this phenomenon was that "executions have become rare among us since the establishment of the Penitentiary system; and therefore the novelty ... excites a considerable interest." Gibson had been convicted in his third trial for the murder of John N. Peatross. In court, when asked why sentence of death should not be passed upon him, Gibson responded: "Had I been rich, and had plenty of money, I should not have been hung. I should have lawyers enough to plead for me — But, I am a poor man, and now I have to die. Such a thing is not usual in Virginia, where there is a Penitentiary house, for a man to be condemned to death upon circumstantial evidence alone.... All I have to say is that I am not guilty." Judge Brockenbrough, in pronouncing sentence, said that "the chain of circumstances provided against you was too strong and irresistible, to leave a doubt of your guilt."

Gibson claimed his innocence of murder until the very last. His final words on the scaffold were to the effect that "his trust was in God only; he had nothing to expect from man."[7] Shortly before his execution, Gibson gave out a confession, one that admitted to robberies but not to murder. He owned up to having picked up the "pocket-book" of a person in Albany, New York, and said that at another time he had stolen "a hat-full of gold." Gibson claimed that he had hidden money somewhere in King William County, and "men were found so credulous and confiding as to work" by a map drawn up attempting to find the "concealed treasure."[8] The *Richmond Compiler* did not report on the hanging, but instead printed an editorial (taken from the *Philadelphia Union*) that denigrated "dying confessions," such as that of Gibson. The reporter said that he expected to see Gibson's confession published because the public avidly expected such fare. Instead of having deterrent value, the reporter insisted, dying speeches "encourage avarice, idleness, and the ambition of getting the dazzling eclat of a daring character, amongst that class of society by which they are most universally read." As "the 'blood of the martyrs was the seed of the Church' so may perhaps the death of the victims of these crimes by

4. "Between the Heavens and the Earth"

these means be the cause of the multiplication of criminals." The reporter compared the actions of criminals with those of heroic characters and the "applause" which they have received. A "weak and silly multitude" are intrigued by "acts of daring villany," which contributes to a disposition devoid of principle, and in combining with avarice and idleness "constitutes the character of a highway robber."[9]

Virginia's law for transportation of condemned slaves outside the state in lieu of execution passed on January 15, 1801. The governor, with the advice of council, had authority to sell slaves sentenced to death, with buyers putting up $500 bond and "carrying" them "out of the United States." Capital punishment could be inflicted if the slave returned to Virginia. The county and hustings sentencing courts had to send to the governor and council the trial records that led to capital conviction, as a basis on which to make a decision granting a reprieve. Owners of the transported condemned slaves, as it was before regarding execution, were imbursed for their loss by the state.[10]

Transportation out of the state for condemned slaves definitely lowered the rate of executions in Virginia. Between 1785 and 1831, of about 141 slaves convicted of insurrectionary activity, 39 were transported, 72 hanged, 14 pardoned, three received whippings, and the rest either died in prison or escaped.[11] For the period of 1785–1865, including the number of condemned slaves transported allowed by private purchase before the law of 1801, for the state as a whole 983 slaves were transported and 626 hanged.[12]

Transportees included mostly persons condemned for some form of robbery (mainly burglary)[13] and to a lesser extent women convicted of arson[14] and infanticide,[15] slaves sentenced for murder of a slave,[16] and persons deemed guilty of horse stealing.[17] Extreme youth was considered grounds for a transportation reprieve.[18] One of the crimes most feared by whites that might be committed by a slave — poisoning — was permitted to be punished by transportation, as long as the victim survived. One case that created quite a stir involved two female slaves, Susan (also known as Suckey) and Kessiah (also known as Kessee), who were convicted of administering to Samuel Cartwright and his wife, Elizabeth, of Henrico County "the seed of the James Town weed, a poisonous substance" with intent to kill. The offending item was placed in prepared coffee. Mr. Cartwright was stricken while traveling to Petersburg; he vomited severely and became nearly blind. Suckey died on January 13, but Kessiah was scheduled to be hanged on a gallows to be erected "near the penitentiary" on March 13, 1829. The sheriff was "to cause the execution of the sentence." On February 12 the sentence was converted to transportation.[19]

Those Richmonders who disapproved of the declining frequency of public executions in the city at least had a steady diet in the local newspapers of coverage of hangings in nearby locations and elsewhere. At Manchester (now part of the city of Richmond across the James River opposite today's downtown section), a slave was hanged on September 11, 1815, at a vacant lot belonging to Francis Smith.[20] Insurrectional conspiracy remained an unpardonable crime. On that account six slaves in Spotsylvania County and two in Louisa County were executed in 1816.[21] Spencer, a slave, went to the gallows in adjacent Chesterfield County in October 1823, convicted of rape.[22] Among the prime execution narratives from places distant from the city several stand out. At a hanging in Warren, Ohio, on December 16, 1816, spectators swarmed forward afterwards to claim pieces of the rope. A report in the *Enquirer* commented on the scene that transpired "in the presence of a large concourse of people." The reporter exclaimed in the article: "What a spectacle: a man loaded with guilt; bowing under the enormous weight of his crime; the victim of folly and cupidity: One moment, he stands before you, the image of health and strength the next you see him stretched, a lifeless corpse, between the Heavens and the Earth. What a crowd of sensations rush into the considerate mind! But all were not considerate; many, on the contrary, were seen, upon whose minds, it is to be feared, no impression was made."[23]

Several months after treating readers to a description of the event in Ohio, the *Enquirer* topped that story with one of the execution of Robert Smith in Philadelphia in August 1816, an occasion which drew "tens of thousands of spectators" of "all ages, sexes, and conditions."[24] The more gruesome the execution the better. Thus readers were told of the burning at the stake in the Edgefield District of South Carolina in February 1820 which produced in spectators "breathless horror": even after death overcame the condemned, the "cry of agony still thrilled in the ear."[25] In October 1818 outside of Nashville, Tennessee, after a hanging at the fork of a road, the head of the corpse was severed from the body "and exposed on a pole, at the place of execution."[26]

Still, Richmonders on rare occasion were treated to their own unmitigated horrors of public death. In 1827 residents witnessed a government mandated killing so gross that it whetted appetites into insatiability for viewing public hangings.

5

"SLEEP IN ALIEN DUST"
1827

Stories of high seas adventure enthralled antebellum Americans. A recurring newspaper item was that of someone spotting the elusive Sea Serpent of the Atlantic Ocean (the equivalent of the modern day Loch Ness Monster or a UFO). Not the least relished were anecdotes of the capture and execution of pirates, in America and abroad.[1] Piratical events of the mid 1820s especially met scrutiny of central Virginians. One incident in particular called for retribution—the piratical capture on October 11, 1824, of the American brig *Edmund de Langham*, out of Bordeaux, in the waters "between the east end of Cuba and St. Domingo." The captain was killed and thrown overboard.[2]

In another incident, when three pirates captured on Virginia shores were tried in a federal court in Richmond and subsequently executed in the city, the events thereof became a gala affair. To hype the hanging "holiday," a local publisher provided for the demanding public a 51-page booklet, detailing the crime and the trial: *A Brief Sketch of the Occurrences on Board the Brig "Crawford" on the Voyage from Matanzas to New York; Together with an Account of the Trial of the Three Spaniards*.[3]

The grand jury hearing and the trial of three Spaniards—Jose (Pepe) Hilario Casares, Felix Barbeito, and Jose (Couro) Morando—on charges of murder and piracy, were held in a special session of the U.S. Circuit Court, in the hall of the House of Delegates at the capitol, July 10–19, 1827. U.S. Supreme Court chief justice John Marshall presided.[4] The hall decorated in "black drapery" contributed to the solemnity of the occasion. An overflowing crowd, including the "general press," attended.[5]

True bills were returned by the grand jury on July 12 containing five indictments. Number one stated two counts of piracy, the accused having acted against the "Law of Nations" and against an "Act of Congress" of

Public Executions in Richmond, Virginia

May 15, 1820. Numbers two through five referred to the murders of Henry Brightman, ship captain, and crewmen Asa Bicknell, Oliver Potter, and Joseph Dolliver aboard the American owned brig *Crawford*. U.S. district attorney Robert Stanard prosecuted the case; Benjamin Watkins Leigh, noted codifier and later a U.S. senator, and Gustavus Schmidt, a Swedish native practicing law in Richmond, served as defense counsel.

The actual trial proceedings for piracy began only on July 16. Each defendant was tried separately and received a verdict during a single day, the trials occurring July 16–18. The court granted a defense motion that the jury be "*de medietate linguae*," to consist of "an equal number of aliens and civilians." One of the ten witnesses (most of whom came from New York City), Adolphus Crozet, "Professor of the French and Spanish languages," acted as interpreter.[6] The testimony at the trial completely revealed the sordid details of the case.

The brigantine *Crawford*, commanded by Captain Brightman, having arrived at Matanzes, Cuba, from Providence, Rhode Island, discharged a cargo and took on board molasses, rum, and sugar to be delivered at New York City. While in port, eight passengers boarded: Ferdinand Ginoulhiac, Alexander Tardy, Felix Barbeito, Jose Hilario Casares, Jose Morando, Norman Robinson (part owner of the vessel), an unnamed American, and an unnamed Irish carpenter. Among the crew, besides those mentioned who were murdered, were Nathaniel P. Deane, Stephen Gibbs ("a colored man, who was a cook"), and Edmund Dodson, the mate. Felix carried aboard a "small iron box" containing $17,000 in coins, which was hidden under the bed of the captain in case the ship should be searched. It was illegal to export specie from Cuba.

Alexander Tardy, fifty-seven years old and "the master spirit," who instigated the ensuing atrocities, had been a wanderer and a failure in business. A native of the island of St. Domingo, he went to the United States, served some time at sea as a steward, and subsequently, in Boston, was an assistant to a German dentist. After being confined for three years at the Massachusetts state prison for pickpocketing, he "executed many a deed of the darkest villany." He "seemed to be possessed with the most invincible hatred against the Americans." On the way to Charleston, aboard a schooner, "after poisoning the passengers," he charged the cook with the crime. The cook, "who was a black man," was "tried, convicted and executed" at Charleston. Soon having misadventures in Charleston, Tardy fled northward. In Boston he was recognized "and chose to retreat." Posing as a physician, as Doctor Tardy, he "again resorted to poison."

5. "Sleep in Alien Dust"

Aboard a schooner headed for Philadelphia, "everyone in the cabin was taken sick except Tardy," who declared that the affected passengers had taken poison. Tardy applied his medicines and a German passenger died "and was committed to the deep. Tardy accused a black man, the steward, of having administered the poison. Tardy, however, aroused suspicion to ward himself by pushing for conviction of the steward and demanding the property of the deceased German passenger. As a result, Tardy himself was convicted of the poisoning and spent seven years at hard labor at the Walnut Street prison in Philadelphia. Afterwards, getting into further trouble at Charleston, he headed for Cuba. On the fatal cruise of the *Crawford*, Tardy had full "ascendancy" over the three Spanish passengers.[7]

The return trip of the *Crawford* began on May 28. Three days out, after breakfast the passengers complained of being ill, except for Tardy and the three Spaniards. Tardy had poisoned the food, but not enough so as to be lethal. The three Spaniards, now the cohorts of the erstwhile doctor, each armed themselves with "a long sharp-pointed knife" and two muskets and went about butchering everyone aboard, except the mate (the only one who knew how to navigate the ship), the cook, and a passenger who managed to hide himself. Tardy drew up a false set of papers for the ship, throwing overboard the real documents; the vessel now had a phony Spanish registration, and the home port was listed as Havana and the destination as Hamburg.[8]

Unfortunately for Tardy and the Spaniards, the *Crawford* had been provisioned only for New York. The pirates took the ship into Chesapeake Bay, seeking a place to restock the vessel. At Old Point Comfort, they anchored about a hundred yards from shore. Tardy had a lifeboat lowered which was expected to be rowed to Norfolk to obtain supplies. The mate of the *Crawford*, Edmund Dodson, was allowed to be lowered alone in the small boat, primarily to pump out the water in it and to take the boat to the other side of the ship. In so doing he quickly took off for the shore, where he informed the authorities of what had transpired aboard the *Crawford*. Seeing the ship's mate ashore, Tardy went into the cabin, and, "giving up every thing for lost," committed suicide by cutting his throat from ear to ear.[9]

The three Spaniards escaped to shore, going to Hampton and crossing from there the eight-mile-wide James River in a small canoe towards Newport News. Then heading inland, they were pursued for twenty miles by a four-man posse. On June 14, overtaking the fugitives seated by the roadside, the pursuers drew their pistols. Felix and Couro "fell to their knees,"

Public Executions in Richmond, Virginia

Murder aboard the Brig *Crawford* (from *Highwaymen and Pirates' Own Book*, comp. Henry K. Brooke [Philadelphia, 1848]).

while Pepe "leaped a fence" and fled. After a chase of about two hundred yards, the exhausted Pepe sat down on the ground and was captured. The three Spaniards were then bound together and hauled on a cart into Hampton. From there, they were dispatched upriver, arriving in Richmond on June 14.[10]

In the trials, the jury took only several minutes to convict each of the prisoners. Allowed to be heard, Felix and Pepe presented a paper to the court (signed with an X) proclaiming their innocence and placing all the blame on Alexander Tardy, "who was not a man, but a demon, and he alone, with his medicines, was capable of killing even a hundred men." The prisoners asked that sentence be delayed until depositions from their friends in Cuba could be obtained to attest to their good character. Chief Justice John Marshall denied postponement, saying that it was "his duty to execute the laws" and that they did not permit him to comply with the prisoners' request. Marshall then pronounced sentence of death and fixed the executions for August 17, 1827.[11]

The day appointed for the triple executions found Richmonders in a holiday mood.[12] About 11:00 A.M. of August 17, several thousand people

5. "Sleep in Alien Dust"

gathered at the Henrico County jail, on 22nd Street between Cary and Main streets, when the prisoners exited onto a cart amidst companies of the Richmond Blues and Artillery and the Public Guard. The condemned men, "clad in purple gowns with hoods covering their heads and faces," were seated on their coffins. The grand parade moved slowly for a mile along nearly the whole length of Main Street, eventually arriving at the gallows, which had been erected in the valley northeast of the penitentiary. The area, surrounded by hills, gave the appearance of "a spacious amphitheatre."

At the gallows, the prisoners were led up a narrow flight of steps to the platform. The gallows, "a novel construction," consisted of two perpendicular posts connected by a horizontal bar at the top, onto which were attached "three strong staples about three feet apart." To the staples the ropes around the necks of the condemned were attached. The platform on which they stood opened downwards, "after the fashion of a folding door," which would "leave them all suspended at once."

Three clergymen of different faiths attended the condemned. These devotions certainly seem to be the city of Richmond's first ecumenical service. The Rev. Thomas Hore, a Catholic priest, spent some time conferring and praying with the three Spaniards. Hore had come to Richmond two years before to set up a chapel on Marshall Street between Third and Fourth streets.[13] Dr. Lemosey and "several gentlemen" who spoke Spanish were allowed on the platform to serve as interpreters. The three Spaniards "were deeply affected at the awful fate" that awaited them "but seemed prepared to meet it with firmness and resignation." Pepe was the "most agitated." He "exposed his face to the crowd more, said more, and prayed with more gesture and apparent despair." Felix and Couro "seemed more tranquil, but were evidently labouring under deep emotions." Pepe was "illiterate, and seemed to follow the example of his comrades in his devotional exercises. They prayed, alternately, kneeling and standing" and holding hands. The devotions concluded and the priest sprinkled them with holy water. After some conversation, Dr. Lemosey, acting as interpreter, announced to the crowd that the condemned men acknowledged their guilt and that they deserved punishment, "but they asked forgiveness of the people, and begged that they would unite with them in prayer for their salvation." Dr. Lemosey then said that the condemned men requested that their bodies be interred and unmolested. With the platform party descending the steps, "several members of the gospel went up." The Rev. John Kerr, pastor of the First Baptist Church, delivered "an eloquent address."

This was followed by the Rev. Stephen Taylor "of the Shockoe Presbyterian church with an appropriate prayer." During this time "the prisoners continued on their knees at prayer."

The two preachers then left the platform, and the deputy marshal and his assistants immediately ascended it. The ropes which all the time had been around the necks of the condemned now were fastened to the staples above. This accomplished, these officers descended. The dreadful moment had arrived: "The breathless suspense of the immense multitude, the supplicating attitude and audible prayers of three human beings standing on the brink of eternity, gave to the scene an awful solemnity."

One of the officers suddenly pulled away the prop which held the door of the platform. The bodies "fell so precipately" that the ropes suspending Pepe and Couro broke, and "they fell prostrate on the ground, where they struggled for a few seconds apparently in great agony." Pepe rose up, and "threw himself in an attitude of supplication to Heaven." Couro stayed on the ground, where "after a few convulsive struggles, he appeared to be lifeless." Felix, "being lighter than either of the others, remained suspended, and breathed his last in a few seconds." The deputy marshal had the platform raised again. "The legs of Felix were placed upon it, his body remaining suspended, and to every appearance lifeless."

Pepe then was led back up the steps. He "mounted them with apparent strength and steadiness and, placing himself under the staple, which he had been before fastened, threw himself again in the attitude of supplication and awaited his fate with extraordinary composure and resignation." The hood remained over Pepe's face all the while "so that his countenance could not be seen." Couro had to be carried up the steps. He seemed to be lifeless, "until put upon his feet, and the rope again fastened to the staple"; he "remained firm." The ropes "were so tied as to leave them but a short space to fall." When the door of the platform again suddenly lowered, the three men were suspended, and "after a few convulsive struggles, their sufferings were at an end."

The accident in the hanging greatly affected the attitude of the crowd. Many of them had arrived at the scene quite earlier than the event, in a reveling temper. There were "young parents, babies, children, old men and cackling hags/ Quarreling and laughing, eating lunch from paper bags."[14] The accident produced "one general burst of feeling and commiseration. Many shed copious tears of sympathy." Some felt that accomplices had come to free the prisoners and fled the scene. None of the officials conducting the hanging faced censure. They had carefully selected the

5. "Sleep in Alien Dust"

ropes and tested their strength at 470 pounds; special attention had been given to the construction of the gallows. The bodies were suspended for a little less than an hour, and then were buried in coffins in a single grave on a hill near the Penitentiary. Thus, as the poet tells us,

> The tragic play was ended, the audience, tired and spent,
> Straggled from the hillside where the weeds were bent
> And littered and trampled. The soldiers marched away.
> The seventeenth of August had been a gala day.
>
> ....
>
> Edmund Dobson, did you watch
> There on the grassy slope,
> The pirates with their hands tight-bound,
> Hanging from a rope?
>
> Remembering how your shipmates begged
> For mercy all in vain
> Aloft amid the rigging while
> Their blood dropped down like rain;
>
> Tardy, face down in the sand,
> Would far rather rest
> Embracing on the ocean floor
> A sunken treasure chest.
>
> Pepe, Couro and Don Felix
> Emptied of their lust,
> Sheltered in a bitter haven,
> Sleep in alien dust.
>
> Captain Brightman, Asa Bicknell,
> Nathan Deane and Potter,
> Do you rest more surely now,
> Floating in the water?
>
> Pale green sunshine filters down
> To your twilight zones.
> Enormous Pulses of the tides
> Cradle your clean bones.[15]

The fateful tale of that multiple hanging day in August 1827 yet had a coda. Only a few hours after burial, the corpses of the executed men were disinterred and removed to the armory, where Dr. Cullen and "other medical gentlemen attempted galvanic experiments upon one or more of them." It was believed back then that electrical shocks could in some instances restore life. The reason given that the electrical experiment did not succeed was because too much time had expired after the executions. The bodies were returned to their single grave.

If Richmond's hanging of the three pirates seemed like a spectacular public show that could not be surpassed, there was a reminder that such events could be staged bigger and better in northern climes. Exactly two weeks after the Richmond pirate hangings, people streamed into Albany, New York, to witness a hanging. All avenues into the city were thronged with vehicles; steamboats and ferry boats, bringing eager spectators from afar, clogged the waterfront. Thirteen military companies from neighboring towns appeared. In all, some 30,000 people attended the execution.[16]

6

"Hideous Curiosity"
1828–1851

The quarter-century between the sensational trials and executions of the pirates in 1827 and Jane and John Williams in 1852 was relatively quiet as to the inflicting of public capital punishment. Still, there were a half dozen hangings, which along with narrative reports of crime and punishment elsewhere was enough at least to satiate partially the public lust for blood. As before, contributing to the reduction in the number of slave executions was the substitution of transportation out of the state for the death penalty. If not executed, slaves were still capitally convicted for crimes against property and assault as well as murder. Only those actually hanged were those sentenced for murder. Further adding to replacement of the death penalty was giving out sentences for confinement to the state penitentiary; for example, instances of burglary and larceny usually resulted in five to ten years' confinement.[1]

It was also expected that capital offenders who had their death sentences commuted to prison time would be placed on penitentiary chain gangs sent to work on community projects. An act of April 7, 1858, allowed "employment of negro convicts on the public works."[2] By the time of the Civil War, the sentence of transportation had been replaced by being put "on the public works for life."[3] Conviction for a third offense of theft could bring a life sentence.[4]

One murder case and execution that particularly caught the public's attention may be designated, in the parlance of a would-be modern novelist, as "The Whorehouse Murder." The sad story had its beginning in early evening of the last Sunday in May 1830. After leaving a church service, a "negro boy" (age 20) named Daniel went to the house of Lucinda Johnson, a black woman, and, upon opening the door, discovered that "there were white men and women in the house, as well as coloured people."

Daniel "respectfully saluted them all, taking off his hat and bowing." He told Lucinda that since she had company he would come again at another time, and "took his departure for home — his master's house." Hardly had he gone beyond the gate when Trower, "a young white man, who had been crawling round the hovel like a cat, watching his motions, pounced on him, seized him by the collar, and demanded his pass and his business at the house." Another young white man, James Drummond, "hearing the fracas, ran out to the assistance of Trower."

Daniel asked of his would-be assailants, "Gentlemen, what are you doing? Have I done any thing to you?" The two young white men inquired why Daniel had come to Lucinda's house. The reply was that he had a right to visit "his own color." Drummond and Trower threatened to take Daniel to the cage (jail), and "by their language and violent conduct, irritated him, and put him in fear." Daniel then broke away and ran towards his home, his master's house, pursued nearly all the way. Once home, Daniel "proceeded to do his usual duty—among other things to clean his young master's shoes. When going into a closet for the shoes, Daniel found a gun, which he well knew how to use, having "attended his young master on hunting expeditions." It occurred to Daniel, "while his blood was up, to return to Lucinda Johnson's house, and show the white men who had abused him that he could shoot as well as they." Daniel loaded the gun and, mounting one of his master's horses, rode to Lucinda's house. Trower came to the door, and, after briefly speaking with him, Daniel, eager to show Trower that "he had him in his power, than to injure him," turned the gun aside and fired at random.

The night was "pitchy dark." Drummond, who had also come up to the house unobserved by Daniel, "received the whole contents of the charge in his head, which killed him instantly." Daniel returned home, and went to bed, not knowing he had injured anyone. The next morning, after his usual shopping at the market, he was arrested.[5]

Daniel's five-day trial, concluding on June 12, 1830, was held before the Richmond hustings court, with a verdict of sentence of death. The courtroom had been "crowded each day with spectators, and the gallery filled with hundreds of blacks." Rumors "implicating a person of respectable standing" were proven "wholly false." A week after the trial, Daniel made a confession from his jail cell that he was the murderer of James Drummond.[6]

The *Daily Richmond Whig* twice reported Daniel's hanging (Saturday, July 31, and Monday, August 2), which occurred on Friday, July 30. The

6. "Hideous Curiosity"

announcements noted that Daniel, "a black slave," had been executed "for the murder of James Drummond, a young white man, at a house of ill fame, in this city." The gallows had been erected in the vicinity of the city's usual execution spot, "at the Powder Magazine, near the Poor House." Daniel "met his fate in a very becoming manner." He "expressed much gratitude for the kindness he had received from his master and mistress, the counsel who defended him, and the officers who had charge of him."[7]

Every now and then in Virginia's past a good murder mystery turns up, one for which there is a logical suspect but who, from adherence to technicalities of the law, remained a free man. Thus is the apparent suicide but actually murder that came to the attention of the city's authorities in November 1830.

One Sunday morning in November 1830 the body of one Reid was found hanging from a branch of a dogwood tree in "a dark and lonely ravine." The death was considered a suicide. But then, several weeks after the discovery of the body, a sailor by the name of Simkins went to the Richmond authorities and purportedly told of the event that had taken place. According to Simkins, who apparently had his information on hearsay, four men, all nautically connected, met at the house of one Ainsworth in Richmond. These persons were identified by newspaper accounts only as Reid, the Swede, a Pilot from Hampton, and Ainsworth. According to Simkins' account, Reid "was struck on the back of the neck with a poker, by the Swede, which brought him on his face," and then the three others participated in choking Reid until he died. The body was hidden under Ainsworth's house until a few days later when it was removed on horseback to the dogwood tree where it was ultimately discovered. Simkins' "loose and rambling" tale left judges at the inquest doubtful of its authenticity, except for one point of corroboration, which regarded Simkins' saying that in "getting the dead body over a fence, they let it fall, the head touching the ground first"; dirt was found on the head of the hanging corpse. An arrest warrant went out for Ainsworth, and he was eventually apprehended. A search for "essential proof," including a thorough investigation of Ainsworth's house, and the offering of a large reward yielded no incriminating evidence, and Ainsworth was discharged from custody.[8] The case was never solved.

No hangings occurred in the city between 1830 and 1837. On December 1 of the latter year, Frank, the property of James Pollard of King William County, was executed for the murder of Michael Daddy in October.[9]

Description of the event is lacking; undoubtedly the location was Richmond's usual death site.

Richmonders in 1845 were enthralled with a reporter's narrative of a homicide and its punishment, aptly titled in the newspapers as "Murder in the Penitentiary." Moses Johnson, a free black who as a prisoner in the penitentiary worked as a cooper, was charged regarding a September 9, 1845, incident with "rebellion in the Penitentiary" and for the murder of Felix Ferguson, an assistant keeper and turnkey at the penitentiary.

On September 29, 1845, a grand jury for the Circuit Superior Court of Henrico County and City of Richmond, meeting in a special term, returned an indictment against Johnson. The trial immediately proceeded in the afternoon and went into the next day. "The prisoner was brought into Court in custody of the keeper of the Penitentiary, Col. Charles S. Morgan, guarded with a file of soldiers from the Public Guard, and accompanied by six of the convicts of the Penitentiary as witnesses." John S. Caskie served as counsel for the commonwealth, and Thomas P. August for the prisoner. After seven peremptory challenges, a jury was chosen from a pool of twenty-four persons.

Philip McLeod, a convict, provided the most substantial testimony. McLeod testified that he was in the prison workshop on Tuesday, September 9, working on a safe near where Ferguson sat at his desk "making some calculations on a small slate." Suddenly Johnson appeared and attacked Ferguson with a knife. Immediately Ferguson jumped up from his seat, the "blood spouting from his neck, and ran forward," shouting, "Who did it?" A response came: "The negro Johnson did it." Meanwhile, the witness, McLeod, grabbed the wound in Ferguson's neck tightly in an attempt to stop the blood flow; but both men fell out the door, whereupon the wounded man was carried to the front gate, where he died. McLeod and several other prisoners went to Johnson's work station, where they secured him until guards arrived.

Asked why he killed Ferguson, Johnson said that the deceased had tried to kill him. Other witnesses at the trial had much the same to say, and most referred to Johnson's having recently been punished by a whipping by the guards, probably at the instigation of Ferguson. Apparently Ferguson had been the immediate supervisor over Johnson. Ferguson had been insisting that Johnson make six barrels a day, one above his usual output. Johnson was so infuriated that he "walked about doing nothing, and said he was not going to make another barrel in the shop for any one, white or black."

6. "Hideous Curiosity"

The jury, in a matter of only a few minutes, found Johnson guilty. The court then ordered Johnson to be taken from the penitentiary on Friday, December 19, and delivered to the sheriff of Henrico County, "who is then to take him to a convenient place of execution, and to hang him by the neck until he is dead." Had Johnson been a white man and possibly also of some standing in the social hierarchy, he probably would not have received a death sentence for a crime committed in the heat of passion and with some provocation. As it was, however, Johnson's past did not work in his favor, his having entered the prison in January 1843 under a ninety-year sentence for burglary and larceny of the home of one of the city's most prominent citizens, John Dooley.[10]

Since the murder drama had played out in the penitentiary, it was decided to stage Moses Johnson's execution in the prison yard.[11] As a preface to the occasion, "a very solemn scene" transpired with all the convicts "assembled in the large workshop of the prison for religious exercises." Also attending were the State Guard ("under arms"), the "Sheriff's Officers, and a few spectators." After the singing of a hymn, the Rev. Moses D. Hoge, minister of the Second Presbyterian Church,[12] "led in an address to the Throne of Grace, which he closed by fervent petitions in behalf of the unhappy man." Next the Rev. Dr. William S. Plumer, pastor of the First Presbyterian Church,[13] gave "an impressive discourse" on Psalms 51:1 and concluded by speaking directly to the prisoner "in a very solemn and affectionate manner." After another hymn, "the convicts, with the guard, withdrew to the place of execution." The two ministers conversed with and prayed with the prisoner. "At last, the appointed moment arrived; the Sheriff entered, the fatal cord was adjusted," and the prisoner was placed on a cart, which was moved to a position under the gallows. Johnson expressed "very little emotion. When the cart moved away from under him, "he hung quivering for a few minutes." The *Richmond Enquirer* had a sharp commentary:

> We are more than ever convinced of the propriety of making these capital punishments private. Not a great number was admitted, but ... even before the poor wretch was taken down from the gallows, among the convicts, who stood in the galleries of the buildings, as well among the rabble who were looking through the front gate, some were seen talking and laughing in the most indecent manner.
>
> The law which condemns the murderer to the gallows is a righteous one, but we believe a deeper impression is made, by simply announcing throughout the community the *awful fact*, that at such an hour and minute, a fellow being *is to die*, than when a promiscuous crowd is admitted, to glut

their hideous curiosity for a time, and then to go away hardened, and more reckless than when they came.

An axe murderer was hanged at Richmond's "usual place of execution" on March 27, 1846. Moses Henry, a slave, had been convicted of inflicting "mortal wounds" on Delila Fisher on January 9, 1846. The trial on January 20, 1846, awarded the slave owner $531.25 and the defense counsel $20. Further details are missing from the public record.[14]

On November 1, 1847, a Henrico County court of oyer and terminer convicted Giles, a slave belonging to Bernard Peyton, for the murder of his overseer, Thomas B. Goodman. The crime took place at the Peyton farm on the James River. The court rendered a verdict of guilty and ordered the county sheriff or one of his deputies to see that a gallows was erected in the proximity of the city's execution site and to hang the prisoner of Friday, December 10.[15] At the gallows, "a promiscuous assemblage of persons, variously estimated from five to ten thousand were present to witness the awful scene." A reporter's somewhat jaundiced opinion described the condemned man: he "was a remarkably stout, athletic man, apparently about 20 years of age, very black, large head, and broad, heavy features—his appearance indicating but little intelligence, and a sullen disposition."

After "two intelligent Clergymen" each gave an "appropriate address," the prisoner's shackles were removed, and he was allowed to speak to the crowd. Surprisingly, the culprit showed "by his language, and general manner of address, that he was a fellow of more than ordinary intelligence, notwithstanding his unintellectual African countenance." In looking at the crowd, "he would occasionally catch the eye of some of his acquaintances, and speak and nod to them with a smirking smile." The speech was "very bold and energetic" and of a religious bent, "warning his fellow servants to shun his career of wickedness, and exhorting them to prepare to meet their God."

Exactly at noon, Giles stood on a coffin in a cart, staying calm and erect while the rope was adjusted around his neck. Upon the prisoner's giving "his attendants a hearty and cheerful farewell," the cart was driven from under him. In five minutes his body ceased any movement. As a final comment, a reporter stated, "The coarse black gallows, the rude black coffin, the sable shroud, with the hood drawn over his face, all together presented a most solemn and awful scene."[16]

A slave by the name of King was convicted in a Henrico court of oyer and terminer on March 6, 1848, for the murder of another slave. He was hanged on May 12, 1848, at a gallows erected at the Richmond execution

6. "Hideous Curiosity"

site, "near the grave yard of coloured persons in the vicinity of the City Poor House." Deputy sheriff Thomas W. Doswell had charge of the execution.[17]

Press coverage of the more prominent executions nationwide continued to attract Richmonders. A nearby example was at the Chesterfield County courthouse, twenty miles from Richmond, where, on July 16, 1830, a soldier by the surname of Wheeler went to the gallows. He had killed his sergeant at Bellona Arsenal in Chesterfield County. Wheeler had intended to murder three other soldiers, two of whom were severely wounded; the motive for the murder spree was that the victims had reported Wheeler for being drunk. Wheeler eventually confessed to the murders of thirteen others. At the hanging, the rope broke, and Wheeler was strung up.[18] Nat Turner's execution and that of cohorts on Friday, November 18, 1831, in Jerusalem, Southampton County were also duly reported.[19]

Sensational reports came in from elsewhere in the United States. For example, Richmonders learned of the July 2, 1830, hanging (for mail robbery) of James Porter before 50,000 spectators in Philadelphia. Despite security provided by all of the city's police, a troop of cavalry, and marines from the navy yard, a "tremendous rush" towards the gallows resulted from a panic caused by the screams of women and girls. Many women had infants in their arms.[20] In August 1835, Richmonders read about the vigilante lynching of twelve blacks and five whites at Vicksburg, Mississippi.[21] At least Richmond executions were not protracted with torture and gore. Such an instance in Cadiz, Spain, on January 13, 1830, came in the news in Richmond. The order for execution called for the prisoner "to be hung, dragged along the ground and quartered, and the quarters placed on hooks on the sea shore."[22]

Spectators attending a hanging in Richmond never left disappointed. In the nineteenth century no last-minute reprieves arrived. Such was not always the case elsewhere. In June 1845 Richmonders read about a situation in Iowa Territory when thousands had gathered, many coming from a great distance, to witness a hanging. "Some informality" was discovered at the last moment in the handling of the case, and the prisoner was reprieved under the gallows. The crowd was bent on hanging the prisoner anyway "for their own amusement" but was prevented from doing so by tight security. Thus the disappointed throng settled on burning "the Judge in effigy."[23]

During the antebellum period, hangings in Richmond followed a not unexpected pattern, being reserved for those impoverished and slaves. No person from the middle and upper strata of society was hanged in Richmond, although in the surrounding counties there were exceptions. Those hanged in Richmond were usually illiterate or nearly so. The Richmond of the antebellum period had a wide reputation as a bipolar society: a haughty elite versus a poor, mostly immigrant underclass. Richmond's vital statistics may not have been too dissimilar from a report given out for London in 1840. Of those arrested by the Metropolitan Police, 23,938 could neither read or write: 37,551 could read or write imperfectly; and only 8,121 could read or write well, in addition to 1,107 who had high literacy.[24]

7

"In Cold Blood"
1852

"Never, in the whole history of the city of Richmond, has an occurrence taken place within its borders, so shocking as the inhuman massacre of the Winston family on the morning of the 19th of July 1852." So declared a specially issued pamphlet of 1852, "and never has any event excited more feeling and interest in a whole community."[1] To Richmonders, "the awful revelation that there were in their midst fiends capable of intruding into the sleeping chamber, and there in silence and in cold blood, slaying a whole family while asleep" was "a fact terrible for contemplation." That "murder will out" is revealed in the printed record.

The crime narrative begins with a description of the horrid intrusion upon the tranquil household of Joseph P. Winston, an esteemed partner in the firm of Nace & Winston, commission merchants. Winston resided with his wife (Virginia B. Winston), their nine month old daughter, and four servants at the northern end of Seventh Street, near "City Spring." The household slaves were John and his wife, Jane Williams, Nelly (the cook), and Anna, who several days before the crime had run away (temporarily).

At about 5:00 A.M. on July 19, 1852, "Mr. and Mrs. Winston, and their child, were all found in their bed, weltering in their blood and butchered in the most horrid manner." When discovered, Mrs. Winston was in the throes of death and Mr. Winston "writhing with pains of his wound." Mrs. Winston had about a half-dozen deep gashes on her face and head; Mr. Winston sustained three major cuts on the top and back of his head. The injuries appeared to have been inflicted with an axe or heavy hatchet. It seemed that the baby had been killed by having her head dashed against the wall or from blows of "some heavy and blunt instrument."

The Winstons had planned to leave the morning of the murders for a northern visit. Mr. Winston had a large amount of money on him, which was untouched, as were household items. A gold watch which had been hanging from a bedpost, however, was missing. There were no signs of forcible entry into the house. Jane, the "house-maid and nurse," who slept in the kitchen with her child of about three years old, claimed to be the first person to discover the mutilated victims. Strangely, she informed Nelly only matter of factly on the fatal morning that "she believed the white folks were dead — she couldn't wake 'em." Nelly ran out into the street and gave the alarm. A hatchet, recently washed and with blood on the handle, was found concealed in the kitchen.

Unlike his wife and child, Joseph Winston lived. For several days he was in a "state of stupefaction" from his wounds and could not utter anything. It was assumed that the household servants were at least material witnesses. All three who were present were whisked away to jail. On the same day the crimes were committed, the Richmond coroner, R.T. Wicker, impaneled a jury and began to take testimony at the Winston home. Numerous witnesses, mostly neighbors, testified. Physicians James Bolton, T.J. Deane, and James Beale evaluated the wounds of each victim.

Jane was soon called to the stand. She said she had been in bed all night, since 10:00 P.M. Jane said she heard loud breathing about 5:00 A.M. that sounded like snoring from the Winstons' bedroom. Going into the room, she "turned the cover down." In taking the baby up, "she felt so limber that I thought she must be dead. I laid her in the cradle, pushed the blind open and saw the bed bloody. I ran down stairs, called Nelly and told her I believed every body in the house was dead. — That was all I saw and know."

Jane explained the blood on the hatchet was from having used it to cut some beef to make soup. As to a "striped dress with blood on it found in her room in the upper story of the kitchen," she said it was the dress she had on when she discovered the bodies and picked up the dead child to put her in the cradle. Jane was interrogated about her activities the day preceding the crimes, with this testimony differing from much of what witnesses said on the subject. Nelly claimed that there "always seemed to be some difficulty between Mrs. Winston and Jane and her husband." John Williams claimed that he had been in his bed all night until dawn; he was awakened by his wife to announce the tragedy. Jane Williams' little daughter was examined, "but nothing of materiality could be obtained from her," she being "too young to understand the questions fully."

There appears to have been some bad blood between Jane Williams

7. "In Cold Blood"

and one of the two other house servants, Anna. Returning home in time to testify at the inquest, Anna, although not outright accusing Jane or her husband, did cast aspersions on them. Anna said that Jane was mad at Joseph Winston because he threatened to sell her without her child. After the examination before the coroner's jury, Jane and her husband, John, were remanded to jail to await trial.

After a few days in jail Jane was visited by her white pastor, the Rev. Robert Ryland of the First African Baptist Church. The all-black congregation, organized in 1842, had obtained its own building, at College and Broad streets, when it separated from the First Baptist Church at Twelfth and Broad streets. The Rev. Ryland, also at the time the president of Richmond College (later the University of Richmond), was very much liked by his black congregation. Ryland had a "plain, instructive, and practical" style of preaching and was viewed as having the best interests of the black church members in mind. From 1841 to 1865 (when he left the church) he baptized 3,832 persons.[2] Ryland asked Jane, a member of his church, "to make peace with God, as she would undoubtedly be hung." This prompted Jane to confess to the Winston killings and the wounding of Mr. Winston; she stated that she acted alone. Jane completely denied any complicity by her husband, saying that he was asleep at the time of the crimes.

The next day, in a more detailed confession to the jailer, Jane mentioned as a motive that she had been "ill-treated by Mr. and Mrs. Winston, and had been brooding over her bloody revenge for some time." In an aside, the writer of the published crime narrative noted that all the "negroes" in the Winston household "were the most indulged in the city of Richmond." Mr. Winston, "to promote the happiness of John and his wife," had purchased him in South Carolina, "where he had been sold to traders, and brought him back to Virginia." The kindness of the Winstons had been repaid by "murderous conduct": "Inhumanly butchering those who had been kind and forgiving to them, and crushing the skull of their innocent child, so that the Physician said, that when he pressed the head to discover its injuries, he heard the broken pieces of bone grating against each other."

On Monday, August 9, Jane Williams was led before the Richmond hustings court, with seven judges attending. Long before the beginning of the trial, the courtroom was packed with spectators: "A deep and painful excitement pervaded the entire assembly." Jane was visibly fearful that she might be taken out and lynched. She pleaded guilty to the charge of killing

Public Executions in Richmond, Virginia

Mrs. Winston. Without calling any witnesses, the court considered Jane's confession ample proof of guilt and sentenced her to be hanged on Friday, September 10, between 10:00 A.M. and 2:00 P.M. Jane's value as a slave was fixed at $500. The charge of killing the infant child was continued for trial until the term of the next court.

The court that tried Jane Williams, despite her insistent denial that her husband, John, had been an accomplice, set the following Thursday, August 12, for a mayor's court to examine him to decide whether he should be arraigned for trial as a participant in the Winston murders.

Meanwhile, Jane awaited her fate. She was described in the court testimony as "a yellow woman of ordinary size, apparently 35 or 40 years of age, hair nearly straight, and with features indicative of great firmness." A gallows of about eighteen feet high had just been built at "the usual place of execution" for the purpose of hanging teen-ager Jordan Hatcher, whose sentence was commuted (see chapter 8). The gallows, as others before it, adjoined the "colored" cemetery and was close to the powder magazine and the almshouse. Local newspapers hyped the impending execution. The *Richmond Republican* observed that hundreds of "negro eyes" would witness the event, and "if Jane Williams, a woman, can stand to be hung they can."[3]

About 9:00 A.M. of September 10, 1852, the Rev. Dr. Ryland of the African Church entered the cell of Jane Williams and proceeded to offer her "practical religious advice in reference to preparation for death." At 10:00 A.M. "she was taken from the jail in an open four-horse wagon, her minister at her side." Dressed in "a snow white shroud," she was guarded by the city sergeant and his deputy, constables, and a detachment of night police. An "immense concourse of people surrounded the procession." The wagon halted under the scaffold. The Rev. Ryland then addressed the crowd of over six thousand persons of "all sexes, colors, and ages." After administering some of "the consolations of religion" to Jane, Ryland had the audacity to say that if she had three lives, "all should be taken to pay the penalty of her wicked and bloody deeds." Ryland then offered an impassioned prayer on Jane's behalf. Jane continued to kneel after the prayer had concluded. Ryland asked her if any one else had participated in the crimes. Her calm reply was a firm "no one."

The halter was then placed around her neck and "adjusted" to the crossbeam of the gallows. Jane aided in arranging the rope about her neck and also "the bandage across her eyes and the white hood which covered her face." The deputy city sergeant then secured her hands behind her

7. "In Cold Blood"

back and placed her on a chair, which was being used to provide a greater drop to insure her neck broke.

At 10:46 A.M., a signal was given and the horses gently moved off. Jane "gradually leaned to the rope, in order to be dragged off her footing, and the knot being pulled around the neck when suspended."[4] After a fall of about twenty inches, Jane was left hanging a few feet from the ground. The knot of the noose had slipped to the back of her neck, so she probably died of strangulation, although the examining physician, Dr. Haskins, asserted that the fall broke her neck. She had kicked convulsively for several minutes. At 11:17 A.M. she was cut down, and immediately the body was interred in a grave near the scaffold.[5]

Newspaper comment was unrelenting in picturing Jane Williams as a horrid villain. The *Enquirer* and the *Dispatch* both commented that "it is to be hoped that her merited and summary execution will operate as a warning to the fractious portion of our negro population."[6] The *Republican* was more charitable: "Never have we beheld such iron-willed determination, such dogged indifference, and indomitable animal courage" from the time of Jane's arrest to her execution.[7]

It was revealed after the execution that Jane Williams may well have murdered another child in the Winston family. The *Enquirer* reported on September 17 that Jane had confided in the Rev. Robert Ryland that she was the murderess of the other Winston child "some weeks" before the Winston killings in July. Jane told Ryland that she "poisoned it by administering a teaspoon of mixture for the destruction of bed bugs." The reason that she "bound the Rev. gentleman to keep the confession a secret until after her execution" was fear "that a mob would seize and destroy her."[8]

The examining court of August 12, after hearing from a number of witnesses, remanded John Williams for trial. It was hoped that Joseph Winston, who was on the mend from his wounds, could testify; but because he was not completely healed, the trial was postponed to the next term. On September 14, before a hustings court consisting of six judges, John was "brought into court in custody of the sergeant set to the bar." John was arraigned on two charges, one for killing Mrs. Winston and her child and the other "for conspiring, aiding and abetting in the murder." Since the evidence against John was vaguely circumstantial, it was decided to proceed with the conspiracy and accessory charge, it presumably not requiring hard evidence.

Contributing to conviction as much as alleged physical evidence were biases against John as a person. His somewhat unruly character as a slave was brought up several times. It was shown that he had motive and opportunity. Not least influential was John's indifferent behavior regarding news of the murders. Nelly, a Winston servant, said that John was "no more disturbed than if there had been a parcel of chickens dead in the yard for dinner."[9] On the material side, the court had presented to it as evidence a hatchet belonging to John as the murder weapon used against Mr. and Mrs. Winston. Also, since John was a skilled carpenter he was the only one in the household who could have fashioned "a wooden roller or one-hand mall [mallet]" which was found near the murder scene and used to kill the Winston baby. Pantaloons worn by John the day before the murders disappeared and were presumed to have been blood-covered. Letters found in John's room expressing a desire to escape to Liberia were put into the trial record.

On the second day of the trial, one of the two prosecuting attorneys, James Lyons, summed up the state's case. John's court-appointed lawyer, John H. Gilmer, then spoke at great length, "dwelling on those points in the testimony which he considered most telling." The other prosecuting attorney, Joseph Mayo, "closed the argument on the side of the commonwealth." The court "immediately announced their *unanimous opinion*" that John Williams was guilty. The sentence was death by hanging between the hours of 10:00 and 4:00 on Friday, October 22:

> The sentence was received with loud applause by the crowd in the court room, who had been there all day anxiously watching the progress of the trial and awaiting with feverish interest the result. Groups of excited men were gathered around the court at its close, 6 o'clock, P.M., who talked strenuously of taking John out and hanging him in advance of his allotted time; but the prisoner passed out through the crowd, in custody of the Sergeant and a guard, on his return to prison, without any violence being offered.

At 9:45 A.M., October 22, John Williams exited the city jail onto a furniture wagon, accompanied by the city sergeant, his deputy, and the jailer. A reporter commented that John's "looks had undergone much change since his conviction. Of a dark gingerbread complexion when tried and convicted, his color had changed to what might with truth be termed a mulatto. His whole appearance indicated that he had been suffering under a great distress of mind."

Three-fourths of a mile away, the death wagon arrived at the same gallows that had launched his wife into eternity. The Rev. Jeremiah B. Jeter, pastor of the First Baptist Church, climbed on to the wagon, and offered the following prayer:

7. "In Cold Blood"

[The first sentence was lost by the reporter.]
We do rejoice, blessed God, that Thou hast had mercy on Thy fallen creatures, and that Thou hast provided for them a great sacrifice, a sacrifice commensurate with the demands of the law, and with the guilt and wretchedness of man; and we do rejoice that Thou permittest us, in our extremity and guilt, to approach Thy throne. O God, we would approach Thee with broken hearts and contrite spirits; we could renounce our own works and ways and put our confidence in Thy precious promises and in the mercy and benevolence of Thy exalted Son.

"We beseech Thee to bless this man, who, this morning, under the law of this land, is to be executed. Great God, his sins are known to Thee; Thou art the searcher of hearts, and only Thou canst search the hearts of the children of men. We pray that he may heartily repent of all past sins, that he may be humbled in the dust before a high and holy God.—And permit him to trust in that mercy which has saved so many of our degenerate race, and upon which all our hopes are based. We entreat Thee to give him grace according to his need. Oh, that he may have that confidence in God, that resignation to His will, that hope in His promises, that will prove his solace in his passage into eternity.

We beseech Thee, O God, to bless this vast throng; and that we may all remember that we are travelling to the tomb, and that whether brought to the grave, by execution of the ordinary hand of death, we must soon reach it. May we remember that we are hastening to the bar of God, and may we be prepared, by Thy abounding Grace, for a place in Thy Kingdom. We ask all for and in the name of Christ, to whom be glory for ever and ever. Amen.

With the religious ceremony ended, John was asked if he had anything to say concerning the murders. Many persons in the huge crowd were "anxious to hear his confession" as well as to witness the execution.[10] The condemned man "almost inaudibly" replied: "Gentlemen, I desire to inform you that the charge alleged against me I am innocent of. I feel myself innocent of the crime." John then started to digress with other remarks, and when asked if he intended to talk only about the murders, he said no. He was then informed that he could not speak on other subjects. He "said no more."

The fatal moment, awaited by "thousands of spectators, densely crowded together ... upon the adjacent hills," had arrived. The city sergeant and his deputy tied John's hands behind him, put on a blindfold, and covered his head with a hood made of black cambric. He was then placed on a chair. The jailer adjusted the rope—which had been around John's neck since he had left the jail—both at the neck and the beam above. Now, at 10:30 A.M., the wagon moved from under the gallows, and John was left suspended in the air. The fall from the wagon did not break his neck. The "knot of the rope lodged on the back of his neck, and his struggles were somewhat violent, and continued several minutes." A reporter in his description of the execution at this point states that John wore a "black cloth dress coat and drab pantaloons" and that he was of ordinary size and about 35 years of age.

After the body had hung for about a half hour, a physician declared John Williams dead, and he was cut down. The body was placed in a "rough black coffin" and buried a few yards away.

From examination of the detailed court testimony, it appears that John Williams died an innocent man. No evidence connected him precisely to the murders. He denied vehemently that the tools belonging to him that were used in the murders and said they had been retained by him merely for his carpentry work. If John had any guilt before or during the crime, from descriptions of his character — unlike his wife, who had a self-destructive attitude — he most certainly would have fled at the first hint of detection. As it was, in the words of a reporter, "thus closed on the 22d of October, the last act in the awful tragedy which had its bloody beginning in Richmond on the morning of the 19th of July, 1852."

8

"The Mob Is Coming"
1853–1860

Despite the foreboding signs of a bloody sectional crisis on the horizon, Richmonders did not find their lives much disrupted during the fitful 1850s. The mounting tensions over current issues such as fugitive slaves and territorial expansion did not much bother Richmonders. There were no slave insurrections, as had appeared in parts of the Deep South, although at the end of the decade John Brown's raid rankled all Virginians. Surprisingly, given the public's lust for immediate revenge in several high profile murder cases, there were no lynchings, although there were close calls.

What concerned Richmonders most was the rise in crime and disorder, owing to a huge influx of poor immigrants into the city. By the end of the decade the city's population stood at one-quarter each German, Irish, African American, and native Virginian. Frederick Law Olmsted, visiting Richmond, noted a prevalence of a "labouring class of whites, among which there are many very ruffianly-looking fellows." There were also many persons of foreign origins, "generally the least valuable class; very dirty German Jews, especially, abound, and their characteristic shops (with their characteristic smells, quite as bad as in Cologne) are thickly set in the narrowest and meanest streets, which seem to be otherwise inhabited mainly by negroes." Added to this mix were rough-hewn wagon teamsters constantly coming into the city, along with "rude, insolent, and riotous" canal boatmen.[1] Although tending to retain their language and old country customs, the Germans, some of whom were definitely middle class retailers and craftsmen, settled throughout the city; the Irish favored their own ethnic conclaves, close to the tobacco and other small factories, particularly in the neighborhoods of "Oregon Hill" and "Butchertown," the latter along the southeast slope of Shockoe Hill. Interestingly, one Irish community was close to the city and county jails and not far from the city's execution site, and the other Irish residency was adjacent to the federal, and sometimes county, hanging locations.

Blacks and whites in Richmond competed not only for space but also for jobs, a factor contributing to some of the violent crimes. The city's free black population numbered 2,400. Nearly half of the total workforce was made up of slaves. Two-thirds of the slaves of working age were hired out, principally in the tobacco factories and Tredegar Iron Works. Riffraff blacks and whites gathered at "grog shops, alleyway gambling establishments, cook shops, and corner store hangouts."[2] It was believed that such spots were breeding areas for crime; many whites called for stricter regulation affecting disreputable places. One of the most explosive issues of the time, which showed what Richmond's citizens were made of and almost led to a lynching, was the Jordan Hatcher case of 1852.

Jordan Hatcher, a seventeen-year-old slave belonging to Chesterfield County widow Mrs. P.O. Godsey, hired out at the Walker and Harris tobacco company at Nineteenth and Cary streets. On the morning of February 25, 1852, Hatcher fell into a violent argument with the factory's nineteen-year-old overseer, William P. Jackson. As a stemmer, Hatcher removed mudribs from tobacco leaves. When Jackson found dirty stems on Hatcher's counter, he beat him with a cowhide thong. At first, Hatcher promised to do better, but when the whipping was renewed, Hatcher grabbed the whip and begged Jackson to stop. With Hatcher letting go, Jackson began with more intensity beating and kicking Hatcher. Picking up a nearby iron poker, Hatcher struck Jackson with it. Hatcher fled and hid out at a stable for three days before being arrested. Jackson died a day after the assault from a skull fracture and head trauma.[3]

Hatcher went on trial on March 12 in the Richmond hustings court for murder. All witnesses were slaves, and one said that Hatcher had acted in self defense. The court unanimously convicted Hatcher and sentenced him to be hanged on April 23. The case was appealed to Governor Joseph Johnson, who, having been out of town and unable to review the case, postponed execution until May 7. In March, sixty of the city's leading citizens signed a petition requesting the governor to commute Hatcher's sentence to transportation. The motive was not only humanitarian but also was out of fear of demonstrations from the black community. Those opposed to clemency were also active, twenty-eight of whom petitioned the governor, noting that "a growing spirit of insubordination amongst the negroes of the city has been manifested for several years and particu-

8. "The Mob Is Coming"

larly amongst those employed in the Tobacco Factories; who number some two or three thousand. This evil has become so great that the managers of those establishments can now rarely correct the negroes for the greatest offences, without hazarding their lives."[4] On April 22, twenty-four hours before the scheduled hanging, the governor commuted Hatcher's sentence to transportation. Hatcher was subsequently purchased by a slave trader and disappeared from history.[5]

The governor's decision incited mob action. Richmonders turned out for an "indignation" meeting at city hall. Several hundred of the attendees rushed out to the capitol grounds, and there besieged the governor's mansion. Most of the crowd were young men, 15–20 years old, chiefly apprentices who competed for jobs with hired slaves. The protestors uttered "the most hideous yells and offensive language." After throwing stones at the mansion's windows, the mob dispersed. To prevent further mob violence, the governor stationed cavalry and artillery troops to protect the governor's mansion, and Mayor William Lambert had the entire police force and night watch on alert for the same purpose.[6]

The gallows prepared for Jordan Hatcher found use later in the year for other executions. A major significance of the Jordan Hatcher case was that it set an important precedent that slaves had a legal right to resist authority.[7] The Hatcher case furthered political animosities between the parties and in the legislature, with the Whigs being accused of antislavery sentiments and the Democrats as being too protective of the slave system.[8]

One factor that may have worked for clemency for Jordan Hatcher was that two and a half weeks before his scheduled hanging, Richmond citizens had witnessed a horrid spectacle staged by the U.S. government at Richmond's "gibbeting ground." The crime, tantamount to piracy, was "murder on the high seas," involving seamen Thomas Reed and Edward Clements. Convicted by a U.S. circuit court in January, the two men were sentenced to be hanged on April 9, 1852. An appeal to the U.S. Supreme Court for a retrial failed, as did a request for clemency from President Millard Filmore. The president acted on a review of the case conducted by secretary of state Daniel Webster. The execution was rescheduled for Good Friday, April 23, the same date reserved for hanging Jordan Hatcher. The two condemned seamen awaited their fate in the Henrico County jail, still not confessing, suffering the restraints of "heavy irons and clanking chains." Comment on the revulsion of public hangings now began to appear in the press. The *Daily Dispatch* noted on April 10: "We think it would be more wise, humane and judicious, as well as in accordance with the enlightened spirit of the age to hang these criminals within the walls of the jail. We consider that public gibbeting exercises a hardening and hurtful effect."[9]

On the day of the hanging, April 23, the *Richmond Republican* advised its readers to expect a carnival atmosphere regarding the occasion: "The morbid appetite for the destruction of life, and the great anxiety manifested to witness the flow of human blood, will be partially appeased today." The condemned men "are to be carried out upon the commons and swung up by the neck like dogs, to expiate a crime of which, in our judgment, they are not guilty." The article continued:

> The execution will gratify the curiosity of the mass who will gather by the thousands to witness it; and as was once in England, it will afford a fine opportunity for "the fancies" to show their dexterity in picking pockets and performing other light jobs....
> Added to those attractions of the morning, five of the Virginia companies—the Dragoons, Blues, Greys, Caledonia Guards and Young Guards—with their fine bands of music, will act as an escort.... The whole forming a grand pageant to one of the most barbarous, inhuman, unnatural and disgusting ... that ever can disgrace an intelligent and refined people....
> If there is truth in history, public executions are demoralizing in every respect, and should be frowned down by every intelligent man and woman in the community.[10]

At 8:00 A.M. people began to gather in front of the Henrico County jail. At 9:30 A.M., with throngs of people now lining both sides of the street, the military troops, who had come by way of the side streets, arrived. A half hour later, the federal marshal and his assistants entered Thomas Reed's cell, where they found the Rev. John Teeling, vicar-general and rector of Saint Peter's Cathedral and a "coadjutor of the Catholic faith," administering "the' last solemn rites." About 11:00 A.M. the prisoners were taken from the jail and placed upon an open furniture wagon. "Over their usual clothing," the condemned men wore "long gown-shrouds, having caps attached, made of black muslin." The "mournful cortege" set out for the gallows, "which had been erected a few hundred yards in rear of the City Alms-House." The Richmond Dragoons led the trek and rode along the sides of the wagon containing the prisoners and the two priests and the carriage carrying the U.S. marshal and his deputies. The "Jailers and their Deputies also guarded the criminal van." The other military troops then fell into line in the procession. The "death-pageant" moved up Main

8. "The Mob Is Coming"

Henrico County Jail (courtesy of Valentine Richmond History Center).

Street, then to Nineteenth, up Nineteenth to Broad, up Broad to Seventeenth, then "directly to the gibbeting ground." The streets through which the procession passed "were thronged with serious and pitying crowds; the ladies, who gazed from the dwellings, in particular, upon the scene, expressing their strong emotions and natural sympathies in tears and saddened features. They viewed the living, moving hastily to the bar of God."[11]

When "the solemn train arrived," all those in the parade found "the hills, surrounding the gallows" were "covered with men, women and children, white and black, to the number of several thousand." One-half of the crowd were blacks, and there were "a great many people from the country present, judging from the number of horses and carriages in attendance." The troops "formed into a square, the infantry occupying three sides, and the cavalry the fourth, into which the criminal-van and Marshal's carriage drove." While still on the wagon, the prisoners had their irons taken off, and the halters were adjusted around their necks. They then "descended from the wagon and walked up the steps upon the traps of the scaffold as composedly as if they were entering the house of an acquaintance." Under the scaffold were the pinewood coffins.

On the scaffold the prisoners conversed with the two priests, who "read to them at length from the Catholic Liturgy," and then the prisoners said they were ready to die. They told the federal marshal that they had no further confession to make. After shaking hands with "the officers and persons upon the traps, the black caps were drawn over their heads, and their hands were manacled behind them." At this very moment, "a horse became unmanageable in the crowd, and some mischief-maker crying out 'the mob is coming,' there was a general breakage of the lines." Soldiers and spectators "seemed to have imagined that their time had come, for they tumbled over one another and ran about in the most frantic manner." As a result, "a number were knocked into the gullies and muddy waters nearby, and completely drenched and plastered with dirt." One of the Young Guards "was fished out from under the feet of the mob in woeful plight."

Order was restored, and the execution proceedings continued. The ends of the "neck-halters were then tied to a cross-beam, over their heads." The platform personnel descended the steps, and the prisoners "were left standing upon the trap-doors." The prisoners then exchanged a few words. Throughout all the proceedings neither one exhibited "the slightest dread or discomposure; indeed Reed very cooly and leisurely examined the ropes to which the traps of the gallows were attached." The prop which held up the platform was knocked away, and the prisoners fell about four feet, thus being suspended about four feet above the ground. The bodies "moved spasmodically only for about two minutes after their fall." The attending physicians said that the necks were broken instantly. After being suspended for a half hour, the bodies were lowered into the coffins, which were then "conveyed to graves, dug near the Poor-House Burying Ground." The corpses were subsequently disinterred and examined and then reburied in more "sacred" ground.

A reporter from the *Daily Dispatch* marveled, given "the immense mass of spectators in attendance," how smoothly the hanging event came off, "during the entire period of the preparation of the prisoners on the scaffold — the hanging itself — and the removal of their bodies from the gibbet." Gratitude was extended to those participants who made the occasion a success. especially to the physicians, Drs. Hancock and Pelticolas and to the federal marshal and his deputies for "courteously" providing "the details connected with this painful tragedy." Praise was extended to W.A. Powell, architect and civil engineer, and "the carpenters work executed by Captain Eppes" for their construction of the gallows, which "was entirely original and different from any ever used heretofore." The edifice "performed its work in the most humane and efficient manner — no slipping

8. "The Mob Is Coming"

or defect inflicting upon the unfortunate criminals a continued series of death-pangs."[12]

The *Richmond Republican* had a more somber last word in its April 26 issue. The hanging represented "only the lowest and most brutal principles of human nature." It served to "satiate a morbid curiosity or a debauched appetite. The occasion was like a "holiday" to the crowd: "Men, women, boys, girls and negroes swarmed to see the most horrid spectacle upon which the human eye can gaze, the spectacle of death — of violent, ignominious death. As lovers hurry to a marriage feast, did the multitude hasten to see two poor, wretched, emaciated creatures worn down with agony, confinement, chains and despair, look their last upon the blessed sun — choke, quiver, and swing helplessly between Heaven and Earth."[13]

What appears to be the only other execution in Richmond during the 1850s stands in contrast to the policy of commuting death sentences for slaves convicted in capital cases other than murder to transportation. In July 1754 the Henrico County court, in an oyer and terminer session, condemned to death a slave by the name of Washington, for arson committed on a "hay house" containing wheat, hay, and straw. The county sheriff was ordered to hang Washington on Friday, November 17, "at such place as the Sheriff may select." The execution was delayed until the governor completed a review. Executive clemency not forthcoming, Washington was hanged on December 12, 1854.[14]

Not all murderers wound up on the gallows. Jurors were quite capable of taking into account mitigating circumstances and showing compassion. A trial of a fourteen-year-old boy who had been in jail since he was twelve for the murder of a seventeen-year-old was finally held in November 1853. William Cudlipp had been charged with killing a youth, simply identified as Thomas, on Broad Street. The first trial ended with a hung jury. Convicted in the retrial, Cudlipp received a sentence of five years in prison, along with a recommendation for executive clemency.[15] Another example of leniency occurred the next year when William Hebden was sentenced to five years in the penitentiary for the murder of John R. Richards.[16]

The murder of a proprietor of a barroom hardly raised any hackles. The victim was Joseph Scott, "keeper of a low grog shop, near Mayo Bridge." He was known to have "living with him a negro woman of bad character." Allegedly, three Irishmen came into the establishment and invited Scott to join them in drinking, which he supposedly did. After several rounds, for whatever reason, one of the visitors stabbed Scott, and then all three fled across the bridge into the village of Manchester. Scott's mistress was arrested and tried as an accomplice. Despite her acknowledgment that she had hid the murder weapon under the floor of the grog shop and witnesses declaring that they had seen no Irishmen crossing the bridge, Scott's mistress was acquitted.[17] It seems that the actual perpetrators of the crime were never caught.

Unusually, an overseer, Thomas G. Smith, was acquitted in a Henrico County court for the murder of his employer, J. Royal Crouch, on November 5, 1856. Crouch had died a few days after an altercation between the men on May 18, 1856, when Smith cleaved him with a hoe. One-half of the jury voted justifiable homicide by reason of self-defense.[18] An accused murderer, George W. Johnson, avoided justice by making good his escape from jail.[19] Lucy, a slave sentenced to be hanged for killing her newborn infant, received an executive pardon.[20]

Transportation was still an option in sentencing a slave convicted of a capital crime. Thus was the case of "an old and infirm negro," a slave who pleaded guilty to second degree murder.[21] Six slaves, ordered to be hanged for assault "with intent to kill" their overseer, John H. Dodd, had their sentences commuted. Two of the criminals were sent to the penitentiary, and the other four, receiving clemency because of their youth, were resentenced to transportation.[22] By the end of the 1850s, more likely than not with the transportation policy soon to be abandoned, slaves convicted of capital crimes experienced the governor commuting their sentences, for women as well as men, "to labor on the public works for life."[23]

Although a vengeful mob mentality on occasion arose in Richmond regarding the high-profile murder cases of the 1850s, fortunately no successful vigilante action resulted. Already mentioned is the almost-lynching of Jordan Hatcher in 1852. Several other instances may also be noted. There was talk of lynching Charles Z. Abrams, a shoemaker, who was convicted of brutally murdering his wife. While beating up his wife, Abrams kicked her down the stairs, resulting in a fatal injury. Abrams cheated any assailants by hanging himself in jail.[24]

A most serious situation arose upon the arrest of Thomas J. Hardy, a free black, for the rape of nine-year-old Laura A. Bennett. The girl's father tried to shoot Hardy. In the night of June 14, 1857, while Hardy awaited trial, a Richmond mob comprising mostly boys gathered at the jail intent on lynching Hardy. It took an entire regiment of troops to disperse the large crowd. As it was, Hardy was sentenced to the penitentiary for a term of twenty-five years.[25] Talk of a lynching also occurred in August 1858 regarding Nathaniel Sutherland, a shoemaker, for the murder in "a

8. "The Mob Is Coming"

small groggery on 17th street" of Patrick Colbert, a thirty-one-year-old cripple. The victim received numerous stab wounds. At trial in October, with the jury considering some extenuating circumstances, Sutherland received a sixteen-year prison sentence.[26]

Richmonders were still fed newspaper reports of major-event executions elsewhere. A few stood out in Virginia, as did carnival-style hangings in other states, not the least being the mass hanging of four slaves in Dover, Tennessee, for "conspiracy for rebellion."[27] Amidst all the morbid interest, once in a while there was a little lighthearted diversion. For example, a report of a "Mock Execution" in Buchanan (in Botetourt County) told of hanging in effigy "on a high gallows" a local physician, Dr. Thompson. An inscription attached to the dummy corpse read: "Thompson the Quack/Seducer and Murderer."[28] A rather gruesome narrative in the press informed Richmonders of the decapitation before 20,000 spectators of a woman in Denmark for the murder of her husband.[29]

Among the spectators at hangings, within a twenty-mile radius of Richmond in neighboring counties, undoubtedly a substantial part of the crowds were from the city. Thus was probably the situation during a two-month period, April–June 1856, in Charles City County, when two, and likely three, separate hangings occurred: two slave men for murder, and possibly a slave woman sentenced to death for arson.[30]

Certainly many Richmonders did not want to miss the multiple hangings in nearby New Kent County. Three slaves convicted for the same murder — two brothers, Henry and Dick Bradley, and another slave named Major Morris — went to the gallows at the courthouse.

"A vast multitude of persons" assembled to witness the execution, and at intervals during the devotions at the scaffold, most of the crowd joined in singing the hymn, 'Hark from the Tomb.'"[31]

One nearby publicized murder case and execution held the attention of many Richmonders. Almost two years elapsed from the first trial to the time of execution. John S. Wormley, sixty years old and a wealthy farmer and lawyer of Chesterfield County, was charged with the murder of his son-in-law, Anthony T. Robiou, in summer 1851. Wormley had become angry when Robiou filed for divorce from Wormley's daughter, who was only fourteen years old when she married Robiou. The complaint had charged adultery on the part of Robiou's wife. Wormley and James Reid waylaid Robiou in the road in front of the Wormley house, at which time Wormley shot and killed Robiou.

The first trial of Wormley in October 1851 ended with a death sentence, but Reid was acquitted. Defense attorneys Samuel Taylor and Robert G. Short succeeded in having the verdict overturned on grounds that the sheriff, George W. Snelling, had taken the jury out for a round of drinks at a nearby home.

For the retrial, in January 1853, there was difficulty in sitting an impartial jury, and hence a new jury was obtained from residents of Richmond and Petersburg. These jurors also proved questionable, and finally a panel was obtained from Amelia and Dinwiddie counties. Again Wormley received the death penalty. There were appeals. At last, the execution took place, on June 24, 1853, at "Gallows Field," a quarter mile from the little Chesterfield courthouse twenty miles from Richmond.

While awaiting his fate in a tiny jail cell, Wormley unsuccessfully asked the court to allow three more links in the chains of his leg irons so that he could exercise. On execution day, more than four thousand spectators gathered at the gallows. About 10:00 A.M. three Methodist ministers entered the jail and stayed with Wormley two and a half hours. Then the condemned man was taken out and placed on a chair on a platform, where he remained for a two-hour religious ceremony that included hymns. Wormley was dressed entirely in black and wore new boots and a silk hat. After the conclusion of the devotions, he was put on a wagon and taken to the gallows, located at the end of a woods, with ample space to accommodate the large crowd. As he moved from the wagon to the cart under the gallows, Wormley affectionately bade farewell to acquaintances, saying he would meet them in heaven. With the final preparations for the hanging made, Wormley spoke for fifteen minutes. Just before he was "swung off," he said, "Lord, have mercy on my soul."[32]

As the Civil War came, Richmonders had their blood lust satiated with a stepped-up rate of public executions. Espionage and military desertion now summoned the ultimate penalty. To some extent the gallows now competed with the firing squad.

9

"To Be Shot to Death by Musketry"
1861–1865

American wars have opened avenues for the death penalty in addition to those already operative for civilians. The Civil War was certainly no exception. In the Confederate states fifteen military crimes were subject to the death penalty. As prescribed in the Articles of War, wartime crimes considered a capital offense included mutiny, desertion, giving aid and comfort to the enemy, breaking parole, and espionage (spying).[1] In Richmond and its immediate vicinity, persons sentenced by military tribunals went to their deaths, regarding special wartime crimes, only for desertion and espionage. A third category of executions in the Richmond area during the Civil War, of course, was the continuation of inflicting death on whites and blacks for premeditated murder, and for slaves, in very rare instances, for other felonies. This chapter treats primarily desertion, and the two Civil War chapters that follow concern espionage and civilian and slave crimes.

Military executions held in posts close to Richmond generally allowed for an unlimited flow of spectators; the several executions held in Richmond prisons obviously had a restricted audience. Whether carried out by firing squad or by hanging, executions were held primarily at Camp Lee (then outside the city but now almost in downtown Richmond); Chaffin's Bluff (near the site of Union spy Elizabeth Van Lew's farm and also a site of a headquarters camp), ten miles further down the James River; Castle Thunder, the military prison in the city where condemned military prisoners were held; and on one occasion the state penitentiary, at the city's then West End.

Camp Lee opened in April 1861 as a cavalry camp as well as an instruction facility for infantry—chiefly, as might be referred to in today's parlance, as a "basic training" post. About two hundred cadets from the Virginia Military Institute in Lexington had the main responsibility of training new inductees at Camp Lee in close order drill and the manual of arms. Confederate soldiers from northern prisons were also processed at Camp Lee.[2] Seventy-five companies of artillery were trained and equipped at this army post during 1861 and 1862. Women and girls frequently visited to bring cakes and other food to the soldiers. The site of Camp Lee was the property of the Virginia Central Agricultural Society and had been known as the Hermitage Fair Grounds and then as the New Fair Grounds.[3]

Desertion was the bane of both the Union and Confederate armies, more so among Confederate troops because they were often fighting close to home. This was especially true during the last two years of the war, the soldiers realizing that the South was losing, not to mention a myriad of other reasons, such as extreme hardships. Also, frequently soldiers left their posts to reenlist as substitutes under assumed names in different units.

By 1862 desertions in the Confederate army were rife, sometimes amounting to 10 percent of troops in service. Of the estimated 103,000 desertions from the Confederate army, only 5 percent were captured. The Confederate government and the generals realized that the military tradition of executing deserters had become necessary. Actually, the number of those executed was not large. Of 1,300 death sentences meted out by Confederate courts-martial during the war, only 229 men were executed—204 by firing squads and 25 by hanging[4] (the latter being those who had gone over to the enemy). This ratio holds true regarding executions conducted in Richmond and its close vicinity.

Persons sent to their death by military justice were convicted by general courts-martial, consisting of five to thirteen officers. Courts-martial had jurisdiction over all offenses committed by persons under military law. Members of general courts-martial were appointed by a general commanding an army in the field or by a colonel commanding a separate department. The jurisdiction applied to all military personnel, regular or militia, and also civilians on hire, including sutlers and retainers at camp. All capital sentences had to be confirmed or disapproved by the president of the Confederate states.[5]

The provost marshal had the responsibility of carrying out orders resulting from a court-martial, including the detention of condemned

9. "To Be Shot to Death by Musketry"

Castle Thunder, Confederate Prison (courtesy Library of Virginia).

prisoners and supervision of their execution. A provost marshal was not hard to single out from the troops. Instead of the grey Confederate uniform, he wore a black suit, a loose black shirt with white collar, and trousers buckled at the knees. He had two Colt .44 pistols in black holsters, one on each side, and carried a short club, a pair of leg irons, and two sets of handcuffs.[6]

The fittingly named Castle Thunder prison in Richmond served as the receptacle of choice for detention of Confederate military prisoners awaiting execution. Capable of holding 1,400 prisoners (at least at S.R.O.— standing room only), the facility was a three-building complex of former tobacco warehouses on the north side of Cary Street between Eighteenth and Nineteenth streets. "Some of the most desperate men in the Confederacy are there," noted one Confederate army captain. Prisoners were horribly mistreated, experiencing floggings and varied tortures, such as being hung up by the thumbs. Condemned prisoners were mainly detained in two cells on the first floor of the main building; a stench arose from the latrine in the middle of the floor. A gallows stood in the "execution yard" at the back of the building.[7]

Almost all military executions at Richmond conducted by firing squad for desertion occurred at Camp Lee. Court-martial sentences calling for a soldier "to be shot to death by musketry" usually made newspaper reportage, but not always regarding the carrying out of the sentence. Since President Jefferson Davis rarely granted reprieves or commutations of sentences, it may be assumed that when there was no mention to the contrary of an execution in a newspaper it most probably took place.

Death by firing squad in the Confederate and Union armies was a gruesome spectacle — but, one might add, not quite as awful as it was back in Revolutionary War times. The difference was that during the Civil War condemned soldiers were usually shot in the chest, while in the earlier executions, members of the firing squad aimed for the head, with the result of brains being blasted out over a distance.

A typical firing squad event started with a procession to the killing field, a military band out front playing the "Funeral March" and followed by the condemned, clergy, and troop units. Coming to the fatal spot, much as in the case of hangings, soldiers formed a three-sided hollow square, with the prisoner at the open side in a kneeling position, with hands tied behind, sometimes at a post. For a single execution, a firing squad of twelve soldiers was used; if more than one person was to be executed, a maximum of twenty-four soldiers made up the firing squad. One or more weapons contained blanks. A blindfold was placed on the prisoner, and a clergyman gave final consolation. An officer, with a sword at his side, stepped up and commanded, "Ready! Aim! Fire!" The corpse was laid across a coffin. The band played a quick march as soldiers filed past the death scene and then went off the field.[8] Civilians who had been admitted as spectators headed for the entrance gate and out of camp.

The first execution by firing squad in Confederate military service was probably that of a soldier named Griffin, of the Polish brigade, on September 23, 1861. Although the exact location is unknown, the event most likely occurred in the Richmond area, as that city's newspapers reported the event without attribution.[9]

On or about July 6, 1862, John Squires went before a firing squad at Camp Lee.[10] Martin Hogan, on August 12, 1862, was taken from the Castle Godwin prison in Richmond a mile or so to the headquarters campsite of General Roswell Ripley's brigade (on Williamsburg Road at today's eastern

9. "To Be Shot to Death by Musketry"

boundary of the city). Here five musket balls pierced his heart "in the presence of his former comrades."[11]

The *Daily Dispatch,* on August 27, 1862, weighed in with a lengthy editorial critical of the Confederate army's execution of deserters, in response to the shooting of Hogan and another unnamed soldier. Although conceding an "absolute necessity of making an example" of deserters in order to deter the spread of escape from duty, as "nothing else will do," the author considered that the Confederate government was remiss in not declaring a clear policy in singling out culprits for execution. The extreme penalty operated like an ex post facto law. Since so many soldiers deserted virtually with impunity, other soldiers did not think they were "doing anything very wrong" in taking off for a while. At the time, there was no distinction between being absent without leave (AWOL) and desertion. The Confederate government, according to the author, should issue a proclamation announcing that the authorities intended "hereafter rigidly to enforce the law." Regardless of the alleged justifiability of any decision to desert, the "salvation of the country" depended upon the implementation of the death penalty for desertion: "Every man in the ranks can with perfect truth present a case full of hardships. All have been called to the service of the country at enormous sacrifices.... To place the question upon individual cases is to dissolve the army.... The rule is positive, absolute, irrefragible [*sic*]. It must be so, or there can be no army." Specifically, the writer called upon President Davis to grant general amnesty to deserters if they returned by a certain date and also to state that he would not interfere to prevent the death penalty upon conviction of a recurring offense of desertion. It was also hoped that the Confederate congress would pass a law enabling Davis to dismiss "unworthy and incompetent officers. It is they who are the really guilty parties in most cases of desertion. It is their criminal neglect of duty that occasions the entire relaxation of discipline which leads to it."[12]

Some town and country folk rose early on the morning of Saturday, October 4, 1862, in order to witness a much heralded affair, the shooting of three deserters and the whipping of a fourth at Camp Lee. Scheduled to go before a firing squad were Patrick McGowan, John Kelleher, and D.W. Rogers; Owen Maguire was to receive a flogging of fifty lashes. At 9:45 A.M. a "large omnibus of the Exchange Hotel" pulled up at Castle Thunder, escorted by the Henrico County cavalry. At 10:50 A.M. the procession entered Camp Lee, where two thousand soldiers were drawn up "in a hollow square." The omnibus carried the condemned men, the superintending officers, and a priest. At the execution site the prisoners and the priest remained some time in the vehicle. A wagon drove up nearby and deposited several pine coffins. The priest performed last rites for those about to die. The prisoners descended and walked to the place of execution. Then the clear voice of Captain George W. Alexander, assistant provost marshal of the Eastern District, rang out, reading the general orders calling for the execution of McGowan and Kelleher and the whipping of Maguire. Rogers was awarded a respite of fourteen days.

The execution of October 4, 1862, then proceeded. The two condemned men knelt down, and white bandages were placed over their eyes and their arms pinioned. The priest came up for the last time, affording final comfort. Asked if they had any last words, Kelleher remained silent; McGowan said, "Good-bye, boys." Then a shooting party of twenty-four men from the Provost Guards, commanded by Lt. Wills, lined up and pointed their firearms at the breasts of the two men. Five musket balls was sufficient to dispatch one of the victims, and three for the other. Kelleher "quivered slightly," and McGowan "struggled" a bit. After this execution Maguire received his whipping; a "stout dragoon" performed this task with a long and wide double leather strap. Interestingly, all three men punished had participated heroically in battles.[13]

Rogers never showed up for his rescheduled execution on October 18. One night he opened a window at Castle Thunder, crawled to the end of a porch used for drying tobacco, and, latching onto a wire, "swung himself to the ground by means of the iron bracket that supported the structure." A sentinel heard Rogers strike the ground and sounded the alarm. Soon "the pursuer was making tracks up Cary Street," but Rogers vanished for good.[14]

Shot to death at Camp Lee on Monday, November 3, 1862, was John F. Parke, a member of the Richmond Zouaves, 44th Virginia Regiment. He had deserted in the face of the enemy in the battle of Front Royal. While confined at Castle Thunder, Parke and two others unsuccessfully tried to escape by digging a hole from their cell.[15]

Several other executions by firing squad at Camp Lee soon followed. Daniel Kennedy was shot on January 23, 1863,[16] and Michael Kearns, also a deserter, went before a firing squad sometime around the end of January 1863.[17] One execution of a deserter stirred substantial public interest. John Mulligan went before a firing squad on January 20, 1863. His was "an aggravated case of desertion," he having been arrested three times for leaving the army. Mulligan almost escaped from Castle Thunder. His friends

9. "To Be Shot to Death by Musketry"

smuggled to him in the prison a pistol, a razor, a file, a large knife, poison, and a bottle of brandy. Mulligan had gained several reprieves, including one by the secretary of war on behalf of the president, while his case was under review.

On execution day, Mulligan rode in a hack from Castle Thunder for Camp Lee accompanied by two "spiritual advisers" and two detectives. All the 1,200 soldiers at Camp Lee, including the City Battalion, formed three sides of a square. The prisoner was brought up, and while conferring with a priest, the execution squad, selected from the President's Guard, now on the scene, had their weapons loaded. Asked if he had anything to say, Mulligan replied in the negative. The prisoner then knelt down, and a bandage was tied around his face. Upon signal by an officer, accompanied by a wave of his hand, the shooting party discharged their weapons; Mulligan fell flat on his face, struck by five balls, three through the breast and one each through the head and mouth. Troops marched by the body in slow time. The corpse was then put in a coffin and handed over to an undertaker.[18]

Army execution-shooters were again on assignment on Saturday, February 21, 1863, at Camp Lee. James Broderick, an artillerist and a deserter, after one respite went before a firing squad at 11:00 A.M. As usual, Captain George W. Alexander, assistant provost marshal, had charge of the arrangements. From Castle Thunder, the prisoner was conveyed in a hack to Camp Lee, accompanied by detective John Caphart, orderly Wiley, and "spiritual adviser," the Rev. Father A. L. McMullan of St. Peter's Church. Several hundred civilians gathered on the parade ground, where a "death spot" was marked off. Caphart put a bandage around the prisoner's eyes, and said, "Good-bye, Broderick." The condemned man then replied, "Good-bye, Caphart." The firing party, consisting of twelve men from the President's

Capt. George W. Alexander (courtesy Library of Virginia).

Guard, lined up to within ten feet of the kneeling prisoner. Broderick's last words were: "Young men, I have a last request to make of you — don't shoot me in the face." Captain Booker, assistant provost marshal of the Western District, gave the order: "Ready! Aim! Fire!" Twelve muskets flashed at once, six loaded with ball and six with blanks. All the loaded volleys struck Broderick's breast. The victim fell on his face and died almost instantly. After a few minutes the corpse was removed, and the soldiers and civilians dispersed.[19]

On June 20, 1863, deserter Charles Kelly faced a firing squad at Chaffin's Bluff. Three bullets pierced his heart, and three his head.[20] At the end of summer 1863 a mass execution by firing squad was scheduled at Camp Lee. Because of the enormity of the event, however, and with the desire to have the execution make a strong effect on the soldiery, it was decided to stage it before a whole division of the army. Thus the mass execution took place at an army camp on Poplar Run, one mile north of Montpelier in Orange County, the site of President James Madison's home.

This tragedy had its beginning in mid–August 1863 when fifteen men from companies H and K of the Third North Carolina Infantry Regiment left the camp of Lee's army at a tributary of the Rapidan River in Orange County. These deserters were among the large number of men leaving the Confederate army as it returned to Virginia from the unfortunate Gettysburg campaign. Squads of soldiers went out to secure places through which the deserters might pass. One such unit from a North Carolina regiment, commanded by Adjutant Lieutenant Richardson Mallett, was dispatched to Scottsville, Virginia, on the James River about fifty miles west of Richmond.

On August 25, the twenty-three-year-old adjutant and his detachment held post near Bowling's Landing, where it was expected deserters would appear. Mullett and his men confronted a band of deserters from the Third North Carolina Regiment. One or two deserters fired. Mullett was mortally wounded. Several deserters were killed and wounded, and a few escaped into the woods. The eleven remaining deserters surrendered. A wounded deserter and Mullett were taken to a hospital in Scottsville, Virginia, where Mullett died. The prisoners, including the wounded deserter, were sent to Richmond and lodged in the Castle Thunder prison to await court-martial for desertion and the murder of Mullett.

The trial of September 2–3, 1863, returned a verdict of guilty and a death sentence of hanging. The *Daily Dispatch* of Friday, September 4, stated that the ten deserters (the wounded man excepted) would be "hung

9. "To Be Shot to Death by Musketry"

tomorrow" at Castle Thunder. But there was an intervention. The secretary of war, James A. Sedden, acting upon President Davis' decision, ordered a change in location for the execution and further ordered that it be by firing squad. The *Richmond Examiner*, on September 4, declared that the execution "was to have taken place at Camp Lee immediately," but instead it would now occur "in the presence of the whole army of Northern Virginia," where "the condemned will be sent" to "expatiate their crimes in the midst of their brothers-in-arms, whom they so basely deserted."

Late on September 4, the prisoners arrived under guard at the army camp on Poplar Run, a mile north of former President James Madison's home. About 9:00 P.M. orders came from Richmond that all ten men were "to be shot to death by musketry" the next day, Saturday, September 5.

On that fateful day, acting adjutant Lt. McHenry Howard and the Reverend George Patterson, an Episcopal chaplain, visited the deserters in the guardhouse, where the "court-martial record" was read and Patterson heard the prisoners' confessions and helped them write letters home. At the site chosen for the execution, a group of soldiers "planted ten posts in the ground, about three feet high and about fifty feet apart, all in a line, boring a hole in each post near the top, and putting in a cross-piece." Afterwards, as Private John Casler observed, "We dug one large grave in the edge of the woods, large enough to hold the ten coffins." By 3:30 P.M. General Edward Johnson's division of four thousand men formed into a hollow square; the fourth side remained open. A column then entered the field and marched up to the execution site. First came fifers and drummers, with the drums muffled, playing the "dead march"; then came, under heavy guard, the prisoners, accompanied by the chaplain and surgeons. An officer then "took each man, conducted him to his post, placed him on his knees, with his back to the post and his arms hooked over the crosspiece, and his hands tied together in front of his body, and then blindfolded him."

One hundred and fifty men made up the execution detail. Ten men from the detail went to six feet in front of each prisoner, thereby making a hundred-man line. One-half the weapons were loaded with ball cartridges, and the other half with blanks. Behind each ten men were five more, as a reserve, to be used in completing the execution for any of the condemned men still alive. "At the command: "Ready! Aim! Fire!" one volley was heard, all the guns in the front rank being discharged. Then a surgeon stepped forward to each prisoner and felt his pulse. They found two of them not dead, when the reserve guard stepped out and fired again. When they were pronounced dead the division was marched by them in two ranks, in order that all might see them." After the troops left the scene, wagons were brought up with the coffins. Most of the victims appeared to have received at least four bullets to the breast. The bodies were then borne away for burial, with the Episcopal chaplain performing the funeral rites. As one soldier witness said, the execution "cast a gloom over the entire army, for we had never seen so many executed at one time before."[21]

Hanson M. Futch, the wounded North Carolina deserter who was condemned to die but was spared inclusion in the mass execution near Montpelier, was scheduled to face a firing squad at Camp Lee on October 2, 1863. His sentence, however, was further respited, and he died of smallpox in December 1863.[22] On January 8, 1864, E.B. Mooney was shot at Camp Lee for desertion.[23]

So far as is known only one soldier was hanged at Richmond for desertion — at Castle Thunder and not Camp Lee, the usual place for execution of deserters in the Richmond area. The case was a compounded one, involving conviction on charges of parole violation and espionage as well as desertion. Captain Spencer Deaton deserted from the Confederate army and joined the Sixth Tennessee "Renegade" Infantry of the Union army. Before the war, Deaton had worked on his father's farm at Strawberry Plains, in Jefferson County, East Tennessee. He was apprehended near Knoxville on August 27, 1863. Convicted by a court-martial convened by General Sam Jones, commandant of Confederate troops in western Virginia, Deaton was sent by the provost marshal of Knoxville to Richmond for the purpose of execution.[24]

The execution, slightly delayed while President Davis reviewed the sentence, occurred on February 19, 1864. In the afternoon of the eighteenth, workmen constructed a gallows in the prison yard of Castle Thunder.[25] Weeks before the fatal event, Deaton slipped into a state of severe depression. It was said that the only way he was kept from "dying from mental prostration" was "by a liberal daily supply of whiskey and laudanum."

"Long before the hour of execution arrived," the houses and fences adjoining the prison were "thronged with scores of people anxious to gratify that curiosity which scenes of such a character seldom fail to excite in the minds of many people," so read a newspaper report.[26] Presumably, most of Castle Thunder's eight hundred inmates were lining up to peer out the windows and doorways on to the prison yard.[27]

At noon a military detachment entered the prison yard and formed into a hollow square around the gallows. The condemned man was then

9. "To Be Shot to Death by Musketry"

escorted out of the prison, accompanied by the "venerable detective" Captain John Caphart, the Rev. J.T. Carpenter, chaplain of the prison, and Mr. Wiley, assistant executioner, the "rear being brought up by the mammoth black dog" (named Nero), a 182 pound Bavarian boar hound "so well known to the visitors of that institution." Caphart has been described as a "tottering giant," the sight of whom "made humanity sick." The condemned man, Spencer Deaton, about forty years old and six feet tall and black haired, wore a mustache and small imperial (pointed beard). He was dressed in a "dilapidated frock-coat, red, dingy homespun trousers, and tall black felt hat, such as Yankee officers usually wear." At the base of the gallows, Deaton, with his hat on, listened to the verdict of the court-martial, read "in a clear and distinct voice" by Captain Dennis Callahan, a prison official. Deaton "gazed anxiously around him, as if expecting some deliverance from his impending doom." The chaplain, the Rev. A.D. Dickinson, then "gave the signal for prayer, when all heads were uncovered, and he delivered a short but impressive invocation to God for mercy upon the unfortunate man's soul." Deaton placed his hat back on his head and "ascended with a slow and tremulous step to the platform." Detective Caphart followed and with the assistance of a "negro," proceeded to adjust the rope over the beam of the gallows and about the neck of the victim. Deaton's wrists (but not the elbows) and feet were tied. He was allowed to sit down for a while. Finally he asked Mr. Wiley to help him to stand up and hold him. Deaton "looked about him in a half unconscious state," and when a "white bag" was placed over his face, he "seemed utterly overcome with emotion, exclaiming rapidly, and in a feeble voice, 'Oh, Lord, have mercy on my soul!' Finally, he said, "I am innocent!"

Deaton was still being supported by Mr. Wiley when the trap "was knocked from under him" at 12:15 P.M. and "he was left dangling in the air." Deaton's "limbs did not quiver, and, after gyrating for some moments, the hands hung still." After the body had hung for a half hour assistant surgeon T.E. Upshur, the prison physician, pronounced him dead. The body "was taken down in the arms of two negro men and deposited in a common flat-top pine coffin, painted red, which had been placed besides the gallows." Upon further examination by Dr. Upshur it was discovered that the victim's neck had not been broken and that he died from strangulation. Besides the civilians admitted into the prison yard, "a large number of the prisoners confined in Castle Thunder" witnessed the execution. The extreme cold somewhat kept down the attendance.[28]

Although many Confederate soldiers were under sentence of death, confined at Castle Thunder in Richmond, it may be presumed that most all of these were not executed, since there appears to be no follow-up evidence to this fact. Fifteen deserters under sentence of death held at Castle Thunder in late March 1864 were given a respite until the completion of a review of their cases had been conducted by President Davis.[29] Further development was not reported. Most likely, however, a soldier from a Georgia regiment, Michael Brander, convicted in an "aggravated case of murder" and held under sentence of death at Castle Thunder, was hanged on December 23, 1864, in "the presence of the Army of Northern Virginia."[30]

With Confederate troops evacuating Richmond and vicinity on April 2–3, 1865, the two soldiers ordered to be shot at Camp Lee several days later, Friday, April 7, most likely never met that rendezvous with destiny.[31] Surely they did not depart with the fleeing soldiers nor were they executed by Union forces.

At war's end, Union troops executed some of their own men in the vicinity of Richmond. Four Federal soldiers were hanged at an Union army encampment near Petersburg, twenty or so miles from Richmond, on January 6, 1865.[32] Two weeks later, a soldier was hanged at City Point (Hopewell, Virginia, adjacent to Petersburg).[33] Thomas Jones, age 21, who deserted from the Union trenches before Richmond, was hanged February 18, 1865 (exact location not designated).[34] Twenty-year-old John Parker, who deserted from the Tenth Connecticut Infantry on Christmas Eve, 1864, from his unit near Richmond, faced a firing squad on the outskirts of Richmond on February 25, 1865.[35] Other Union soldiers executed on the outskirts of Richmond were a twenty-one-year-old Connecticut infantryman, William Cooper, who was shot March 16, 1865.[36] Frederick W. Brandt, a twenty-seven-year-old Prussian immigrant and private who deserted from a New York infantry company, was shot for desertion near Richmond on March 27, 1865.[37]

While most military executions in Richmond or vicinity were for desertion, other military executions occurred for espionage, and, of course, there were the usual crimes meriting death under civilian jurisprudence.

10

"Farewell, Brave Spirit"
1861–1865

Four men convicted of espionage died on the Confederate gallows in Richmond during the Civil War. They were Timothy Webster, Alfonzo C. Webster, Spencer Kellogg Brown, and Spencer Deaton (see chapter 9). This is quite a small number, considering the proliferation of enemy agents on both sides of the conflict, a war within a nation, and the casualness and amateurism of the espionage operations. Spies were also executed elsewhere, several instances in mass hangings.

Richmonders did not quite take to spy hangings like they did hyped events featuring murderers and slave felons. Perhaps the contradictory emotion of witnessing someone being executed who did no physical injury and yet who was so callous as to betray his own people to the enemy might have accounted for the less celebratory status of the espionage hangings.

Timothy Webster, the war's first double spy and first American spy hanged since the Revolutionary War, went to his death at Camp Lee on April 29, 1862. Webster's story is one of cloak-and-dagger. He became the star performer for Allan Pinkerton's Chicago detective agency, enlisted in secret service for the U.S. president and General McClellan's Union army, all the while on assignment from the Confederate War Department. As one author notes, the surprising thing about Webster as a double agent was that he evaded capture so long; "his downfall after glowing successes came about because Tim went once too often to the well—in this case, Richmond."[1]

At age twelve, Timothy Webster came with his parents from Sussex County, England, to Princeton, New Jersey. After working for some time as a machinist, he hired on as a policeman for the World's Crystal Palace Exposition in New York City. There he met Allan Pinkerton and joined the detective agency at age thirty-two. As his first major assignment, Webster,

Public Executions in Richmond, Virginia

in order to prevent the assassination of President-elect Abraham Lincoln, infiltrated a band of conspirators who had ostensibly formed a cavalry company. The plot was to accost Lincoln on his trip to the inauguration as he changed trains in Baltimore. Webster secured the incriminating evidence that crushed the scheme.[2] As Pinkerton stated afterwards, Webster "more than myself deserves the credit of saving the life of Mr. Lincoln."[3]

Webster made trips behind Confederate lines in Kentucky and Tennessee, posing as a merchant and rabid secessionist. Back in Baltimore he successfully infiltrated the pro–Southern Knights of Liberty. During four excursions to Richmond, Webster hung around the Confederate war office and secured passports to reenter Union lines, primarily serving as a courier between the Confederate War Department and Southern sympathizers in Washington, D.C. Federal authorities at the nation's capital opened the correspondence and resealed it on similar paper for delivery. In effect, as an employee of the Confederate War Department, Webster was able to obtain information on rebel troop strength, sources of supply, and forts.

Timothy Webster (from William G. Beymer, *On Hazardous Service* [New York, 1912]).

Webster's cover in Richmond was as an English merchant seeking financial opportunities.[4]

In his last two trips to Richmond, Timothy Webster had as a companion fellow secret agent Hattie Lawton, wife of another agent. On his fourth and last jaunt to Richmond, Webster came down with severe rheumatism and confined himself to a room at the Monumental Hotel. Mrs. Lawton, assisted by John Scobell posing as a black servant, attempted to nurse him back to health. Meanwhile, not hearing from Webster, Pinkerton sent two agents, John Scully and Pryce Lewis, to inquire into Webster's situation in Richmond. Upon arriving in the city, the two agents were tailed by Confederate provost marshal personnel. Scully and Lewis found Web-

10. "Farewell, Brave Spirit"

ster at the Monumental Hotel. On their second visit to Webster, Captain McCubbin from the provost marshal's office dropped by. All went fine, with Scully and Lewis convincing McCubbin they were natives of England, having come to Richmond to arrange smuggling through the Union blockade. Next day, the two northern agents, returning to Webster's room, discovered there another provost marshal detective, George Clucken, accompanied by George Chase Morton, whose house in Washington had been searched by Scully and Lewis. Sensing trouble, Scully and Lewis immediately left the room. As they paused on the hotel stairway, Clucken came up and ordered them to accompany him to the office of the Confederate military commandant of Richmond, General John H. Winder. There Morton arrived and identified the two arrested men as Federal agents. Lodged in the Henrico County jail, Scully and Lewis escaped, but getting only as far as the Chickahominy River, just beyond the city. While making a fire, they were apprehended by Confederate soldiers. Back in Richmond, the prisoners, secured by double chains, were put in separate cells in Castle Godwin, another of Richmond's military prisons.[5]

Scully and Lewis were tried separately by courts-martial held at city hall; they were sentenced to be hanged on April 5, 1862. Their lives were spared just moments before execution in return for testimony against Webster as a Union spy.[6] The trial of Webster as a spy, instead of occurring by the usual practice of court-martial, was held under civil authority. Because of Webster's grave illness, part of the trial, which dragged on for three weeks, was held at his bedside, presumably at his cell in Castle Thunder. The verdict called for death by hanging at Camp Lee on April 29, 1862. Many witnesses had testified at the trial.[7]

Allan Pinkerton, who was serving with McClellan's army in northern Virginia, accompanied by Colonel Key of McClellan's staff, hastily went to Washington to confer with President Lincoln. Lincoln expressed sympathy for Webster and called a cabinet meeting that evening to consider Webster's case. The result was the decision that nothing could be done other than seek commutation of the sentence from the Confederate government by diplomatic contact. The message subsequently sent reminded President Davis that the Federal government had hitherto pursued leniency toward rebel spies and that none of these had been sentenced to death; furthermore, execution of Webster might ignite "a system of retaliation" of death on Union-held rebel prisoners.[8] Hattie Lawton equally had no success in appealing to President Davis' wife, Varina. Given an interview at the Southern executive mansion, Mrs. Lawton was informed that the First Lady refrained from matters of state and therefore could not help.

Suddenly, on April 29 at 5:15 A.M., footsteps were heard outside Timothy Webster's prison cell. The heavy bolts slid back, and in the doorway stood Captain George Alexander, the provost marshal official in charge of the hanging. Allan Pinkerton describes the ensuing scenes:

> "Come, Webster, it is time to go."
>
> "To go where?" inquired Webster, starting up in surprise.
>
> "To the fair grounds," was the laconic reply.
>
> "Surely not at this hour," pleaded the condemned man; "the earliest moment named in my death-warrant is six o'clock, and you certainly will not require me to go before that."
>
> "It is the order of General Winder, and I must obey," answered Alexander. "You must prepare yourself at once."
>
> Without another word Webster arose from his bed, and began his preparations. Not a tremor was apparent; and this hand was as steady and firm as iron. When he had fully arranged his toilet, he turned to Mrs. Lawton, and taking both her hands in his, he murmured:
>
> "Good-bye, dear friend; we shall never meet again on earth. God bless you, and your kindness to me. I will be brave and die like a man. Farewell, forever!" then turning to Captain Alexander, who stood unmoved near the door, he said:
>
> "I am ready!"
>
> As they went out through the door a piercing shriek rent the air, and Mrs. Lawton fell prostrate to the floor.
>
> Arriving at the entrance to the prison, they found a company of cavalry drawn up before them, and a carriage, procured by Mrs. Lawton, awaiting their appearance. Webster crossed the pavement with unfaltering step and entered the vehicle, the order to march was given, and the procession started for the site of the execution.[9]

When Webster arrived at Camp Lee, the "scene was one of hustle and bustle." Detachments of soldiers were marching, and some spectators were already present. A twenty-five-foot high gibbet towered from the north side of the parade ground.[10] As the morning wore on, two hundred mostly "negroes and boys" sought a perch on the camp's trees and rooftops.[11] A group of prostitutes in the city rented hacks to take them to the hanging.[12]

Upon entering Camp Lee, Webster was placed in a room on the ground floor in one of the camp's buildings for several hours, with his only companion being the Rev. Moses D. Hoge, the city's preeminent Presbyterian minister.[13] At the prison, Webster had been attended to by the Rev. Dr. George Woodbridge of the Episcopal congregation of Monumental

10. "Farewell, Brave Spirit"

Timothy Webster Receiving His Death Warrant (from Allan Pinkerton, *The Spy of the Rebellion: A True History of the U.S. Army During the Rebellion* [Hartford, 1885]).

Church. This clergyman abandoned Webster when the condemned man requested that at the hanging he read "the psalm of David, invoking vengeance on his enemies." Woodbridge refused, and "Webster grew indignant, causing the clergyman to take an early departure."[14]

At 11:10 A.M. Captain Alexander came to escort Webster the two hundred yards to the scaffold. Still quite infirm, Webster slowly climbed the steps of the gallows. The rope was adjusted around his neck, and his arms were pinioned behind him and his feet tied together. There was a slight pause. The Rev. Hoge then gave "a prayer of solemn and touching eloquence." A black hood was draped over the prisoner's head. Then "followed a moment of solemn silence. The entire assembly seemingly ceased to breathe."

Upon a signal, "the trap was sprung, and, with a dreadful, sickening thud, Webster fell from the gibbet to the ground beneath. The hangman's knot had slipped," and Webster "lay in a confused heap, limp and motionless." He was lifted up and "again placed upon the readjusted trap. The rope was again placed around his neck, this time so tight as to be excruciatingly painful." Webster said, "I suffer a double death." When someone noticed that the rope was too short, he almost inaudibly commented, "You will choke me to death this time." Now, at 11:22 A.M. the condemned man again was launched into eternity. Even in death Webster suffered ignominy. General Winder refused requests to send Webster's body to the North for burial by friends and also to be placed in a vault in Richmond. Instead, Captain Alexander ordered the body to be buried in the pauper's burial ground.[15]

Hattie Lawton, herself a spy, had stayed with Webster during his illness and during his final hours. A newspaper account said that Webster, "who had plenty of gold and C.S. Treasury notes," gave it all to Hattie Lawton. She was imprisoned at Castle Thunder for a year, and then released. Scully and Lewis served twenty-two months of confinement before being set free.[16] Allan Pinkerton, Webster's mentor and employer, gave a fitting tribute to Webster: "Farewell, brave spirit! Brave, tender and true; thou hast suffered in a glorious cause, and died a martyr's death. Thy memory will long be green in the hearts of thy friends. When treason is execrated, and rebellion is scorned and despised, the tears of weeping friends will bedew the sod which rests above the martyred spy of the Rebellion — Timothy Webster."[17]

Coincidentally, the second spy hanged in Richmond was also named Webster — Alfonzo C. Webster, born in New Hampshire or Maine. At age twenty-three, on October 3, 1861, he was appointed a first lieutenant in the Ninth Pennsylvania Cavalry. Webster tried to persuade some of his comrades to desert and go with him to Boston to form a new company. For this he was court-martialed and then resigned. Going to Louisville, he was again arrested for "inciting soldiers to desert." Webster escaped and enlisted as a private in the Confederate Eighth Virginia Infantry. In March 1862, Webster deserted from this unit, and, with an accomplice, began to carry mail across the lines.

In Virginia Webster joined Captain Samuel Means' Union cavalry company. He was made drillmaster for new recruits during July 1862. With two comrades, Webster was sent to Loudoun County, Virginia, to capture Captain James R. Simpson of the Eighth Virginia Cavalry, who was on a recruiting mission. Webster killed Simpson, probably to prevent him from telling anyone of his desertion from the Eighth Virginia Infantry. Subsequently Webster enlisted as captain in the Third Cavalry Regiment of Virginia Volunteers, a "band of desperadoes" formed by Governor Francis Pierpont of the breakaway state of West Virginia. On October 20, 1862,

10. "Farewell, Brave Spirit"

he married Alice Downey, daughter of a former speaker of Virginia's house of delegates.[18]

In December 1862 Webster was arrested in Washington, D.C., for stealing horses and placed in the Old Capital Prison there. Since it was determined the horses were stolen in northern Virginia, outside the jurisdiction of the capital, Webster was let go. Webster and several other men then went to a camp of the 35th Virginia Cavalry, which was commanded by Major Elijah V. White, expecting to persuade members of this unit to raid the Union camp of Captain Means, whom Webster thought had been responsible for his arrest. White, thinking that Webster intended to kill him, had Webster taken into custody.

Webster was sent to Richmond and imprisoned in Castle Thunder. He was held on grounds of being a deserter, parole violator, spy, horse thief, and murderer of Captain Simpson and also John Jones. Convicted only of murder, horse thievery, and parole violation at a court-martial in Richmond that lasted from March 11 to 26, he was sentenced to be hanged, on April 3. Because April 3 fell on Good Friday, President Davis postponed the execution until April 10. In an attempt to escape from prison, Webster fractured an ankle and injured his spine.[19]

The usual procedure for a hanging at Camp Lee was activated on Friday, April 10, just past 10:00 A.M. Captain George W. Alexander, an assistant provost marshal, again in command of an execution, had guards at Castle Thunder convey the disabled Webster on to a carriage, which then headed to Camp Lee at Richmond's West End. Riding along with the condemned man was Alexander, detectives John Caphart and W.W. New, and Presbyterian minister William Brown. The Henrico County Dragoons, commanded by Captain B.W. Green, Jr., flanked each side of the carriage. The procession moved very slowly, taking almost an hour to reach its destination. At Camp Lee another hour passed while everything was readied for the execution.

Once at Camp Lee, Webster, dressed in a Union army uniform, was seated in a chair near the gallows. While waiting to ascend the steps to the platform, he prayed with Reverend Brown. Webster "shook hands with all who approached him," giving "a cordial grasp" as if "stepping on board a steamer from a foreign country." Webster asked Captain Alexander, "What do the people say about me?" "They are saying a great many hard things, but say you die game," said Alexander. Webster responded, "It is hard, hard, hard."

At 12:35 P.M. Webster was carried up to the gallows and placed in a chair. There were a few minutes more of "religious ministrations." Captain Alexander read the death warrant. Webster, who was described as a stout man, 5'10", fair complected, and with blue eyes, then had the noose adjusted around his neck and a black cap placed over his head. Someone handed Webster a black hat, which, although he was pinioned, he was to drop to signal his execution. At this moment, Webster said, "Hold a minute while I pray," which he did. At 12:47 P.M. the condemned man dropped the hat, and the trap fell. Webster descended four feet, and the chair toppled to the ground. The body swung three times as the rope unwound. It took only one and a half minutes for death to occur. At 1:23 P.M. drums "beat to quarters," the military troops "massed in review," and the crowd "broke for the camp entrance."[20]

Spencer Kellogg Brown, just past his twenty-first birthday, was the third spy to be hanged in Richmond during the Civil War. The son of a staunch abolitionist, Spencer had moved with his family from New York City to a location near Osawatomie, Kansas. From the family's log cabin on 160 acres, Spencer dreamed of obtaining a good education and finding a better life.

Mistaken as one of firebrand John Brown's sons, Spencer Brown was seized by a mob as his home was burned down. After being imprisoned for a while in Missouri, the teenager was reunited with his family. Because of bad times caused by severe drought, Spencer's mother and sisters were sent back East. At age seventeen, he secured a job as a teacher, but this employment lasted only a few days; he fled for his life when local vigilantes ordered him to leave Kansas. He showed up as a laborer in St. Louis. He let it be known that he was assuming a new name, Spencer Kellogg.

In January 1861 Spencer Kellogg enlisted in the Union army at Newport Barracks, Kentucky. He was stationed in St. Louis as a company clerk and took on the role of army scout. In a few months he received an honorable discharge, and General John C. Frémont, Union commander in the West, appointed him a first lieutenant to recruit a Missouri regiment of volunteers. Soon Frémont was replaced, and Spencer Kellogg was out of a job. He entered Union naval service and was assigned to the *Essex*, one of the new ironclads in the Mississippi River. Needless to say, Spencer Kellogg was a hard man to track. In January 1862, he deserted from his river duty and was rumored to have joined the Confederate army. Actually he had gone downriver with a companion as a Union spy to explore Confederate batteries and fortifications. He posed as a day laborer, working up and down the Mississippi, all the while collecting intelligence. Though

10. "Farewell, Brave Spirit"

suspected of being a spy, he was allowed to join a Confederate volunteer unit. During the battle of Shiloh, he deserted, bringing to General Grant significant information that helped the Union general to gain advantage in the battle. Spencer Kellogg then went back to duty on the *Essex*, participating in the sinking of a Confederate supply vessel.[21]

Deciding to return to being a spy, Spencer Kellogg went ashore in Mississippi and was arrested, suspected of being a deserter and a spy. After several months' confinement in Jackson, Mississippi, he was taken under guard to the Castle Thunder prison in Richmond, in late May 1863. Several months passed without a trial; during which time he sought to further his education and underwent a religious experience.[22] Kellogg became quite an intellectual, as attested to by his diary and frequent letter writing of his last years to his father and his sister, Kitty.

At Castle Thunder, Kellogg found his captivity now more relaxed and comfortable than his previous imprisonment in Mississippi. As fellow prisoner Captain John H. Sherman noted, Kellogg was lodged in a large room among eighty other inmates. He kept busy and worked in the "manufacture of bone rings, buttons, tooth-picks, slides, and breastpine, and coarse and fine combs of bone." Since he was "an expert at such work, he was able to live and to get many articles of needed food." Kellogg "entered heartily into all our games and sports for exercise and recreation, and excelled at most." Sherman also observed that the young spy prisoner "was a Christian in every sense of the word."[23]

Spencer Kellogg received a speedy trial by court-martial (lasting one day) on September 18 and was convicted of desertion and espionage and sentenced to be hanged a week later, Friday, September 25. On execution day at 11:00 A.M., a detail of one hundred militia cavalry and infantry (two companies) under Captain Potts called at Castle Thunder and placed Kellogg in a carriage. Already in the vehicle were Reverend J.L. Burrows of the Broad Street Baptist Church, Reverend J.T. Carpenter (chaplain at Castle Thunder), and Detective John Caphart. A procession of a drum corps in front was followed by the troops, on the flanks and behind the carriage, and a gathering crowd. The cavalcade headed up Main Street and then made a right turn on to Governor Street, left to Tenth Street and again to the left, up Broad Street on to Camp Lee (the New Fairgrounds). Arriving at the destination at 12:35 P.M., the carriage halted one hundred yards from the scaffold for about ten minutes. Already "a vast crowd of people, of both sexes and all ages, was congregated."[24]

No time was wasted. Captain Alexander read the charges against Kellogg and the sentence of the court-martial. Reverend Burrows gave a brief prayer. Newspaper reports commented on Kellogg's appearance at this time. He was about five feet nine inches tall, his eyes were "sparkling, bright blue." His hair, "which they call sandy, was rich brown, and curled at the tips." He had "well trimmed whiskers." His skin, "from long confinement, had become as fair as a woman's." The condemned man wore "a neat Federal uniform."

The prisoner mounted the scaffold unattended. Detective Caphart, acting as hangman, followed and once on the platform proceeded to adjust the rope around Kellogg's neck and to pinion the arms behind and also the ankles. All the while, Kellogg was talking. He took off his hat to admit the noose over his head. He then "threw it to one side, and falling off the scaffold, it struck a gentleman beneath, when the prisoner turned quickly, and bowing, said, 'Excuse me, sir.'"

A "negro man" then "ascended, and, placing one end of the rope through the hook at the top, began to draw it through, till, getting it within about a foot of the neck," Kellogg said he wanted a greater fall. Addressing the surgeon present, he declared, "One foot, doctor, won't break my neck. I wish, doctor, you see that it is arranged properly." After glancing at the readjusted length, Kellogg said, "There, that will do it." Caphart again ascended to the platform and placed the "cap" over Kellogg's head, and, upon the condemned man's request, the rope's knot was brought closer to the ear. Kellogg "then bowed his head and engaged a few seconds in prayer, at the conclusion of which he raised himself, and, standing perfectly erect, pronounced in clear voice, 'All ready!'" Caphart now left the scaffold. Two minutes later, the props from under the trap were knocked loose. As "the body swung in mid air" for two and a half minutes "a few convulsive movements passed over his frame, and then the body relaxed, and all was over." The body hung another fifteen minutes, then it was cut down and placed in a coffin.[25]

At the time of Spencer Kellogg's death, his wife, Mary, was ill. Just before his hanging, he wrote her: "Dear wife: I do earnestly long to see you once more before I die, but we must not complain, for God has done it.... We had happy hours together, darling; God grant they be not the last.... I have always loved you, dear one, and love you to the last...."[26]

Among the Confederates there were "many who regarded his execution as inexpedient and unjust."[27] One Confederate army private who witnessed Kellogg's execution afterwards commented, "What is the death of one man, when thousands fall in a single battle? Truly, war has many

10. "Farewell, Brave Spirit"

repellent phases, many horrors, many tragedies, and there are many secret foes and many betrayals, [and] when or what the end, no man knoweth."[28]

Only twenty-one years of age (born August 17, 1842) when he died,[29] Spencer Kellogg may be regarded as the Union spy who most resembles Nathan Hale of Revolutionary War fame, who also was twenty-one years old when he was hanged as a spy. He may also be considered a counterpart of the nineteen-year-old Sam Davis, the "Nathan Hale of the Confederacy," whom Union troops hanged in central Tennessee on November 27, 1863.

Another Union spy marched along in the execution procession that made its way from Castle Thunder to Camp Lee. Elizabeth "Crazy Bet" Van Lew overheard Kellogg, in what may be his most fitting epitaph, tell one of the persons accompanying him: "Did you ever pass through a tunnel under a mountain? My passage, my death, is dark, but beyond all is light and bright."[30]

11

"Certainly Horrible to Look At"
1861–1865

A reign of terror did not seize Richmond during the Civil War. But the social and economic instability in the city might have provoked one. The mood was somber. Sallie Brock Putnam reported in July 1862 that because of all the mortally wounded soldiers being brought into Richmond "death held a carnival in our city."[1] With the war raging around the city, invasion was always imminent. A large number of prisoners of war were incarcerated in vacant tobacco warehouses and outdoors on Belle Isle, situated in the James River across from downtown. A volatile mix of riffraff permeated the city: thugs from out of town, pickpockets, campfollowers, unruly soldiers from nearby army camps, prostitutes, and criminals. It seemed more crime than usual stemmed from the black population, with freedom now within reach. Burglaries and assaults by the general population were on the rise. Spiraling prices and acute food shortages plagued the city. Impatient housewives went on a major riot in April 1863 to purloin food supplies. Even boy gangs increasingly became troublesome with their rock fights near the capitol grounds. A lightly administered martial law, starting in March 1862 and then fizzling out, offered little relief. A smallpox epidemic in the winter of 1862–63 underscored the precariousness of the public's health.[2]

Citizens were still tried in the regular courts, despite the fling with martial law. Considering the rampant crime, it is surprising that there were not more hangings. Of course, with the war going on, military justice, with its hangings and firing squads, took up some of the slack. The Confederate Articles of War added death penalties for military desertion and espionage. The Confederate congress also made counterfeiting a capital

11. "Certainly Horrible to Look At"

crime. Civil authorities were now tempted to enforce the death penalty for arson and burglary under the old slave laws.

Just as the Civil War got underway, Richmonders witnessed the execution of William D. Totty on November 16, 1860. Totty had been convicted of the murder of Catherine J. Thorn, his wife's sister. Age twenty-five and handsome, he had a fine reputation in the city and had never been in any trouble or "altercation" before the murder. Totty served on Richmond's Night Watch until October 1859, when "he became addicted to intemperance." From about November 1859 to July 1860, Totty kept "a small grocery" at the corner of Grace and Monroe streets at the city's western boundary (located today at the center of downtown). Totty, his wife, her father, and her sister all resided at the workplace.

On the morning of July 18, Totty found in the kitchen Miss Thorn, a Mrs. Adams, and a young man eating breakfast:

> [Totty] drew up a chair near to where Miss Thorn was sitting, and was asked to participate in the meal, but declined. He then asked her whether she would go away with him. She declined to do so.—With this he drew two pistols, placed them on the table, and again demanded to know if she would leave with him. On her again declining, he told her to take one of the pistols and shoot him, and that he would shoot her with the other. Supposing him to be joking, Miss Thorn told him not to act so foolish, and on seeing him pick up the weaponry and aim one at her, she attempted to seize it. Just at that instant the pistol exploded, the ball entering her stomach about three inches above the navel, and passing entirely through her body, lodged in the muscles of her back near the spinal column, producing death that night.

Totty fled to "an old field," just west of the city, where he stayed a few hours. On the morning of July 20 Totty was arrested at the Mount Vernon Hotel in Richmond. That afternoon he was examined before the mayor and remanded to custody pending further investigation. Tried in the city's hustings court on September 8, with Judge James Lyons presiding, Totty was found guilty and sentenced to death.

The Totty trial was unusual because he was tried and convicted in hustings court rather than in the normal venue for capital cases, the circuit court. A lengthy period followed as the defendant sought a writ of supersedeas from the state court of appeals that would set aside the verdict. The court of appeals refused and confirmed the original date for execution, November 3. Three days before the scheduled execution, upon application of the Rev. Francis J. Boggs, chaplain of the Grand Lodge of Virginia,

Public Executions in Richmond, Virginia

Governor John Letcher granted a reprieve until November 9 and did so again, for November 16. For two weeks before the execution Totty was allowed a private room in the "upper part" of the city jail during daytime but was confined to his cell at night. He talked and prayed with other prisoners.[3] On Sunday, November 4, several Richmond churches offered prayers, "by request, for the spiritual benefit of the prisoner."[4]

On the morning of the fatal day, William D. Totty, in his cell at the city jail at Fifteenth and Marshall streets, was visited by his stepmother, brother, and friends. Totty told them that his situation had brought him to Jesus. He said all his troubles came from the "use of ardent spirits." Totty asked the visitors to kneel in prayer and assured them that he would soon be "in the bosom of God." At 10:00 A.M. the visitors left, amid the screams of his stepmother and "tears and sobs of his brother." Totty then met with the Rev. F.J. Boggs and the Rev. D.S. Doggett, who administered communion and baptism for the prisoner. They stayed until 11:00 A.M., at which time Totty requested they leave. Totty then wrote letters of gratitude to the jailer and his assistants. Newspaper reporters dropped by.

Just after noon the prisoner was escorted from jail by two assistant jailers. At the gate they climbed onto a wagon, which contained a coffin. Totty took a seat with his back to the horses. He was joined by the Rev. Boggs, deputy sergeant Brady, jailer F.W. Hall, and assistant jailer Mr. Brooks. A military escort of twenty-four men, supplied by the governor, accompanied the wagon on each side and "kept back the immense throng which had gathered in the streets." City sergeant Thomas U. Dudley and physicians Dove and Peachy rode in a carriage. Also in the procession were "a large number of the night and day police." On the way, the Rev. Boggs read passages from the Bible, while the prisoner at times glanced at the "multitude of people, who followed him, bowing to such as he recognized."

The execution site had shifted slightly northeastward from the "usual place of execution," now near Victor's Old Mill, up Shockoe (Valley) Creek. Hundreds of spectators crowded around the gallows. The wagon halted thirty feet from the scaffold, and Sergeant Brady announced they were "ready to proceed." The prisoner, "looking pleasantly around him," jumped off the wagon, and, with "the passage way cleared by soldiers," walked swiftly to the gallows, running "lightly up the steps." After surveying the crowd, he inspected the crossbeam, the rope, and the trap. The military escort then formed around the gallows to keep back the crowd. Sergeant Dudley, on the platform, read the sentence of the court, and, saying

11. "Certainly Horrible to Look At"

that he had a painful duty, shook hands with Totty, finally declaring, "May the Lord have mercy on your soul." Totty then grasped the hand of the sergeant, and "thanked him for his kindness and begged him to meet him in Heaven."

As soon as Sergeant Dudley left the platform, the Rev. Boggs in a loud voice read the Twenty-Third Psalm and several passages from John 14. Totty gave a brief response. The Rev. Boggs then read the prisoner's favorite hymn, commencing: "Jesus, to thee I now can fly, On whom my Help is laid." The Rev. Boggs gave "a fervent and eloquent prayer, the prisoner kneeling by him and composedly joining him in his devotions." Afterwards Totty stood up and requested the Rev. Boggs to say a few words on his behalf. The Rev. Boggs simply said that Totty acknowledged the justice of the sentence, warned others of "the error of their ways," and in bidding "an affectionate farewell" called upon persons to meet him in heaven. The Rev. Boggs then shook hands with the prisoner, "urging him to put his trust in Christ" and bidding him "good-bye." Totty grasped the minister's hand, and said in a loud voice, "God bless you, Mr. Boggs, for your kindness to me. God bless you. Meet me in Heaven." The condemned man then "turned with a pleasant smile on his face to receive the rope."

At 12:35 P.M. jailer F.W. Hall proceeded to pinion the prisoner's arms behind, tie his feet together, and adjust the rope to the cross beam. All the while, the Rev. Boggs read from the Bible, with Totty responding by saying again that he believed in Jesus and addressing the crowd: "Let us all meet in Heaven." Totty asked jailer Hall to make the rope tight, so "that he might die easy." With everything now ready, the "black cap was pulled over the face of the prisoner." While waiting for the fall, Totty's last words were, "God bless you all — meet me in Heaven."

At precisely 12:40 P.M. the drop fell. The three and a half feet descent "instantly dislocated the neck," and after three or four "slight muscular convulsions," Totty died without a struggle. After twenty minutes the body was cut down and given to friends for burial.[5] For expenses of conducting the execution, the Richmond hustings court credited $110 to the account of the city sergeant.[6]

Newspaper reportage reflected contrasting views of the execution drama. The *Daily Dispatch* said that "no noise was to be heard, and no confusion witnessed." The only regret was that "children of tender years were permitted to see a sight so shocking, and, we fear, demoralizing."[7] The *Richmond Enquirer* of the date of the execution (and hence printed before the fact) declared:

Public Executions in Richmond, Virginia

Execution of the Negro William Johnson at Petersburg, Virginia, June 20, 1864 (courtesy Library of Virginia).

> This morning in health and vigorous life; at its setting this evening it will behold him a cold and strangled corps—strangled by the law, because he has killed another—strangled as a warning to the wicked; killed as an atonement to offended justice. It is an appalling mode of execution this hanging. A man stands on a trap, his eyes blindfolded, his arms pinioned, a rope round his neck; there is a moment of most fearful, appalling suspense; a bolt is sprung, and with his tremendous fall the living man drops thro' the length of the rope, and at the instant there is a cracking sound of broken spine, a horrid shudder and convulsion of limb, a wriggling and writhing in agony, and a heaving of the body to and fro, and then, ere many moments elapse, the spirit wings its way before the throne of Him, who said, "Thou shall not kill."

Hinting perhaps of an awareness of a mounting opposition to public hangings, the *Richmond Enquirer* added: "Hanging is a horrid spectacle, one which certainly no woman should go to see. We hope for the honor of our city and the character of our women for sensibility and humanity, that they will not be seen at the dread tragedy which is to be enacted in the Valley as the sun crosses the meridian today."[8]

Of the many executions in Richmond, probably the one most over-

11. "Certainly Horrible to Look At"

looked by the citizenry was the hanging of a slave girl, Clara Ann, for the murder of her mistress. Although the crime occurred in Culpeper County, the prisoner, three weeks before the execution, had been brought to the penitentiary in Richmond for "safe keeping." The governor ordered that she be executed at the penitentiary. She went to her death on Friday, May 23, 1862, on a gallows erected in "the interior yard" of the prison. Just before the hanging at 2:15 P.M. the Rev. Sweeney offered a prayer at the gallows. Peter Phillips, deputy sheriff of Henrico County, served as executioner. Clara Ann's body remained suspended for forty-five minutes, until 3:00 P.M. There were only a few spectators.[9]

Early in the Civil War, the Confederate congress enacted the death penalty for counterfeiting. Among the large-scale bogus money activity in the Confederacy, only one person was singled out to pay the extreme penalty. The crime was stealing, forging, and passing Confederate treasury notes.[10] The Confederate government limited prosecution mainly to counterfeiting paper money; there was not much counterfeiting of postage or small change.[11]

The person who bore the brunt of full force prosecution for counterfeiting as a capital crime was John Richardson, alias Louis Napoleon. Richardson (the name used here) was a thirty-year-old Italian (probably an immigrant) who had been a street peddler selling "fruit in a basket around the city."[12] At the time of his arrest, he was described as "an Italian of bad countenance, and until recently was the proprietor of a little confectionary, as a blind for the illicit sale of poisonous liquors in the rear."[13]

A night of drinking led to the crime for which Richardson expiated with his life. Richardson ran across George Elam, and the two walked towards the market, stopping to take several drinks on the way. Elam turned towards Richardson, and said, "Let's go and make some money." The pair headed to Howe and Ludwig's bank. Elam broke down the door and gave Richardson a pistol, with directions to shoot anyone who might come up. Inside, they found on the table eight sheets of already printed ten-dollar notes. They put the one hundred-dollar plate on the floor and struck $800 for Elam and another $800 for Richardson. Richardson thought this amount was enough, but Elam struck off more. The two men left and went to a shop kept by an acquaintance of Richardson near Mayo's Bridge. A woman who let them in gave Elam an authentic note, from which they forged the signatures needed for the notes they had stolen. The crime spree ended when the two men were tripped up in passing the bogus notes in local stores. They were tried separately. Richardson, on April 7,

Public Executions in Richmond, Virginia

1862, was convicted by a Confederate States (Henrico) Circuit Court, presided over by Judge J.D. Halyburton. Richardson was sentenced to hang on a day in late April. Elam's trial in early May ended in a hung jury. After waiting in jail for over a year he was again tried, in August 1863, with the outcome unknown, but presumably he received a prison sentence.[14] Richardson's execution was postponed by President Davis three times, to May 9, May 22, and finally to August 22, 1862.[15]

The *Daily Dispatch* of August 22, 1862, announced that the execution of Richardson would take place "near the Poor House gulley, to-day" between 11:00 A.M. and 1:00 P.M. Colonel John P. Wily, Confederate States marshal for the Eastern District of Virginia, and his assistants were in charge. "Having been sentenced by the County, the military properly have nothing to do with the execution of the sentence."[16] The actual gallows attendees were deputy marshals Henry Meyers, Bass, and Baker. The surgeons were Doctors Cabal, Beli, and Broock.[17]

At 11:00 A.M. the prisoner was picked up at the jail by a furniture wagon, which carried the coffin; he was accompanied by a Catholic priest, the Rev. Barratta, and Deputy Marshal Meyers. A company of the City Guard Battalion provided escort to the gallows. Richardson was dressed in a grey summer coat, a dotted linen shirt, brown linen pants, and a "light drab slouch hat." Having served in the army, under the name of Louis Napoleon, he was permitted to address the spectators for twenty minutes. He was eloquent, although illiterate, even though he could speak three languages. The condemned man still claimed his innocence. He closed his remarks by saying that he hoped to meet the audience in heaven. His coat having been removed and his hands manacled, the prisoner knelt and consulted with Father Barratta for ten minutes. Then Richardson was moved to the center of the trap, his legs pinioned, and a cap drawn over his face. At exactly noon the trap fell. The rope did not slip as planned, and there were "several violent struggles." The body was left hanging for a half hour.[18]

One of the several slaves who suffered death by order of the Richmond hustings court during the Civil War was a twenty-year-old mulatto woman, Margaret Ann Butt (Butter). She was among the eighteen women throughout the country, North and South, hanged during the Civil War.[19]

Margaret Butt was the slave of Mrs. Mary M. Butt of Oxford, North Carolina. What brought Margaret to Richmond is not known. She had the reputation of being a "very zealous member of her church." Allegedly, on December 31, 1862, she murdered Frances Deane Tardy, infant child of

11. "Certainly Horrible to Look At"

Samuel C. Tardy. Justice was swift. Margaret was scheduled to die on a gallows on the same spot where John Richardson (alias Louis Napolean) had been hanged, at the usual location, near the new city almshouse.[20]

At 1:00 A.M. on the appointed day, January 9, 1863, the somber procession from the city jail to the gallows began and covered the short distance in a half hour. The dreary parade escorting the prisoner to the scaffold consisted of a detachment from the City Guard Battalion, "surrounding the wagon," which contained Margaret, sitting on her coffin, and jailer Frederick W. Hall, followed by a carriage conveying Dr. Dove, city physician, and several others. On the sidewalk, "following the cortege were promiscuously mingled civilians, soldiers, and negroes by hundreds all pushing forward. Meanwhile the prisoner was assisted in "devotional exercises" by the Rev. Watkins, pastor of the Second Baptist African Church, and the Rev. L.W. Seeley.[21]

The "cortege" having arrived at the execution site, there was a brief interval while Margaret paused to converse with several persons before ascending to the scaffold. This done, city sergeant Dudley read the sentence of the court and told Margaret that she could say anything she wanted. In a "clear voice and perfect enunciation," Margaret spoke briefly, criticizing the governor for not allowing enough time for her mother to see her and saying, though she was innocent, her fate might be a warning to others. She expressed her expectation of reaching heaven. A "brief interlude" followed, after which the Rev. Seeley, who was on the scaffold with her, read from a short address which Margaret had composed for the occasion. "I die perfectly innocent" and "forgive those that have condemned me" were words that rang out. The Rev. Seeley himself then presented an address, ending with a prayer. Finally, Margaret again spoke. She claimed to be a "victim of injustice," and if allowed "half a chance in Court" she could have proven that a woman who testified against her was the actual murderess.

Margaret's hands were now pinioned by jailer Hall, "the rope (a cotton cord) affixed to her neck, the black cap drawn over her face." The jailer and the preacher then left the scaffold. "A heavy thud against the side of the scaffold announced to the thousands assembled that the fatal drop had fallen." There were "a few spasmodic struggles." After thirty-five minutes (at about 12:38 P.M.), Dr. John Doyle pronounced Margaret Butt dead, and she was taken down and buried close by in the Colored Burial Ground (Fifteenth and Broad streets). Again the local press issued a negative comment about public hangings. The *Daily Dispatch* noted that

Public Executions in Richmond, Virginia

it was doubtful "whether an exhibition of this kind is either instructive or edifying. It is certainly horrible to look at, especially when the victim is a woman."[22]

It is reasonable to assume that another execution closely followed the hanging of Margaret Butt. Michael Bucton was sentenced to die at "the usual place of execution" for the murder of John Delaney a few days before Christmas. It is not known whether Bucton was white or black, but, with his conviction coming in hustings court, it is likely he was a slave. The city sergeant and his deputies were charged with conducting the execution. The governor gave Bucton a respite until February 27.[23] There is no mention in the press that the execution occurred then or at a later date. Normally a sentence of death for capital murder was decisive.

Toward the war's end it seemed that the old practice of bringing capitally convicted felons from jurisdictions outside of Richmond to the city for execution was beginning to be revived (a practice that would be mandated in 1908). A slave named Richard, owned by Mrs. Rosalie P. Sampson of New York, went to the gallows erected in the Henrico jail yard at 12:34 P.M., May 29, 1863. The sheriff of the county and his assistants had charge of the execution. The victim had been convicted of murderous assault on Atwell F. Pitts, a farm manager; the trial on April 21, 1863, was conducted at the King William County courthouse. Because of security reasons, the prisoner had been brought to Richmond for safekeeping and execution. Since only a few people knew of the execution only about a dozen persons were present.[24]

On October 7, 1863, another "imported" prisoner was hanged in the courtyard of the Henrico jail. Henry, a slave owned by William O. Day of neighboring Hanover County and employed by the Virginia Central Railroad Company, was sentenced to death by the Hanover County court on September 2, 1864. He was convicted of "setting fire to the wheat and straw stack of Mr. Day" and "afterwards arming himself and waylaying him on the highway." Allegedly Henry acted the way he did to avenge himself of having been shot in the leg by Day's young son. A serious threat of lynching of Henry in Hanover County caused the transfer in custody. Henry's execution in Richmond "was witnessed by a very small concourse of persons, and his death was unaccompanied by any incident of interest."[25]

The increased crime rate during the war years seemed to contribute to the city and county's judicial systems becoming less compassionate.[26] The death penalty for slaves committing crimes less than murder, customarily commuted to imprisonment or being transported out of the state,

98

11. "Certainly Horrible to Look At"

were again implemented. Thus Henry, mentioned above, went to the gallows for arson. Similarly, a double execution of slaves for burglary occurred.

In July 1864, slaves Ben and William were condemned by the Richmond hustings court to be hanged for burglary. Ben, a slave of John H. Gentry, was convicted for breaking into and robbing the James T. Butler & Company store. William, a slave of Samuel Fauntleroy of King and Queen County, received the death penalty for breaking into the home of Mrs. Mary Harris, on Grace Street between Eighteenth and Nineteenth streets, and stealing several women's dresses, valued at $500. The double execution was scheduled to take place "on the hill back of the Poor House, the usual place." The date for the hangings was extended from August 19 to September 23, October 10, and finally Friday, October 21, 1864.[27]

At 10:15 A.M., October 21, Ben and William, handcuffed, exited the city jail and climbed onto a wagon, taking a seat on their coffins. Heading toward the execution site, they were followed by the Rev. J. Lansing Burrows, pastor of the First Baptist Church, who had frequently visited them, Dr. John Dove, city sergeant Thomas Dudley, jailer Frederick Hall, and several jail employees. A "crowd of persons collected outside, consisting chiefly of negroes and children, scampered away at a rapid pace towards the place of execution," some "taking one route and others another." When the newspaper reporters reached the gallows site, "every available housetop, tree and hill in the vicinity were packed with spectators, and around the scaffold thousands were standing curiously gazing upon the gallows."

At 10:30 A.M. the condemned men and their "attendants" arrived at the scaffold. Ben and William "jumped from the wagon, and, being uncuffed, ascended the ladder leading to the platform in a rapid and cheerful manner." Ben, "who was a tall, well-formed mulatto, was dressed in a handsome suit of light woolen goods, and wore on one hand a white military-glove, carrying in his right the other, with which he saluted the crowd around him." William, "a short, stout negro, very black, was commonly dressed and barefooted." Neither of them displayed any fear.

"Uncovering their heads, as if in token of respect and reverence for the occasion," they listened to Sergeant Dudley's reading of the death warrant "in somewhat an agitated and feeling manner." Sergeant Dudley then asked if the condemned men had anything to say. "Ben promptly responded that he should like to address the crowd and sing a hymn. He then went on in rambling sort of speech, the point of which seemed to be that he had gone 'on and on in badness until de cotch me,' and that now he was going to suffer for it. He felt that he was going to Heaven, and pressed all his 'friends, brothers and sisters' to meet him there." The Rev. Burrows, after Ben finished speaking, gave a "feeling and eloquent prayer"; the minister then shook hands with Ben and left the scaffold.

Next, Nelson, who had ascended to the platform, delivered a speech. He was an "old grey-haired negro clergyman," who had spent much time counseling Ben and William. Nelson exhorted the crowd to abide by the warning of the fate pending for the two men standing near him. He declared, "My friends, sin and Satan is now howling through dis land more than I ever hearn of afore. I'se been preaching de gospel of de Lord dis forty years, and I neber see so much bad doins afore. Our poor old commonwealth is suffering with sin of every kind. Our jails, our courts, our law offices, is all full of wicked bad people, who have violated de law; an it seems dat de devil am let loose. Dese boys (pointing to the negroes beside him) am truly pent of dar sins, and I believe am going up to God." Nelson then shook hands with his "unfortunate brothers," and desired himself to be "remembered to Father Abraham in Heaven."

William then made a short speech. He was satisfied with the verdict and the punishment. He said that "he was not afraid to die; believed he was prepared, and hoped all his friends would meet him in heaven." During these proceedings, the African Americans, who amounted to four-fifths of the spectators, "wept bitterly, and many of them shouted and ejaculated so violently that the officers several times were compelled to quiet them."

At 10:55 jailer Frederick Hall ascended to the platform. William fell upon his knees, and Ben leaned against a scaffold prop and prayed aloud. "Just then a negro in the crowd obtained permission and ascended the scaffold for the purpose of shaking hands with Ben." This was done, and Ben requested the man to care for his family. Then turning to the crowd, Ben exclaimed, "Good-bye! don't fail to meet me in Heaven." Hall then adjusted the ropes around the necks of the condemned men, placed the caps over their eyes, and then descended from the scaffold. Underneath, he knocked away the supports from under the platform.

In the fall, neither of the necks of the two men were broken. They "suffocated, dying in the most violent manner":

> Owing to the stiffness of the rope, the knot did not slip close to the necks of the criminals, consequently they died very hard, and near a half hour elapsed before life was entirely extinct. For about one or two minutes they hung perfectly motionless, but then their bodies commenced twitching and

11. "Certainly Horrible to Look At"

heaving, and they could be heard breathing for some distance off. William struggled desperately, several times swinging till he could throw his feet upon the top of the platform, which was hanging by hinges edgewise to the scaffold, upon a level almost with his head, by which means he would raise himself up in such a manner as to lessen the strain upon his neck. Several times he supported himself in this manner, and would remain in that position till the executioner would pluck his legs off, and then he would violently reel round and round till he could again strike the scaffold with his feet. Finally, however, his movements became weaker and weaker, and death put an end to his sufferings.

Dr. Dove examined the pulses of the two hanged men, and pronounced them dead; the bodies were cut down, placed in the coffins, and hauled off for burial.[28]

Thus the war years drew to a close amidst horror at home as well on the battlefield. One fortunate aspect of the story of capital punishment in Richmond was that the situation could have been much worse. President Davis stayed or commuted many military executions. Among the vast horde of deserters from the Confederate army only a very few went before firing squads. Also fortunate was that the planned hangings of captive Union officers selected by lot from Libby Prison in retaliation for the summary execution of Southern prisoners of war by Yankee officers[29] never materialized.

12

"The Last Carnival of Death"
1865–1869

Just after the war, Virginians continued to witness at least a minimal army presence in their lives. There was first a semblance of martial law during the military occupation of 1865–66, then the brief military support of the Johnson Restoration government, and finally the establishment of the Reconstruction military government of 1867–70. Despite only a skeletal force of Union troops remaining in Virginia, until the state could have a new constitution military government intervened in the judicial system.

In February 1866, Isaac Chaney, an African American, was tried and convicted by a federal military commission, sitting in Staunton for the "brutal" murder of Mr. and Mrs. Gerald of Rockbridge County. Granted several reprieves, Chaney, under sentence of death, was confined for several months in Staunton and eventually transferred to Libby Prison in Richmond. Finally the execution date, with no reprieve, arrived; it was set for Monday, July 16, 1866.

Isaac Chaney, age 32, 5'10" and weighing 180 pounds, was a native of Ohio. He enlisted as a volunteer in General Philip Sheridan's cavalry. In a raid on Burbridge in southwestern Virginia, he was captured, and carried to Lynchburg, where he was sold as a slave to Mr. Gerald, with whom he remained after the war. On October 6, 1865, Chaney, while working in a field, picked up a hoe and struck Gerald on the head, killing him instantly. Chaney then went into the house and murdered Mrs. Gerald, then set the house on fire. When apprehended, he confessed to killing Mr. Gerald, but not Mrs. Gerald. With the prisoner in federal custody, the execution was held at a place other than the city's "usual place of execution," namely inside Libby Prison.[1]

12. "The Last Carnival of Death"

The execution was "strictly private," witnessed inside the prison only by the guard and a small number of persons who held tickets provided by either General Alfred H. Terry or Gordon Granger. This arrangement, however, "did not prevent the gathering of an immense throng around the prison seemingly inspired by a curiosity to gaze at the walls, within which was to be enacted the fearful tragedy" or "possibly hoping to get a glimpse as he made the fatal plunge."

The morning of the execution, Chaney ate a hearty breakfast "with apparent relish." Visited by clergymen James H. Holmes and Nelson T. Vandervaughn, the prisoner confessed to the murder of Mr. Gerald, expressing "feelings of animosity" towards the victim.

At 11:15 A.M. Chaney, dressed in a black coat, white pants, and a white vest, came out of his cell on the second floor, accompanied by the two black ministers, and headed to the trapdoor of a scaffold, "fixed in the hatchway on the third floor, the rope being attached to the windlass." The condemned man, as described by a biased reporter, had "a countenance brutal and sensual, expressive of much low cunning and ferocity," the face "that of a bold, bad, passionate revengeful man, and a physiognomist would have pronounced him capable of any crime."

With his hands tied behind him, Chaney mounted the scaffold steps without assistance. The two ministers were allowed to accompany him, and when they reached the third floor of the prison, Chaney was out of sight "until he was dropped." The prisoner's last words included these: "I owe a debt to the Government. I'll pay it to God. I am certainly going to Heaven.... I want everybody to meet me in Heaven." The rope was attached to a "stationary windlass over the trapdoor," and "the black cap was drawn over his face." As the rope was being fixed, Chaney "bade farewell to the group around him."

At 11:20 A.M. all was silent, and then there a was click of the bolt of the trap being sprung. The prisoner "fell with lightning rapidity through the drop." Then the rope, "which had been thoroughly tested, gave way," and the prisoner fell fourteen feet from the third-floor level to the second floor. For a moment Chaney was stunned, but then he rose, apparently not much injured: "He was led up-stairs, and a new rope being procured, the murderer was swung off again at 11:40. His neck was broken instantly and he died without a struggle, only a few convulsive tremors of his limbs being visible." After twenty minutes, Drs. Brown and Tremaine pronounced death, and the body was cut down and delivered to the Freemen's Bureau for burial. A Richmond newspaper concluded

Public Executions in Richmond, Virginia

its coverage of the event: "For once military law has awarded justice. 'Stick a pin there!'"[2]

For the next three years Richmonders were not treated to any gallows festivities. This may seem ironic because the city experienced "an unprecedented crime wave in the postwar years," and boasted a "large number of criminals both native- and foreign-born."[3] Probably to make for more jail room rather than from any benevolence, President Andrew Johnson issued a "general jail delivery" for the penitentiary in July 1866, emptying that institution of all its prisoners, except for those convicted of rape and murder.[4] In three years, however, everything was back to normal. As the *Daily Dispatch* reported on January 1, 1869, "The hospitable doors of the Valley Inn have been opened during the last twelve months to receive 884 prisoners."[5]

At the end of the decade, largely because of the rowdy behavior and excessive showmanship of a Richmond execution, the legislature declared that executions would henceforth take place in jailhouse courtyards or the like, thus greatly reducing the number of spectators. "The last carnival of death, public execution," in the words of William A. Christian, occurred on Saturday, May 29, 1869.[6] Let Herbert T. Ezekiel, who became a prominent Richmond newspaperman, introduce this grand finale:

> Providence ... must have intended me for a newspaper man. My initiation, so to speak, took place at the tender age of five "going on" six.
> A connection of the family started out with me to see Albert Taylor [Tyler], a negro who had poisoned a woman, hung. These pleasant functions in those days were generally held near the Central (now C & O) shops. Disappointment and my old nurse overtook me before we had gone a block. College Hill, named for the Medical College of Virginia which overlooked it, at Fourteenth and Marshall Streets, afforded a bird's eye view of the impending festivities, for as such were hangings then regarded. A crowd of some size had gathered on the brow of the declivity, largely made up of professors and students from the nearby halls of learning.
> "Mr. Sim (Hart), do you want that child to have brain (!) fever?" shouted my old mammy. Such a prognosis from without their ranks elicited a roar of laughter from the assembled medicos. It is needless to say I did not join in the merriment, being led away in disgrace. This Hanging took place on Saturday, May 29, 1869. Hangman's Day in Virginia had before and since been Friday, and why Judge Burnham, of the Hustings Court, violated this precedent never became known.
> The features attending this execution were particularly disgusting. Taylor, sitting on his coffin, in a wagon, guarded by forty-eight armed policemen, was paraded through the streets. Four or five thousand people viewed

12. "The Last Carnival of Death"

the hanging from the surrounding hills. The dead body swung in the air, in full view of all, for twenty minutes. This seems to have been the first appearance of John Jasper before the public, he attending the condemned man and offering prayer on the scaffold. The minister did not "have much" on Taylor, who delivered a rambling address of thirty minutes. The scaffold had been built for Jeter Phillips. This hanging, possibly the last public one in Virginia, helped hasten the passage of a law forbidding executions in the open.[7]

Tyler came to his end for committing murder at a house on the eastern boundary of Richmond where he lived with his two stepchildren and Henry and Paulina Hubbard, man and wife. It seemed that this was a harmonious household. Albert Tyler, about thirty years old, was viewed by his "employers" as "industrious and obedient, and of a very peaceful disposition." He "was a very black negro, about medium height, and had a countenance indicative of sheer ignorance more than of malice."

The tragic turn of events began on Saturday night, February 20, 1869, when Paulina and Henry Hubbard discovered Albert Tyler "in the act of committing a most violent outrage" upon Mary Ann Billups, his stepdaughter, who was almost twelve years old. Henry beat up on Albert, and both Henry and Paulina threatened to "inform on him." On Tuesday, Paulina, as usual, cooked dinner for the household. When she gave the children biscuits to eat, they refused them, saying that their "father" (Tyler) told them not to eat them as they were made for someone else. Tyler had slipped arsenic into the flour. Paulina ate part of a biscuit and "remarked upon their peculiar taste." She then left to take her husband's dinner to his workplace. "She had nearly reached him, when she was taken violently ill. She suffered in great agony for several hours, and died."

At the inquest, Dr. McCaw testified that he and Dr. Knox conducted a postmortem examination that revealed that "the mucous membrane of the stomach was violently congested, and it contained but a small quantity of a bloody secretion of some kind. This secretion contained arsenic, and the walls of the stomach, on being boiled, also showed traces of the drug." Arsenic in large quantities had been found in the flour. Albert Tyler was arrested. At his trial on March 31 he was convicted and sentenced to be hanged.

During his incarceration, Albert Tyler was a model prisoner, so much so that "the irons usually placed upon condemned men" were omitted. Occasionally religious leaders dropped by, namely J.C. Granberry and P. August of the Methodist church, John B. Crenshaw of the Quakers, and

Public Executions in Richmond, Virginia

Peter Randolph (an African American minister), but "his apparent regardlessness of his future gave them but little encouragement." Moreover, Tyler's "foolish, rambling conversations about his visits to Heaven and to hell, and of his visions of the murdered woman, seemed more like the vagaries of a crazed mind than the sober reflections of one doomed so soon to meet his God."

On Tuesday morning before the execution, Tyler was interviewed by a newspaper reporter:

> [Reporter] "Tyler, do you know that Saturday next is the day on which you are to be hung for killing Paulina Hubbard?"
> [Tyler] "Oh, yes, I knows it."
> [Reporter] "Did you kill Paulina Hubbard?"
> [Tyler] "I wants to tell you about it. You see I hadn't nothing agin Paulina, and didn't want to kill her. I fixed the pizin for her husband, Henry Hubbard; and I wanted to give it to him, case he beat me almost to death de night befo. I had nottin agin Paulina, she always treated me as a lady; but jis as soon as Henry beat me I sent dat gal to de doctor shop to git de pizin. I told her to tell de doctor I wanted to kill rats. When she cum back I took it from her, and next morning, after breakfast, Paulina axed her what dat was she brought me de night befo, and the gal tole her it was pizin. Paulina den call her husband out in de yard and tole him what de gal tole her. While dey was out in de yard I went to de kag whar dey kept dar flour and put de pizen in it. Dey had done eat dar breakfast. When Pauline went to git dinner she got flour out of de kag, and made de bread, and eat it."
> [Reporter] "Was what Paulina said about you and the girl true?"
> [Tyler] "Yes, sir dat was the truth; and Paulina told me I oughtn't to do so; but she never quarrelled with me, and never said she was gwine to tell anybody about it. I ain't gwine to tell you any lie about it."
> [Reporter] "How do you feel about what is to take place on Saturday?"
> [Tyler] "I don't feel oneasy about it. I'm perfectly willin' to go at any time. I'm sorry for what I've done, but I can't help it now."

During the whole interview the condemned man manifested a great disposition to talk and indulged in a great deal of the irrelevant, rambling conversation of which negroes are so fond.

On Saturday morning, May 29, Albert Tyler, after eating a hearty breakfast, "waited calmly for the coming of the hour of his execution." About 11:00 A.M., five clergymen arrived at Tyler's cell. They were the Rev. James Holmes of the First African Rev. Church; the Rev. Charles Bowe of the Fifth Baptist Church; the Rev. John Jasper of the Sixth Mount Zion Baptist Church; and D.P. Smith, a seminary student. All of these were

12. "The Last Carnival of Death"

African American, and the Rev. A. Gladwin was a missionary with the American Baptist Publishing Society in Virginia. Tyler joined in with the singing of a hymn, "Show Pity, Lord," he himself singing the tenor part "with a sharp, shrill voice." The Rev. Jasper prayed. In "between the praying and singing," Tyler conversed "with great coolness, and wore a perpetual grin upon his face." Asked how he slept the night before, Tyler replied, "I rested well. I slept in de faith."

"Oh, very good. I ate well. I has been very well."
He was asked: "Are you sure you appreciate your situation? Don't you think you are mistaken in the idea that you do?"
"Oh, no; I ain't mistaken. Not much. I'm gwine to heaven, I am."
With this remark he broke out into a loud laugh. There was nothing about his demeanor that would indicate that he felt his end approaching, but there was that about his appearance and conduct characteristic of a total want of humanity, and an entire ignorance of the horrors of death.

All the while, a large crowd gathered outside the jail. Also waiting was a police detail of forty-eight men. A furniture wagon with a black coffin was brought up to the gate. At 12:10 P.M., the condemned man was led by jailer J.E. Brooks onto the wagon and seated on the coffin. Tyler was accompanied by Brooks, deputy-sergeant Bowie, and the Rev. James Holmes. The wagon set off to the execution site, surrounded by a police squad, with the rest of the policemen following behind; completing the cortege were "hacks containing the officers of the law, ministers, and members of the press." As the procession made its way from the jail on Twenty-Second Street to the "valley field," east of the city almshouse and near the powder magazine (in the vicinity of Richmond's "usual place of execution"), Tyler "continued cheerful" and spoke to persons he recognized in the crowd, "using such

John Jasper (1812–1901), minister, Sixth Mount Zion Baptist Church (courtesy Library of Virginia).

Public Executions in Richmond, Virginia

expressions as 'I feel first-rate,' 'How are you?' 'Good bye, I am going above.' The crowd that had gathered in front of the jail increased as the procession went on, and by the time it reached the scaffold it had swelled into thousands. From every side, and through every avenue they came, young and old, male and female, white and colored, the latter predominating, however. The windows were filled with human beings. On every hilltop commanding a view of the ground gathered knots of people, and the sidewalks were lined with them. Around the scaffold it is estimated that there were about three or four thousand persons."

Policemen formed around the scaffold to keep back the crowd, and "none but the privileged few were allowed to come within the lines." Tyler was taken from the wagon, and he walked "nimbly" up the steps of the scaffold. Dressed in a blue checkered shirt and dark pants, he was accompanied by jailer Brooks, city sergeant Mills and his deputies, and his "spiritual advisers." Tyler bowed to persons in the crowd whom he recognized. City sergeant Mills read the death sentence and commended Tyler for his good behavior as a prisoner. Mills offered Tyler a drink of whiskey, which was refused. Asked if he had anything to say, Tyler stepped forward, and responded:

> I am glad to see dis large congregation here to-day. My brothers and sisters, I am glad to see you before me dis day; my last day here. I, should tell you all around me I am prepared to meet God. I say I'm prepared to meet God You hear me? I has no doubt I'm gwine home. My way is clear. I'se sorry for what I done, but it can't be helped now. God has forgiven me. Brothers and sisters, I want you all to forgive me, and to know that I'm ready to go. I wants every one around me in dis large congregation — white, and colored, and all — to forgive me. (Voices in the crowd: "Ask God to forgive you; don't ask us.") I'm happy to see you. My way is certingly clar. I'm gwine to God. Who gwine wid me in dis congregation? (Voice: "I won't go wid you, but I'll meet you dar.") I ain't gwine no whar else but heaven. I'm not ashamed of God. You hear me? For He has said dat whosomever is ashamed of Him here He won't own in de kingdom come. I say I'm sorry for what I've done, but it can't be helped now. You hear me? I look to de future, and not to what has been done. I'm prepared for de day dat's com'n, and I won't be dead. You hear it? Well, my last word is dis: I has fout de good fout. You understand me? I has kept de faith I has found in heaven. Hear me! Didn't I tell you dar was a crown in heaven for me? You will honor me. Farewell (Voice: "God deliver you.") I've got a hymn I want you all to sing — every brother and sister here; and while de Christians sing I wants de sinners to look to God. You hear me! If you don't hear me, I'll make you hear me. I want God Almighty to holp de people to sing. I ain't

12. "The Last Carnival of Death"

got no time to look at you any more, for if I do I'll go to hell. Brethren and sisters, sing regular.

Tyler then led the crowd in a hymn that began with "death don't make my soul afraid of God." The African Americans assembled joined in, singing "to a wailing air with considerable effect." With each verse, the condemned man exclaimed, "Brethren, sing regular!" Upon conclusion of the singing, Tyler said, "Thank you all, brethren, for dat hymn."

Next the Rev. Gladwin "gave out" a hymn, "Show Pity, Lord." As he read the words someone called out," Good-bye, Albert." Tyler replied, "Good-bye; tell Mass Jim I'm gwine home; make all your folks pray, children and all."

The hymn was "sung in the same wailing tune." The Rev. Holmes then read verses from the third chapter of John. The Rev. Bowie then spoke briefly of Tyler's pending execution as an example. Finally, Tyler bade farewell to his "spiritual advisers," his defense counsel, Mr. Thomas, and one of his former masters, Peter Lawson. At 1:07 P.M. all these persons left the scaffold, "leaving the condemned man alone with his executioners."

The "murmers of the great crowd were hushed, and all was as still as death." Jailer Brooke removed the handcuffs, and with the assistance of deputy sergeant Bowie bound the hands and feet. A rope was then placed over Tyler's head, the knot adjusted, and a black cap pulled over his face. All the while, the prisoner maintained a "stupid stare," not moving a muscle, still as a statue. Jailer Brooks and Sergeant Mills descended from the platform, leaving deputy sergeants Bowie and August on the scaffold with the condemned man.

Let a spectator comment on the concluding moments:

[T]he crowd waited in breathless suspense for the signal that was to deprive a fellow-being of his life. The dark figure upon the scaffold has not moved a muscle, and all eyes are turned upon it. Suddenly, at exactly ten minutes past 1, a sharp click is heard, followed by the noise of the falling trap, and a heavy thud. The form of the condemned swings for a while to and fro like a pendulum; but no movement was perceptible save the slightest twitching of the left thumb. The indifference of the creature's body to the great shock of the execution seemed to have accorded with the indifference of his mind to his approaching death. The body was left swinging until half-past 1 o'clock, when it was examined by Drs. James Dove and E. H. Smith, and found that death had been produced by the breaking of the neck. The fall given was about nine feet. The body was soon afterwards cut down and buried near the spot where Jane and John Williams were buried.

The crowd dispersed, and the execution of Albert Tyler was over.[8]

13

"YOU'RE GWYNE TO HELL!"
1870–1882

The movement to require that executions be concealed from the general public was slow in coming. Mississippi was the first southern state to end such displays, in 1839. The Virginia legislature came in line at the end of the 1860s, but left the matter discretionary, with the trial judge or sheriff deciding whether to make an execution public.[1] For all practical purposes, by 1870 all executions in Virginia were conducted in jail yards. Although viewing was now drastically curtailed, crowds could press upon the scene or watch executions from elevated places adjoining a jail. If one were lucky, he could secure a ticket to a hanging, although most tickets were reserved to members of the press, clergymen, and officials.

It seems that one effect of the steep reduction in the number of spectators permitted to witness hangings was that the press media began serving up tantalizing narratives of hangings that occurred elsewhere. For example, the hangings of two blacks, William and Warner Taylor (William in June and Warner in August 1870), in Fredericksburg, Virginia, drew wide attention. The murder victim was William Jett, a seventeen-year-old store clerk. The *Daily Dispatch* reported that a "large number of spectators" from the counties of Essex, Westmoreland, and Stafford and "the entire Northern Neck" attended the execution.[2] Lynching was also reported, such as in the case of George Peck, an African American, who was arrested for attempted rape of a "small girl" in January 1870 in Bealesville, Maryland. Peck was taken to Poolesville and "lodged in the Odd-Fellows Hall." Before he could be taken on to the Rockville jail a mob seized him and lynched him from a locust tree, with rope secured to a fence.[3]

Determined Richmonders could ride out of town and witness infrequent hangings in nearby counties. One such occasion took place twenty

13. "You're Gwyne to Hell!"

miles from the city, in New Kent County on February 11, 1870. The event featured the execution of Alexander Gardner for the "horrible double murder" of John Baker and a Mrs. Stewart in September 1868. Actually Lewis Kennedy, who would be sentenced to a "lunatic asylum," was the main perpetrator of the murders. The facts of the crime were simply that Mrs. Stewart, age thirty, after her husband's death ten years before had become enamored with "a Half-breed," John Baker, who lived on an adjacent farm. Eventually Baker became a field hand for Mrs. Stewart; he then moved in with her and "took possession of the place." Baker, part Negro and Indian, had been previously married to a slave and had four children; Baker's second marriage was to a "free Negress," whom he divorced. Baker and Mrs. Stewart frequently quarreled. It was not unusual for Mrs. Stewart to receive a "sound drubbing." For two weeks before the murder Baker and Stewart did not speak to each other. Gardner, "a full-blooded negro" about thirty-five years old, and Kennedy (along with his wife) worked for Baker. Baker and Kennedy fought, and Kennedy was discharged from his employment. On September 8, while Baker was calling his hogs, Kennedy shot him, Gardner staying concealed in bushes nearby. Kennedy then went to the farmhouse and raped Mrs. Stewart and then "beat her brains out with a fire-iron." The house was set afire. Gardner denied any role in the killings but acknowledged helping to burn down the house. Gardner was tried and convicted of murder.

On the scaffold, one hundred yards to the rear of the county jail, Gardner was asked if he had anything to say. He turned "to the assembled negroes, who were laughing and carrying on as if witnessing a horse race or a circus," and said that he did not know whether he was going to Heaven or Hell, but for sure, "before God," he was innocent. "You're gwyne to hell!" yelled out a black woman. This caused laughter from the crowd. Gardner replied, "Yes; you laugh at poor me now, with these limbs tied, but the devils in hell are laughing at you!" He then proclaimed his innocence of the murders.

Gardner was "shrouded in black, and the cap was drawn over his face." A black preacher "uttered a few words of exhortation" and gave a "fervent prayer." With the drop, there was no struggle or other indication of suffering. After twenty-four minutes, doctors Slater and Williams examined the body, which was cut down, placed in a pine coffin, and buried in front of the scaffold. Thus, "the show being over, the negroes went their way in high glee with the entertainment and with something to talk about for a month."[4]

Public Executions in Richmond, Virginia

Richmonders had been disappointed that two candidates for the gallows had not been turned over to the hangman. The trial of John Bowler for the murder of Charles H. Rodgers on Westham Road in Henrico County on December 4, 1869, was postponed until mid April 1870. Though residents had expected a hanging would be the result, the jury deadlocked over a capital conviction, and decided upon murder in the second degree, with a nine-year prison term.[5] The execution of James Jeter Phillips for a murder committed in February 1867 was in abeyance for three and a half years because of two trials, appeals and respites. Besides the exhaustive defense maneuvers and the prolonged media hype the case has significance because it resulted in an execution under the new state policy of displacing public with private or semiprivate hangings. When the execution finally occurred, on July 22, 1870, local newspapers reported the event with as many as six full columns, which touched upon topics such as the condemned man's biography, forensic analysis, and scenes at the scaffold.

The facts of the case had all the ingredients of a modern mystery novel. On February 28, 1867, George F. Drinker, walking through the woods of his farm a few miles from Richmond in Henrico County, came upon the partially concealed body of a woman. There was no immediate identification. The corpse exhibited a bullet wound to the head from a small parlor pistol. The skull was not pierced, and it appeared the woman had died from having been beaten and strangled. A coroner's inquest declared "death by violence at the hands of some person or persons unknown." For several months the public was treated via the press with speculation as to the identity of the victim. The body was buried. Richmond detectives, nevertheless, continued their investigation, with support of the governor, who awarded imbursement for their expenses. One important clue did emerge. The toll-keeper on the Williamsburg turnpike, a Mr. Dowden, reported that a few days before the body was found, he had seen a man and a woman pass the tollgate and go down the Darbytown Road. The man soon returned alone. Mr. Dowden could not describe anything about the woman, but the man was of small stature and young, dressed in a black coat and cap. Dowden also described the suspect's wagon (red with white running gear). Questions were now being asked about the victim's wearing apparel as if these items would yield information. The body was exhumed and this time was correctly identified at that of Mary Emily Pitts.[6]

On June 13, 1867, Detective Knox and Constable Cole brought to the Richmond jail James Jeter Phillips, twenty-four years old, whom they had

13. "You're Gwyne to Hell!"

arrested at George Turner's farm for the murder of Phillips' wife. The brother and sister of the victim identified clothes belonging to the deceased found in a trunk, at the Turner farm, that belonged to Phillips. Other incriminating evidence included a Bible, inscribed with "Emily," a photograph of a "Miss Gerdy Pitts," and a six-shooter with three spent shells (Phillips said that he used the weapon to shoot at a dog). Phillips was examined in a hearing and remanded to be tried for murder in the Henrico County Circuit Court presided over by Judge Joseph Christian.[7]

James Jeter Phillips came from a prominent Henrico County family; his father had been sheriff. During the Civil War Phillips won esteem as an officer in the Thirteenth Virginia Infantry. At the time of his arrest he claimed to never have been married. This assertion was put to the lie when investigators turned up the fact that the Rev. W.A. Bayman, on July 13, 1865, had married Phillips and Miss Emily Pitts in Caroline County. Phillips at the time was on sick leave from the army, and Emily, ten years older than he, nursed him back to health at the Pitts home. Pitts brought Emily to Richmond on February 16, 1867, promising to take her to her father's house. Although James and Emily were observed together at the Virginia House and on Franklin Street on February 17, Emily was never seen alive again.[8]

The trials of James Jeter Phillips, according to one historian, "excited greater and more continued interest than any that ever had been held in Richmond, as to that, in the State." Moreover, it proved to be "in many respects the most remarkable criminal case in Virginia."[9] The first of two trials, both held in the chamber of the house of delegates at the capitol, lasted nineteen days (Oct. 30–Nov 20, 1867), and ended in a hung jury.[10] The second trial was held June 15 to July 10, 1868, before Judge George L. Christian, a Confederate veteran who, having lost a leg during the war, depended upon the use of crutches. The court sentenced Phillips to be hanged on November 6, 1868.[11]

Expert defense counsel challenged the conviction on several technicalities, chief of which was faulty commitment to trial procedure. Governor Wells and then Governor Walker granted respites; in all, Phillips received a death sentence thirteen times. The case went through the Virginia Court of Appeals and the U.S. district and circuit courts. Finally, in June 1870, the chief justice of the U.S. Supreme Court, Salmon P. Chase, for the Supreme Court decided that Phillips' death sentence was legal.[12]

All the while, Phillips was confined in a 16' × 18' cell on the second story of the Henrico "new, or granite," jail. He was "lightly ironed": his

Left: Mrs. Mary Emily Phillips (from James G. Watson, "The Jeter Phillips Murder Case...," *The Virginia Trooper* [Richmond, 1953]). *Bottom:* Jeter Phillips (from James G. Watson, "The Jeter Phillips Murder Case...," *The Virginia Trooper* [Richmond, 1953]).

arms were unmanacled, but a leg was chained at seven feet. In a rare newspaper interview a reporter found Phillips seated in a chair, a Bible and a Baptist hymnal on the bed. The Bible was opened to Romans, chapters 3, 4, and 5. On a stool, there were several religious books and tracts and a newspaper. The condemned man received visits from ministers Rosse, of the Methodist Church, and Jeter, Dickinson, and Taylor, who were Baptist.[13] On the eve of the execution, Phillips was consoled by the Rev. Woodward of the Union Station Methodist Church, who left about 10 P.M.[14]

The local newspapers provided coverage of the execution with about three times the space normally used for such occasions. It was as if the public, denied direct access to the death proceedings, wanted vicariously to obtain all the details and more. Times had greatly changed since the reportage on the Gabriel slave conspirators of 1800–1801, when even mass hangings only merited several lines in the local press. The *Dispatch* announced on Monday, July 25, 1870 that because of the great demand for the *Dispatch* on Saturday (July 23, the day after the execution) "with our graphic and thrilling account," the coverage would be republished in the next semiweekly edition.[15]

13. "You're Gwyne to Hell!"

At 2:00 A.M. on the day of the hanging, Phillips went to bed and rose at 5:00 A.M. He washed, trimmed his mustache, and gave special attention to his curls. At 8:00 A.M., upon request of the prisoner, the attached seven-foot chain was removed.[16]

A large crowd had gathered around the jail, "lining the sidewalks and filling the several yards" of the facility. Just before 11:00 A.M. a group of reporters, officials, and clergymen who had been issued tickets signed by the sheriff entered the very small paved, interior yard of the old jail. A police squad kept back would-be spectators gathered in the other yards of the jail. Some without tickets pressed their way into the execution compound. "At one time it became necessary for the officers to use their clubs, and a free fight seemed imminent."

The scaffold was the same that had been used to execute Albert Tyler at a different site. Reconstructed on the jail yard, it was made of plain white pine, twelve feet square and twelve feet from the ground. The platform had a trap door of about four feet square in the center. On a crossbeam, about ten feet above the platform, was an iron hook, one-half inch in diameter, "from which was suspended the fatal rope." This cord, about eight feet long and one-fourth inch thick, had been specially made by one W.E. Simons two years previously and cost six dollars. Besides the numerous persons at ground level, sightseers were perched on the roofs of the jail and nearby houses, even on chimneys a block away. Many viewers, becoming weary "of looking at the scaffold and its surroundings, exchanged rude and crude jests."

Reverends Dickinson and Jeter stayed with the prisoner until 1:00 P.M., when Sheriff Smith arrived and announced the execution would proceed. Phillips emerged from the jail with deputy sheriffs Magruder and Walsh on each side of him, the clergymen behind, and in the rear deputy Sheriff Childress and the prisoner's counsel, G.W. Thomas. As soon as Phillips reached the gallows, a crowd in the adjacent jail yard tried to push past "officers for a sight of the gallows," and "for several minutes there was considerable disorder, but at length silence was secured by the closing of the door."[17]

The clergymen accompanied the prisoner onto the scaffold platform. After "some preliminaries," Phillips rose from a chair where he had been seated, and the Rev. Dickinson read the following paper prepared by Phillips:

Richmond, July 22, 1870.

I, James Jeter Phillips, condemned to be hanged on the charge of murdering my wife, and expecting soon to appear in the presence of my Creator and my Judge, do make the following confession and statement: I acknowledge that I am guilty of the crime for which the law pronounces against me. I need not detail the circumstances of my crime; they are mainly as they were presented in the testimony on my trial. I lived unhappily with my wife. I scarcely know when I formed the purpose of getting rid of her. While on my last visit to her mother's I resolved the subject in my mind. After I brought her to Richmond my purpose was settled. I borrowed a pistol on Sunday evening, took her from the boarding house, and we walked to the place where her body was found, and murdered her. I confess the greatness of my guilt, and I don't understand how I could have been led to commit such a deed. I have confessed it with sorrow before God, and hope He has forgiven me through the merits of Jesus Christ. Acknowledging my sin before the world, I hope that all will forgive me now. I die in peace with all men, but with a deep sense of my guilt and unworthiness. I wish to say distinctly before God and all persons present that I am alone in my guilt. No one suggested my crime to me, knew my purpose, or gave me the slightest countenance in my deed either before or after the act. All the rumors that I was engaged to be married or that I was in love, are entirely false. I had not motive for the commission of my crime, but escape from a connection which seemed to destroy my prospects for happiness in life. I bid you all farewell, hoping we may meet again where sin and sorrow are unknown. Let others be warned by my example and fate. And now I yield my body to the dust in the hope of a joyful resurrection, and I command my soul to the God that gave it, and to the Lord Jesus Christ, who I think redeemed it by his precious blood, and fitted it through grace for his eternal kingdom. (Signed), Jeter Phillips.

The Rev. Dickinson then read a postscript, which he said had just been given to him by the prisoner just a half hour previous, and was in Phillips's handwriting: "As to the judge and the Commonwealth's attorney I have no unkind feeling, nor have I towards any other human being. As to the officers of the law, they have been very kind to me, especially the jailor and guards. As for the Governor he acted right. I justly deserve all I have suffered. (Signed), James Jeter Phillips."[18]

Dr. Knox, the physician who had testified against Phillips during the trials, was also on the platform and threw his arms around the prisoner. Both men burst into tears. Knox and the two preachers then exited the platform. Deputy Walsh stepped forward and said, per the prisoner's request, that Phillips held no ill will towards anyone, especially the sheriff. Sheriff Smith then said, again at the prisoner's request, that Phillips was "at peace with all mankind."

Deputy Walsh untied Phillips' hands from the front and pinioned his

13. "You're Gwyne to Hell!"

arms behind his back. Walsh then put a "black cambric cap" over Phillips' head and adjusted the rope over the cap, fixing the knot over the left ear; the legs were tied together. After Walsh stepped down from the scaffold, Sheriff Smith conversed briefly with the prisoner. Shaking hands with the condemned man for the last time, Smith waved his handkerchief. Walsh drew the bolt at 1:20 P.M. For five to ten seconds the body swayed to and fro. Then Phillips "commenced the most violent contortions. His legs were drawn up suddenly and were kicking through the air, and his arms were drawn up in a most violent manner"; his elbows "rested high up his back." After three minutes the convulsions partially ceased; muscular spasms lasted for eight minutes, and then there was no movement. At 2:00 P.M. the body was taken down and examined by doctors Knox and Walker (Walker was the surgeon for the penitentiary). Though there had been a lengthy drop of 5' 10", because the knot had slipped there was no dislocation of the neck, and death was by strangulation.[19]

The Phillips execution, with the long-drawn-out case that led to it, seems to have satisfied Richmonders's blood lust for a while. The next execution in the city did not occur until 1883. Meanwhile, condemned prisoners from neighboring counties were jailed in Richmond until the time of their execution; this was for security purposes, to provide them safekeeping from lynching. Thus in 1871 four such felons spent their last days in Richmond before being hanged: William Henry Johnson and Richard Green (a double execution), Thomas McGiffin, and Dick Head. Nothing is known about the latter (an African American), including the reason or for his odd name, other than that the *Dispatch*, in its New Year's Day edition of 1872, mentioned he had been hanged the past year.[20]

William Henry Johnson and Richard Green had waylaid and murdered Charles Friend, "an old and respected citizen" of Prince George County (near Petersburg), on March 24, 1871.[21] On the night before the execution of the two on July 28, 1871, the sheriff of Prince George County and four deputies arrived in Richmond on the 8:30 northern bound train. On the 3:45 A.M. return train, the law officers, with Johnson and Green in tow, journeyed back to Petersburg (25 miles from Richmond), arriving there at 5:00 A.M. The escort, now numbering thirteen men, and their two prisoners headed the seven miles to the Prince George courthouse and jail, followed by a large number of African Americans who had gathered at the Petersburg train depot. During the one and a half hour ride from the depot to the gallows, the road swarmed with "white and black humanity.... [T]o one uninformed it would seem that there was some grand

Public Executions in Richmond, Virginia

festivity to take place. Wagons and vehicles loaded with living freight, pedestrians, and persons on horseback, were all bound in one common way."[22] Undoubtedly some Richmonders were among the anxious throng.

Detained throughout the morning, the two prisoners received spiritual counsel from two black preachers, Atwell (Episcopal) and Givins (Methodist). With their arms pinioned in front, the two prisoners went up the steps to the scaffold, accompanied by the sheriff and his deputies. Each prisoner was placed in a chair. The burial service of the Episcopal Church was then read. The doomed men rose and made to stand upon the drop. With the assistance of "some expert volunteers" the noose was adjusted to the necks and the rope tied to the crossbeam. At the time the legs were fastened and the black caps placed over their heads, Green shouted, "I am Innocent! I never killed Friend, or no other man!" At 12:48 P.M., "a sharp click" was heard, followed by a "heavy thud." The fall was five feet. Green's neck broke, but Johnson was "strangulated." Commented one reporter, "The contortions of the bodies were awful to behold."[23]

In the same month as the Green and Johnson executions, another condemned criminal held in the Richmond jail was sent back to the county of his conviction (Greensville County) and hanged there. Thomas McGiffin had been sentenced to death for the murder of Constable Drummond of Brunswick County in 1869. The actual murderer, a Dr. Lewis ("a desperado from the North"), also was incarcerated in Richmond, but he was eventually ruled insane and sent to a "lunatic asylum." In Richmond, McGiffin was "double-ironed" and placed in "one of the strongest cells of the jail."[24]

McGiffin claimed that he had been riding along with Lewis, not knowing that a posse that accosted them, led by Drummond, had a warrant for Lewis' arrest. Lewis shot Drummond with a Spencer rifle at a distance of one hundred yards.[25] On the morning of the execution day, July 21, 1871, McGiffin was brought from Richmond to Hicksford in Greensville County.[26] The *Dispatch*, in reporting the execution, said that McGiffin was "the boldest, most careless man apparently that ever went to the gallows." Also it was noted that the rope broke and the condemned man, "half-dead," fell to the ground, whereupon he was picked up and hanged again.[27]

Richmonders almost had one of their own hanged several years later. Horace Venable had been sentenced to death for the murder of Mary Holmes. After several reprieves while the case was contested in higher court on technicalities, Venable's sentence was commuted in 1874 to eighteen years in the penitentiary.[28]

13. "You're Gwyne to Hell!"

The hanging of a prisoner held in the Henrico County jail (in Richmond) in Chesterfield County greatly excited Richmonders, if the extensive newspaper coverage in the city is any judge. Two things especially stand out. One, the culprit was a much respected black teenager. Furthermore, the crime was arson, which had not been a capital penalty for whites before the war and had long since not been used under the slave code. Anticipating the hanging on September 1, 1876, the *Dispatch* predicted that "a large crowd of persons will go from this city to attend the execution."[29]

In commenting on this case, the *Dispatch* further noted that "the history of the crimes of Hillary Page is one of an unprecedented nature in the annals of incendiarism." The persistence in the perpetration of Page's crimes "finds no better excuse than in his own utterance: 'I had the devil in me.'" In at least a dozen attempts to burn down buildings, beginning as early as March 1874, Page succeeded in five arsons. A major fire was the total destruction of Summer Hill, the "beautiful homestead" of Colonel F.G. Ruffin, Jr., located in "a large and thick grove" two hundred yards from the Richmond and Petersburg Turnpike, three miles south of Richmond. Page was a servant at the Ruffin estate; most sadly Ruffin Sr. had raised him almost since infancy. Shocked by the fire and finding out the perpetrator was his affectionate and loyal servant, who was like a son to him, Ruffin moved to Richmond with his family, where he lived to the end of his life.

It was quite a while before the serial arsonist was arrested, although Page had been early suspected. What cracked the case was an informer, "a negro boy named Wesley" admitted into the confidence of Page. Wesley enticed Page, who told Wesley that he had set many fires to burn down a barn belonging to a Mr. Johnson, who "turned out to be none other than Detective John Wren." On February 15, 1876, Hillary Page was arrested.

Charged under four indictments at trial February 19–22, Page was found guilty under the third indictment, relating to the Ruffin arson. The state supreme court set aside this verdict and remanded the case for retrial on the third count before the Circuit Court of Chesterfield County, held in Manchester (today part of Richmond) during the November 1875 term. Despite "numerous exceptions ... taken during the progress of the trial," the jury returned a verdict of guilty and sentenced Page to death; the execution date, however, was suspended to permit time for an appeal. The supreme court was unanimous in upholding the second trial judgment. During the May 1876 term of the Chesterfield County Circuit Court, the day for the execution was fixed in July. The governor, "at the earnest solicitation of some humane gentlemen," postponed the execution until the first Friday in September. The superintendents of three "lunatic asylums" examined Page and unanimously pronounced him sane.

During the morning of the day of the execution, "the road leading from Manchester to the court-house was lined with vehicles of all descriptions," and "it seemed that all the whites and blacks of the county were going to witness the saddest act of a poor unfortunate's career." Page, heavily guarded, set out for the execution site in an ambulance. It had already been announced that he had started on his way; this was done for the purpose of preventing a crowd to gather at the jail. An escort, commanded by Captain "Dinks" Lipscomb and Henry Fitzgerald, accompanied the ambulance. At the courthouse Deputy Sheriff Gill took charge of Page and put him in a cell. A "number of reporters" arrived, and interviewed the prisoner:

> "Hillary, do you feel any better prepared to die than you did yesterday?"
> "Yes, sir. I feel a heap better."
> "Do you acknowledge yourself guilty of everything that has been charged against you?"
> "Yes, sir, all but one thing, and that is young Mr. Ruffin's house. I didn't burn that. It caught fire by itself. I didn't burn that."
> "Hillary, why did you say that Colonel Ruffin and his son came to you and desired you to make statements implicating other parties?"
> "All that was false. I just said so because I thought it would do me good. I was put up to it. It's natural that I should try to save my life."

At this point two ministers, Binga and J.E. Brown, arrived and the reporters left.

The scaffold, about a half-mile northwest of the courthouse, was "built in a most primitive manner. The platform was three feet ten inches above the ground, and was supported by a post with a binge in the middle. It was by a general verdict accorded to be as mean a scaffold as was ever erected for the execution of a human being. It measured ten feet by four. The sheriff of the county was even more nervous than the condemned." Hillary entered the scaffold, and the sheriff asked him if he had anything to say. Hillary gave this reply: "I have, but I would rather have Mr. Binga say it for me." The Rev. Binga declared:

> I wish to say to the friends of the poor condemned man that he is free to acknowledge that he is guilty of all the crimes of which he has been found guilty, and for which he is to suffer death. He had declared himself prepared to die, and I am glad to hear him say so. I did not know until a short

13. "You're Gwyne to Hell!"

time ago that he wanted me to preach his funeral, or else I would have prepared myself. I cannot under such painful circumstances say all I would wish to say. I say to you who meet to witness the execution of our unfortunate brother, that as he has committed one of the highest crimes under our State laws so he will have to meet the law. He feels that he has violated the divine as well as the civil law; but he feels also that he finds more foregiveness in Christ than in the civil law. He also feels that he finds favor in the sight of God. He is able to say to you, as he has said to me, that he is ready to die. He said before he left his cell that he would rather die than live, because he had such an all-abiding faith in the blood of Jesus Christ. Take warning, young men. Though you may mean well, remember that the way of the transgressor is hard. What better proof do you want of this than is contained in the scene before you to-day? But I feel consoled, because he told me to-day that he felt that he was saved by the blood of Jesus. We behold him here to-day as a man ready to leave this world, and who feels that he has the assurance that he will join that immortal band that will praise the Lord eternally in Heaven.

The Rev. Brown next prayed, after which Rev, Binga led the assemblage in singing the hymn "Death Cannot Make Our Souls Afraid If God Be with Us There."

The final arrangements were made. Hillary Page stepped upon the trap "with great fortitude." He was allowed a fall of only eighteen inches. When the trap was sprung, at 1:17 P.M., for a few moments "he remained dangling in the air without motion." Soon "he commenced springing about in a desperate manner, and at one time it looked his feet would lodge upon the platform." At 1:43 P.M. he was declared dead by Dr. T.J. Cheatham. "He was cut down as though he had been a beef, and his head struck heavily against the trap-door of the scaffold. Poor fellow, as he proved to be, this made no difference to him." The body was buried about twenty yards from the scaffold.[30]

14

"WAIT, I'M NOT DONE YET"
1883

The semiprivate hanging of Charles Henry Lee, a twenty-year-old black man, on August 3, 1883, was reminiscent of the rowdiness of the public hanging days of the past. A newspaper account revealed the commotion at the scene of Lee's execution:

> It was well understood both in city and country that on yesterday at some hour between sunrise and noon a negro boy named Charles Henry Lee would be hung in the jail-yard at Henrico court-house, in this city. There is nothing that attracts the morbidly curious more than a hanging, not even a circus or a game of base-ball; and the result was that early yesterday morning crowds of people from the country were making their way to the city and thence to the county court-house. City people also flocked toward the same place, and by 10 o'clock in the morning a dense crowd, composed mostly of colored people, had wedged themselves into the lots around the court-house and county jail.
> And this, too, when it was well known that the execution must, according to the law of the land, be private.
> But curious people thought they might be able to get a glimpse of the criminal, or possibly prevail upon the authorities to make exceptional rulings, and admit them to the scene of the hanging.
> The doors were closed, however, and only those who were armed with tickets were admitted. Outside the pressure continued, and the hum of voices roared with a dull sound above the jingling of street-car bells or the rattling of wheels over the stony pavement. Now and then the scream of a vender of lemonade, or the mellifluous drone of the owner of a cart filled with watermelons, could be heard in distinct tones. Each newcomer was besieged by the motley crowd with appeals of "Get me in"; and now and then could be heard offers of money to any one whose influence would secure a permit. On top of high piles of lumber adjacent to the jail-yard were groups of people. Others, with more boldness, secured a long ladder,

14. "Wait, I'm Not Done Yet"

and upon this mounted to the top of the jail-walls, and there perched themselves, resting for two hours under a blazing sun, just to see a man hanged.[1]

Charles Henry Lee, along with his mistress, Barbara Miller, who was the wife of the victim and who would be hanged on September 14, had been arrested for the murder of Daniel Miller, "an inoffensive sort of darky, who lived near Hungary station on the line of the Richmond, Fredericksburg and Potomac road." The "old man" was found dead along the railroad track on February 14. At first the death was ruled an accident. The body was buried, but upon the persistence of a suspicious Constable Solomon, the corpse was exhumed, and strong evidences of homicide was discovered. Charles Henry Lee and Barbara Miller stood trial separately in the Henrico Circuit Court for the murder of Daniel Miller. Lee's death sentence was overturned because a newspaper account of the trial had been made available to the jury. A second trial also resulted in a death sentence. Lee was convicted mainly on the testimony of Barbara Miller.[2]

Subsequently Lee had a conversion experience and was baptized in a bathtub in the jail yard by a black preacher, the Rev. George H. Boswell, of the Eighteenth Street Church. Lee also made a confession, accusing Barbara as the murderer of "poor old Daniel." Actually the court had already established Charles Henry Lee only as an accessory, but under the law he was equally as guilty as the one who performed the fatal act.

A brief description of the gory murder will suffice. Charles Henry Lee resided in the home of Daniel and Barbara Miller; Charles and Barbara were lovers. Barbara, "a middle-aged negro woman," was perhaps close to twenty years older than Charles. Daniel, the victim, seems to have been much older than Barbara.

"The night before the deed was dark and rainy." Before the three principals retired for the night, the murder plan was hatched. The murder took place at dawn, as "old Daniel, like any other good old darky, heeded not the rain and roaring wind" and slept "like a log" in one corner of the cabin. All the while, a fire blazed from "the ample fireplace." The "wind roared around the rude log cabin," and "gusts of rain pattered against the sides of the house with force sufficient to penetrate the chinking and daubing and send dirty streaks of water to the rough pine floor." When Barbara awoke Lee and thrust an axe into his hands, her young paramour was reticent to commit murder. Barbara then grabbed the axe, and going to her husband's bed, brought the weapon down on Daniel's head with deadly force. Charles, a "powerful man muscularly," easily "shouldered" the body and placed it on the railroad track beside the house. Almost immediately a "fast mail mail-train from Washington thundered past, scattering fragments of Daniel Miller's body for a distance of sixty yards along the track."

On Thursday night before his execution, Charles Henry Lee received permission from Sheriff J.W. Southward to hold a midnight prayer meeting. Thus, "by the light of flickering lamps, in the company of his father and mother and a half dozen friends," Lee listened to "the words of counsel let fall by ministers of the Gospel of his own race." Mention may be made of Lee's parents. His father, Sandy Lee, was nearly seventy years old, was described as "a well-behaved, old-fashioned darky." He was once a slave belonging to a prominent citizen. Sandy owned eighteen acres of land. Charles Henry Lee's mother was about fifteen years younger than Charles' father and was considered "to be a woman of remarkably good sense." At the prayer session, which lasted for about an hour, the worshippers lifted their voices "in songs of praise in that weird manner so peculiar to colored people."

Lee arose early on the execution day, ate a "hearty breakfast," and then dressed himself in a white shirt, dark pants, and vest, leaving off his coat and shoes. At 9:00 A.M. the prayer meeting renewed in his cell, now in the presence of seventeen men and seven women, including his condemned partner in crime, Barbara Miller. Barbara sat on the floor in the cell "at the feet of Charles Lee, thrusting her ugly presence upon the father and mother of the boy of whose destruction she had been the author and finisher." Charles' parents did not approve of Barbara's being present. His father said that "she takes more authority over Charles than his own mother, or me either; I never saw such a scand'lous woman."

After many songs and ministerial prayers, Charles Henry Lee "fell upon his knees and broke out in a loud voice into a wild prayer." He called upon Jesus to forgive those who had brought him to justice, and also prayed for his defense lawyer, his mother, who knelt next to him, his father, and for Barbara. He ended the prayer by entreating the Lord "to have mercy upon him and stand by him when he came to die." The sheriff then announced that since Lee had only a few more hours to live, his cell would have to be cleared of all persons, except for the ministers and Lee's parents. Lee's parents declined to stay, and, after a final good-bye, they went into the jail yard, "where they rested a few moments." Then they took up their "carpet-bags, and moving out disappeared in the dark cloud of colored people that lined the boundaries of the jail-yard and courthouse." The three ministers stayed in the cell until 11:45 A.M.

14. *"Wait, I'm Not Done Yet"*

The sheriff came in the cell and told Lee that he had only a few minutes to live and to prepare himself for death. Lee stood up and put on "a thin black alpaca coat." At this moment Barbara Miller was conducted into Lee's cell. With permission from the sheriff she took from a brown-paper package a pair of white cotton gloves, which she "in quite a lover-like manner proceeded to stretch over Charles's hands—the gloves being a size or two too small." She then whispered for half a minute in Charles's ear, after which she kissed him and was brought back to her own cell. Meanwhile, with the execution now soon expected, the crowd outside the jail began loud shouting, yelling, "Time's up!" "Here he comes!" and the like.

The time had come to go to the gallows:

> [I]n his sock-feet, escorted by the sheriff and jailer, and followed by the three colored ministers and a half-dozen reporters, the march to the gallows commenced. As soon as the *cortege* reached the jail-yard, in pursuance of the programme adopted by the colored clergy, a mournful hymn was sung, commencing with the words "Dark and thorny is the desert through which the pilgrims make their way." With a firm step the condemned man marched, up the seventeen steps to the top of the scaffold. Close behind him followed the sheriff, the colored jailer, the Commonwealth's attorney, and the three colored ministers.

On the scaffold the sheriff read the sentence of death. Asked if he had anything to say, Lee moved to the edge of the platform and spoke briefly: "Well, I don't have anything much to say; I only want to advise my friends to take warning, and not to be persuaded and led off like I was. I would advise that you all that has got children growing up to raise them up right, so that they will not be led off as I was led off. I think I am prepared to make my peace with God. I trust that I will be able to meet you all in Heaven. I don't have much to say, but I go prepared. I feel that I am fitted to die."

Lee seated himself in the only chair on the scaffold. Religious services followed, conducted by two black ministers, Reverends Binga and Boswell. The latter "delivered an exhortation," telling his audience that there nothing "to frolic over." He said that God forgives sins and that the condemned man would be "perhaps in ten minutes be in glory." In concluding, Boswell said that this was his first hanging, that he came only because he was called upon. Reverend Boswell then shook hands with Lee, and said, "If you get to the kingdom of God before I do, look out for me, for I am coming, too." While the two men shook hands, the colored jailer wiped the perspiration from Lee's face. The other ministers also said their good-byes, and when all three had left the platform, Sheriff Southward adjusted the black hood and placed the halter around the prisoner's neck. Lee appeared to be praying silently. At 12:25 Sheriff Southward stepped to the railing of the scaffold and "gave the signal by dropping his handkerchief. Constable Neurehr pulled the prop from under the trap and the body shot through the opening like a flash. The fall was about nine feet, breaking the neck, causing instant death. There was not the slightest movement of the body from the time the trap was sprung until it was taken down. Drs. Hawks, Carter, May, Hinchman, and Burfoot were present, and examined Lee's pulse, which ceased to beat in eleven minutes, and in fourteen minutes the doctors pronounced Lee dead."

When someone said something about taking down the body. Sheriff Southward declared, "No, wait a minute; I wish to speak to the crowd." Addressing the some hundred people in the jail yard from the scaffold platform, with Lee still dangling beneath, Southward said that Lee's parents were very poor and were in need of enough money "to convey the remains of their son to their home, in Lunenburg county, for burial." Southward said that any amount would be greatly appreciated. Commonwealth's attorney Thomas removed his straw hat and passed it around to receive donations; it is not known how much money was raised. The body was cut down and "placed in a neat pine coffin and delivered to friends, who carried it to the depot," from whence it went to Lunenburg County for burial.

In six weeks, on September 14, Barbara Miller had her own rendezvous with death on the same gallows that had claimed her young paramour. Again the local press gave wide and lurid coverage. Barbara had been convicted as the actual murderer largely on her own confession. A week before her execution she repudiated that confession and trial evidence and named the executed Charles Henry Lee as almost the sole perpetrator of the homicide of Daniel Miller. In the second confession, Barbara said:

> This is the last statement about the death of my husband, Daniel Miller.... The first time I ever consented for Charles to kill Daniel was on the 13th day of February, and he killed him on the 14th. As we both agreed to it, I never talked to Charles about the killing after I consented to it until he killed him. When Charles left the house that morning I knew it was to kill my husband, as, Charles and myself had talked the matter over the night before, and Charles acted with my consent when he killed my husband. When he got back to the house he had blood on his coat, vest, and pants. I

14. "Wait, I'm Not Done Yet"

washed all his clothes afterwards. If Charles and myself had not been arrested we would have been married between that time and Christmas. Charles worried me to let him kill my husband until I consented to let him do it. He killed him at my suggestion. I was not present when he killed him. I am willing to die for my guilt, as I am going to Heaven.

her
BARBARA MILLER[3]
mark

During Barbara's last days,[4] curious Richmonders learned from the local press how she was holding up. "She is in good spirits, sleeps well, and laughs and talks freely with all who visit her," commented one news release. Her children, mother, and Reverend George H. Boswell, who had counseled Charles Henry Lee, frequently came by. Two nights before the execution, Barbara underwent an epiphany of sorts. As she told Sheriff Southward, "I dreampt last night that when I went upon the gallows three angels came down from heaven and took me up before Mr. Southward could put the rope around my neck. Mr. Southward cried out, 'Wait, I'm not done yet'; but I didn't wait. One angel was in front of me, and beckoned to me and said, 'Come on, Barbara,' and I went flying over the jail-walls with the other two angels on each side of me to my eternal home in glory." When asked if she had seen Charles Henry Lee, she said,

> "Oh, yes. I forgot to tell you about it when you were in here this morning. I was lying on my bed fast asleep when Charles came and touched me on the shoulder and said, 'Barbara, you have only got one day before you will be with me,' but when I awoke he left me. She said she knew Charles was in heaven, because he came in the shape of a spirit and wore an eternal robe. When the reporter asked her if she had seen her husband she hung her head and replied: 'Yes; but Mr. Miller ain't at rest. I have seen him in my dreams, but he is very miserable. I have prayed for him, and hope he will yet be happy.'"

Barbara's request, as had that of Charles' earlier, that a late night-early morning prayer meeting be held just prior to the execution was granted. Several black ministers, church officials, and friends attended. "Prayers of the most fervid and incongruous were offered up," and "hymn after hymn, sung in the style peculiar to the colored race, followed each prayer." Words were "improvised to suit the occasion," and the "exercises" lasted until 2:00 A.M. Then everyone left, except several women friends, who "rolled themselves in blankets and slept soundly on the floor of the cell." At 9:00 A.M. the cellmates awoke and ate a hearty breakfast. The ministers, "several officials from the colored churches, and a crowd of curious spectators, mostly colored, came into the cell, and the prayer-meeting was resumed."

Meanwhile, Barbara put on her "death dress," which had been specially made according to her request. The garment, made of white Swiss muslin, "fitted nicely." It seemed the condemned woman was making a fashion statement:

> The skirt was long and flounced near the base, the flounces being trimmed with broad bands of insertion. The sleeves of the body were similarly ornamented, and the dress made plain, no attempt at sacque or overskirt being made. Her short, nappy black hair was carefully combed, and ornamented with an inch-wide band of white ribbon, tied in a bow on the left side of the head. Around her throat she wore an immensely wide collar made of cheap thread-lace. On her breast was pinned a small bouquet made of artificial flowers, representing lilacs and orange-buds. She wore no shoes.

As the religious service played itself out in Barbara's cell, the condemned woman "stood in the centre of the sable throng" and "almost continuously kept up a swaying motion of the body." At intervals Barbara's voice sounded out above the prayers, singing in "a wild ejaculation or an appeal for mercy." One hymn which seemed to greatly affect her was one given out by "a little short, stumpy black man, evidently a preacher." One verse of the hymn, as noted by a reporter, "chanted in mournful but musical cadences, ran as follows":

> Come, let us turn our back to the shore
> And leave the world behind;
> Fix our boats, and tie our sails,
> And our souls shall not be drowned

The chorus became personal:

> Barbara is nearer her home,
> Nearer her home to Thee;
> Barbara is nearer home, where Jesus is,
> Nearer her home to Thee.

All the while the prayer service continued, Barbara's mother was out in the jail yard, "circulating in the crowd for the purpose of raising a subscription to defray Barbara's burial expenses." She seemed to have been "a pretty good collector," apparently raising more than enough money.

At 11:00 A.M. Barbara's sister entered the cell to say good-bye. Mr. Waddill, clerk of the court, and Mr. Thomas, commonwealth's attorney, were in the cell at the time. When they left, Barbara told her sister that

14. *"Wait, I'm Not Done Yet"*

they had been present for the prayer service; "it was necessary for them to pray, and pray hard, as they were lawyers, and mighty few lawyers ever entered the kingdom of heaven."

Exactly at noon Barbara was moved out into the jail yard. The sheriff and the black jailer walked in front of Barbara, followed by four black preachers "chanting a hymn." Barbara moved slowly up the steps of the scaffold, holding on to the railing. She tried to join the "droning words of the hymn," but her voice was hardly audible. On the platform she was seated in a chair. Sheriff Southward read the death sentence, and asked her if she had anything to say. Barbara came forward, and "stretching wide both arms, sang, rather than spoke, something like the following, which she repeated again and again: 'Thank God. I bid you all good-bye. Farewell, farewell to you all. Thank God! I'm going to my long home. I want you all to get a lesson from Barbara. Farewell.'" She seemed rather "dumbfounded with fright," much like that of a rabbit "when a regiment of soldiers jumps it from its bed and yells after it in pursuit. The rabbit always stops in its flight and permits capture."

The four preachers, the black jailer, and the sheriff remained on the scaffold platform while another hymn was sung and a prayer given by the Rev. George H. Boswell. During this phase of the ceremony, the jailer "turned his back to Barbara and the others" and "puffed vigorously at the very short stump of a cigar which he had taken to the scaffold." The jailer "eyed savagely some dozen or more people who had climbed to the top of the jail-yard walls and were sitting high above him." These spectators began to create a disturbance, whereupon the jailer, in a much louder voice than that of the Rev. Boswell, who was still praying, yelled, "Silence!" The Rev. Boswell, "catching the spirit of the negro jailer ... fired a shot at the bad boys by saying in his prayer: 'Oh, Lord, bless those people on the wall, and let them understand that while they are on the walls that every one of them could be sent to hell.'" After concluding the prayer, Reverend Boswell, "a man of nervous temper," in a loud voice further berated the wall-sitters. He then "shook hands with Barbara, delivered himself of some prayerful abjurations, and abruptly descended the scaffold steps, holding tight to the railing with one hand and his umbrella with the other."

The fatal moment arrived. Sheriff Southward "adjusted the noose, pinioned Barbara's arms and feet, placed the black cap over her head, and stood ready to give the signal for the springing of the trap." Just as he was about to drop the handkerchief, Barbara said, "Farewell to all." Just then the deputy sheriff yanked the rope connected to the trap door, and the body fell. "Death came slowly; the body writhed and twisted, and was dreadfully convulsed. The neck could not have been broken, and death, no doubt, was produced by strangulation." After twenty minutes, "Drs. W.D. Burfoot and J. Knox pronounced life extinct, and the body was cut down, placed in a poplar coffin, and turned over to friends for interment in Henrico County."

Thus concluded a sad morality tale, as old as the story of Adam and Eve, in this instance one of an older woman leading a youth to the coils of sin and damnation. Charles Henry Lee's mother said of him that he was "a mighty good boy while at home." But, as a reporter noted, "the immodest and outrageous conduct of wicked Barbara Miller" had brought about the "destruction" of Charles Henry Lee as well as that of herself.

15

"CLUVERIUS'S DAY"
1884–1887

Richmonders learned from the newspapers of January 14, 1887, that the time for the long anticipated hanging of Thomas J. Cluverius was about to take place at the city jail:

> The murder for which Thomas Judson Cluverius (pronounced here Kla'veers) will to-day suffer the death-penalty was committed about 10:30 o'clock on the night of March 13, 1885.
> The victim was his second cousin, Fannie Lillian Madison, daughter of Charles J. Madison, of King William county.
> The scene was the Old (or Marshall) reservoir, which is in the western confines of the city about a hundred yards beyond Hollywood cemetery.
> The motive alleged was that Cluverius had betrayed the girl, and that as her time approached she became importunate; that he having engaged himself to marry another girl saw no way to avoid the exposures which it was in her power to make but to kill her.
> ....
> The hanging will be done with a rope twenty-three feet long, made in Richmond of fine silk thread. The silk is of different bright colors. The noose part has been greased with olive oil to make it slip easily.[1]

Although Richmond, in its past, had spectacular murder cases and executions that put the public into a feeding frenzy—for example, the three pirates (1827), Jane and John Williams (1852), and James Jeter Phillips (1871)—the Cluverius-Madison case surpasses them all as to both the public animosity and sympathy towards the condemned man, compassion for the murdered woman, and, not the least, the extensive reportage of details of the crime investigation, trial, and execution. As one historian notes, the murder of Lillian Madison allegedly by Thomas J. Cluverius was "the most famous criminal case in the annals of Virginia; a case that was given

Public Executions in Richmond, Virginia

more newspaper notoriety and that stirred the people more than any to that time."[2] Cluverius was the most prominent person to be executed in Richmond since John Posey in the 1780s. An 1883 graduate of the new law school at Richmond College (University of Richmond), he was a practicing attorney. Of special interest, the sole reliance on circumstantial evidence against Cluverius called into question the court's reliance on this kind of evidence, of which Cluverius, who made no confession, stated that he had been placed on earth by God to bring about a curtailment of the use of circumstantial evidence. Adding more fuel to the speculation, Culverius' book-length autobiography was published several months after his execution.[3]

One of the two principals in the crime, Tommie Cluverius was twenty-four years old at the time of the murder, 5'6" tall, and weighed only about 130 pounds; he had dark auburn hair and a "quiet and reserved" disposition. The "frequency of his smiles caused him to be dubbed by some of the college boys 'Smiling Moses.'" Fannie Lillian Madison was "a short and stout little woman," about twenty-two years old, only 4'11" tall and weighed 125 pounds. She was eight months pregnant, although her condition was never suspected by anyone.

Tommie Culverius grew up near Little Plymouth in King and Queen County, and Lillian (she went by this name) Madison grew up near Manquin in King William County. Near Little Plymouth lived Mrs. Jane Tunstall, a wealthy, childless widow. She was the aunt of Tommie and a great-aunt of Lillian. Both Tommie and Lillian lived for a while with Mrs. Tunstall; both had their education paid by her: Tommie at Richmond College, and Lillian at the Burlington Academy in King and Queen County. At home Tommie exhibited piety, and in college his behavior was "unexceptionable." Upon graduation, Thomas Cluverius returned to King and Queen County, and in Centreville he had a law office. He was superintendent of a Sunday school. During this time he and his brother, Willie, lived at Mrs. Tunstall's. Culverius' character was different when he was in Richmond, where he "kept company with some dissolute women." In 1884 Lillian was living at her grandfather's home near that of her parents. Culverius visited Lillian at this residence, where on many occasions they were alone. In October 1884, Lillian, now aware of her pregnancy, accepted a teaching position in the western part of the state at Mr. Dickerson's little log schoolhouse, near Milboro. In January 1885 she visited Culverius in Richmond, each staying at different hotels. In March she was again lured back to Richmond at Culverius' insistence that she accompany their aunt to Old Point Comfort.

15. "Cluverius's Day"

On Friday, March 13, Lillian and Tommie looked for an abortionist in Richmond, but were unsuccessful because of her advanced pregnancy. They searched for a backroom abortionist and were seen at various places in the city. At night they set out to visit one more would-be abortionist. Taking a streetcar to Main and Reservoir streets, they then headed on foot near the Marshall Reservoir.[4]

On March 14, about 7:00 A.M., Lysander W. Rose, keeper of the reservoir (on Richmond's West End, at today's Byrd Park), while making his rounds spotted a woman's glove and a piece of shoestring. Along the sharp picket fence surrounding the reservoir he discovered the footprints of a woman and a man, appearing as if there had been a struggle. Looking beyond the fence into the water he saw a woman's dress floating; investigating further, Rose and an assistant pulled a woman's body out of the water. The fence gate had been bolted; a question that later would arise was whether Cluverius, with his puny size, had the strength to hurl a body over the fence. The same question could be asked, if it ruled a suicide, whether Lillian could have lifted herself beyond the fence. The body was brought to the Almshouse, where it was identified. From extensive blows to the head the death was ruled a homicide.

Three factors especially suggested a link of Cluverius with Lillian Madison's murder. The pair had been seen together at different places in Richmond on the eve of the homicide. A note had been found in Lillian's hotel room from Cluverius that read: "I will be there as soon as possible; so do wait for me." The most telling piece of evidence was the finding of a gold watch key at the scene of the crime. A local jeweler testified that he had repaired one such item for Cluverius, who, however, vigorously denied that the key had belonged to him. Detective John Wren gathered much of the evidence against Cluverius.

Cluverius was arrested and lodged at the Richmond city jail at Marshall and 15th streets, in Shockoe Bottom. Great difficulty occurred in obtaining jurors for a trial. Only six jurors from a large venire qualified in Richmond; six more jurors were secured from Alexandria. The trial began May 13, 1885. The prisoner rode between the jail and the courtroom between Ninth and Tenth streets and Capitol and Broad streets in a carriage hired by himself. Huge crowds turned out at the entrances of the jail and courtroom.[5] The best of the Richmond bar represented each side of the case. Defense counsel denounced roundly that at the time Virginia law prevented the defendant in a capital case from giving testimony.

During the trial Dr. William H. Taylor, the city coroner, who was

Public Executions in Richmond, Virginia

convincing in declaring that the victim died from murder and not suicide, occasionally lent some levity to the proceedings. One of the attorneys for Cluverius, A. Brown Evans, sought to discredit Taylor's testimony by showing that Taylor was nearsighted.

"Now, Dr. Taylor," said Evans, "without quibbling, will you please tell the jury in a direct answer just exactly how far you can see?"

"One hundred and ninety-six million miles," came the reply. After brief hesitation, Taylor continued, "I can see the sun, and the scientists tell us it is the distance from the earth."[6]

On June 4, the jury delivered a verdict of guilty. There was breathless silence in the courtroom, while applause burst out among the curious crowd in the street. On June 19, Judge Thomas S. Atkins sentenced Cluverius to be hanged at the city jail on November 20, 1885. Largely with the skill of Cluverius, execution of sentence was delayed through the appeals process and respites for a year and a half. Governor Fitzhugh Lee refused to further respite beyond January 14, 1887, which finally would become "Cluverius's Day."

During his long incarceration, Cluverius, who insisted on his innocence to the end, hoped for commutation of his sentence or an exoneration. (Indeed, about the time of the execution a Richmonder then in New York City came forward to declare he was the murderer of Lillian Madison, but no one paid attention.)[7]

The authorities made Cluverius' ordeal as comfortable as possible. They even spared him the noise of building the gallows. It was constructed in the shop of J.E. Farrar, a "colored council-man," and was pieced together from 11:00 A.M. to 5:00 P.M. the day before the execution, at the east end of the jail yard facing Marshall Street. The trap door and the trigger were not installed until the morning of the fatal day in order to prevent corrosion from possible rain. Several sheriffs were in town to put in a bid to borrow the gallows for use in their counties. The scaffold consisted of a platform, eight feet square and 11½ feet from the ground; fifteen steps in the rear; and a crossbeam, 7½ feet above the platform. The structure was made of pine, except for the crossbeam, which was of Virginia black walnut.

As the fatal day neared, Cluverius had a steady stream of visitors. His younger brother, Willie, who took a hotel room nearby, was at the jail nearly every day. Cluverius felt a special attachment to his spiritual adviser, the Rev. William E. Hatcher, a prominent Baptist minister. Although everyone thought that Hatcher could elicit a confession from the con-

15. "Cluverius's Day"

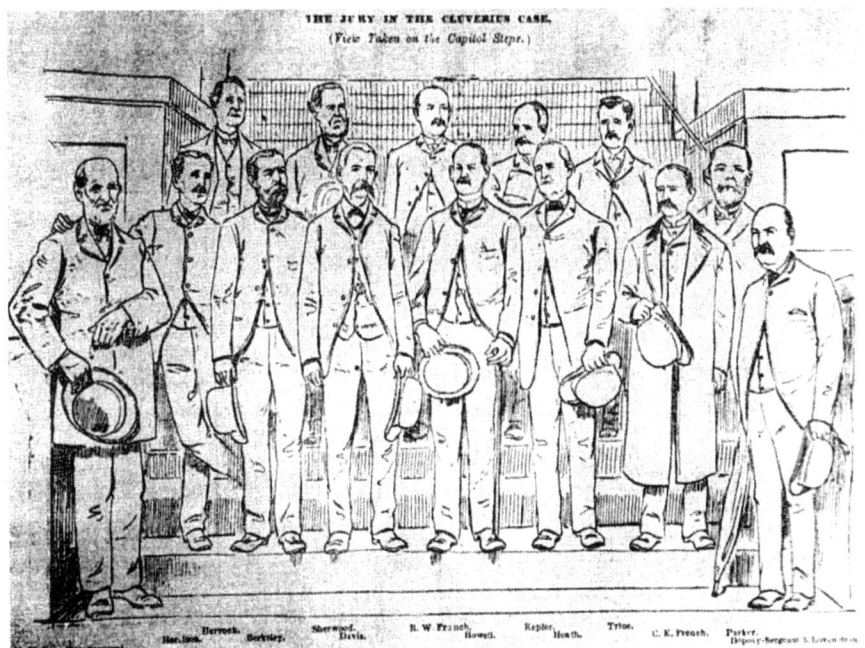

"Gentlemen of the Jury" of the Cluverius trial, in G. Watson James, "The Famous Cluverius–Lillian Madison Murder Case." *The Virginia Trooper* (October 1852).

demned man, he failed to do so. Hatcher, as did some others of Richmond's elite, became convinced of Cluverius' innocence. Hatcher consented to a lengthy interview by a reporter of the *Dispatch*, the day before the execution, which was published the day after the hanging.

Hatcher reluctantly accepted the role of counseling Cluverius. He did so primarily because both men were alumni of Richmond College, and, as Hatcher said, "for the dozen years I have lived in Richmond I have taken a deep interest in the general welfare of the students; and I may add that the fact that a young man is a Richmond College boy enkindles my brotherly interest in him." Although Hatcher acknowledged that it was not his duty to try to obtain a revision of the penalty, he was party to a petition for a respite and visited the governor for that purpose. The preacher also encouraged the prisoner to write an autobiography, which he did. Hatcher advised Cluverius that he needed to prepare to meet God, that innocence of the crime was not sufficient in itself to merit absolution of sin. Hatcher attested to the cordiality and sincerity of Cluverius. He was "open, simple, and natural," and "on no human face have I ever seen a more real or contagious laugh than on his." The young prisoner's "consistency was wonderful, and if he was an actor his art was transcendent." In prison "his deportment not only commanded respect, but to a large extent disarmed prejudice."

Hatcher was quizzed as to Cluverius' religious faith. Asked if the prisoner had any doubts concerning religion, the Reverend replied:

> He had one staggering doubt. He said that the promises of God to hear prayer were very many and full, and that he thought he had pleaded those promises faithfully for deliverance from his cruel fate. He had hanging on the wall of his cell a number of placards on which were printed various Scripture promises. One day while we were talking on the subject he arose rather nervously and went to the wall and uncovered the promise in Matthew xviii, 19 and 20, and said: "How is this, Doctor? There is the promise that God will hear the prayer of two or three. I know that many more than that have been pleading for me, and yet no answer seems to come." The act betrayed intense feeling and a painful doubt. I gave him such an explanation as seemed necessary, and with brightening face, he said: "I see it. We must not expect to understand everything. I try to feel as the old colored man said he did in reading the Bible — that is, when I find anything that is too deep for me I turn to what I can understand."

Culverius "never had a handcuff on him from the day of his arrest to the hour of his death." He received kind treatment in jail. His meals came from an outside "cook-shop." A barber came to his cell twice a week to give him a clean shave. On the eve of the execution the city jail buzzed with persons coming and going. Some were on legal matters traveling back and forth from the governor's office, where after much wrenching a reprieve was denied; there were also reporters, relatives and friends, and the curious inquiring if the scheduled event would indeed transpire. Culverius himself remained calm, conversing, writing, and sleeping. Captain Frank Cunningham, of whom "the prisoner had become very fond," stayed until past 1:00 A.M., and sang, upon the prisoner's request, hymns and secular songs, including "How Firm a Foundation, Ye Saints of the Lord," "Jesus Is Calling for Thee," "Rock of Ages," "Home Sweet Home," and "Home of the Soul."

About 9:30 A.M., Friday, January 14, 1885, Culverius had breakfast with city sergeant James C. Smith and "ate heartily of tenderloin beefsteak, with mushrooms, fried potatoes, egg omelet, hot rolls, and coffee." Frank Cunningham, on the same morning, gave an interview to the press, saying that he was much depressed over the impending event. He also said he asked the previous night: "Tommie, tell me on your honor as a man, and

15. "Cluverius's Day"

in the fear of God, are you guilty of the murder of Fannie Lillian Madison?" The reply was, "I am not guilty."

Cluverius said that he would only say a few words on the scaffold. He promised Cunningham that, being innocent, he would walk onto the scaffold "without a tremor." Cunningham added: "He then asked me to sing him 'Home Sweet Home.' I did so. My feelings were such that I forgot the last lines of the first verse. He repeated them for me." As Cunningham took his leave, the two "heartily" shook hands, with Cluverius helping Cunningham in putting on his coat. Cluverius expressed appreciation for Cunningham's frequent visits. He asked that Cunningham come by for a final farewell the next morning.

Colonel W.R. Aylett (courtesy Library of Virginia).

"Did you see him in the morning?" asked the reporter.

"Yes. I called to bid him good-bye. I again asked him if he was innocent, and he maintained that he was. I then told him, 'You must pray to God to help you, and put your trust in Him.'"

Cluverius answered, "I have, and I have no fears of the scaffold."

"Then he requested me to sing for him. I sang three verses of the hymn, 'How Firm a Foundation.' I then said good-bye."

Shortly after noon, Beverley Crump, one of the defense lawyers, returned from a visit with the governor, who again rejected executive interference. At 12:30 P.M., Sergeant Smith went into the corridor of the jail and told Mr. Richardson, a friend of the prisoner, to bring in the suit of clothes the doomed man was to wear. Cluverius, with a little assistance from A.W. Dunn, the "deathwatch," dressed himself; he washed his face and brushed his hair. The occupants in the cell now were the Rev. Hatcher, Sergeant Smith, Deputy Macon, Mr. Dunn, and Cluverius. After several prayers, led by the Rev. Hatcher, Deputy Allen came in with "the black waterproof gown and a couple of stout ropes." The prisoner's hands were tied in front, and "the gown was wrapped around him, covering him from the neck to below his knees. His soft, drab-colored hat was placed upon his head slightly to one side."

An enormous crowd was waiting for the big event. Despite the law requiring only twelve witnesses for an execution, hordes of people gathered in and around the jail. The jail, located only a block from the "usual place of execution," sat on low ground in Shockoe Valley, and the surrounding hills served as a natural amphitheater, on which there were now thousands of people. Moreover,

> Jail alley was packed. Broad Street and the houses that could command a view of any part of the jail were dotted with people. The hill up Marshall Street to College Street was covered with black faces. On College street an enterprising person named Foster made quite a considerable sum renting out standing-room on his house-top at 50 cents per head.
> At the Medical College the students, standing on the roof, of the building, contrived, with the aid of telescopes and field glasses, to get a good view of the scaffold.
> Six men with spurs on ascended the very tall telegraph poles on Marshall street, hoping from that elevated perch "to get a glimpse over the walls at the scaffold."

At the jail itself, white prisoners from their cells peered through iron bars at the execution courtyard. Prisoners on the upper floors had a full view. At first it appeared that the women prisoners on the top floor would not be able to see because the broad iron slats in the window frames were at such an angle as to cut off view; this was remedied by holding outside the window bars mirrors that reflected the full scene. In the small jail yard — a walled-in space of 15 × 120 feet — hundreds of people were jammed, having obtained tickets issued by the city sergeant, James C. Smith. Because this yard was very damp, Smith spread sawdust over it.

In late morning, a police squad of twenty-five men were marched to the jail and posted there to prevent disorder. Just before 1:00 P.M. the door to Thomas J. Cluverius' cell swung open, and he joined a small procession in the corridor formed in the following order: first, Deputy Sergeant Macon; second, Sergeant Smith and the prisoner; and third, the Rev. Hatcher and Deputy Sergeant Allen. As the group went down steps into the jail yard, those gathered outside let out a "loud yell." Passing through a cordon of police, the death party reached the scaffold. With Deputy Ser-

15. "Cluverius's Day"

geant Macon leading the way they ascended the sixteen steps. Culverius stood in the center of the trap door. Sergeant Smith then read the death warrant. Asked if he had anything to say, Cluverius said, "No, I do not wish to say anything."

"Not a word?" inquired the Sergeant.

"No, sir," was the reply,

Sergeant Smith motioned to the Rev. Hatcher, who stepped forward and said, "Let us pray." The reverend then, with his hat in his hand, knelt and gave a rather fervent four-minute prayer. He then conversed briefly with the prisoner. The preacher then announced to the crowd that "I am requested by the prisoner to utter just one word. That is that in this the moment of his death he carries no ill-will to any man on earth." The Rev. Hatcher addressed the prisoner: "Is that all?" The response was simply, "Yes." The two men then shook hands, with Hatcher uttering, "God bless you." Upon Sergeant Smith's request a policeman escorted the Rev. Hatcher through the crowd and through an exit door.

After Sergeant Smith bade the prisoner farewell and left the scaffold, Macon held the skirt of Cluverius' cloak while Allen pinioned the prisoner's legs with a rope just below the knees. Allen then put the black hood over the prisoner's face and adjusted the silk rope about the neck, leaving the knot just back of the left ear. Allen descended from the scaffold, leaving only Macon with the prisoner.

At 1:08 P.M. Deputy Sergeant Macon gave a signal, and Deputy Sergeant Johnson, from inside the jail (inside a cell at the east end on the first floor, located next to the scaffold) pulled the chord. A dull thud "broke" the deadly silence. Many people looked away from the scaffold, but most of them "gazed upon the victim and watched every movement of the body" without being the least moved.

As the trap door fell, Cluverius' body "shot through the opening made by the springing of the door like a bullet from a rifle." The victim "whirled around about seven or eight times until the rope was straight, and then for about five seconds stood suspended in midair as if life was extinct. Then there commenced a slight twitching of his feet and legs, which became more and more violent until they became like a severe spasm. His limbs would first draw up and then stretch out, and he kicked fiercely. The most horrifying sounds of choking and strangulation could be heard clearly all over the yard. This was kept up for several minutes, when it begun to die down, and finally the body hung lifeless." Three minutes after the drop "Dr. W.T. Oppenheimer found that his pulse was 96; at six minutes it had increased to 130; at eight minutes it had fallen to 30, and at ten minutes it ceased to beat, and he was pronounced dead.

Drs. Thomas Jackson and J. Grattan Cabell, "at the request" of the jail surgeon, Dr. Beale, also made examination and confirmed Dr. Oppenheimer's judgment. Dr. Beale, the physician to the jail, is so blind that he had to be led to the body by a colored man. Some one lifted the cloak and directed his hand to Cluverius's wrist, and he felt for his pulse, but it had stopped beating." One flaw emerged quite obvious. The silk rope used demonstrated that it was "not good for hanging." It had been calculated that the fall would be seven feet, leaving the body four feet above the ground. The rope, also having been greased, had stretched so much that when Cluverius was pronounced dead his right toe was touching the sawdust on the ground.

The body remained hanging for twenty-six minutes. It had taken eleven minutes for Cluverius to die. When Deputy Sergeant Allen and several others cut down the body, they had to pull very hard to pull the noose out of the flesh of the right side of the neck, which had borne most of the weight. Now suddenly the crowd dispersed. There was a rush for the outer yard. "Men descend from their perches; the crowd about the jail breaks." The body was placed in a coffin, and a covered wagon brought it to L.T. Christian Undertakers, at 1215 East Broad Street. The wagon was followed by hundreds of persons. A few hours later the body was placed on the "York-River train," accompanied by brother Willie, aunt Mrs. Tunstall, and several friends. It was interred at the family burial ground on Mrs. Tunstall's farm near Little Plymouth, in King and Queen County.

Thus concluded the tragic end of a promising young man, just out of college and already established as a lawyer, admired by many for his excellent qualities. Judgment still weighs in that he may not have been guilty. A punctuation came to the whole horrid affair a month after the execution when city sergeant Smith was fined fifty dollars for admitting a large crowd into the jail yard for the execution.[8] An irony, too, is that the execution, supposedly private, drew thousands of the morbidly curious, in a festive atmosphere, just as in the old days of the "carnivals of death."

16

"Good-Bye, Boys"
1888–1899

Hangings in Richmond proceeded at the average of about one in six years (more if adjacent counties are considered). This may seem a bit meager with the city's population reaching 85,050 by 1900 (127,628 in 1910).[1] In some ways it is surprising that there were not more capital felons, as the city had been long distanced from being a paragon of virtue.

By the standards of any age, the city exhibited horrors.[2] A large degree of societal dysfunction (simply check police court reports) and unsanitary conditions afforded a sure breeding ground for crime. Violence was much the way of life. Garroting, which was mugging at the time, and other assaults and robberies were common. Alcohol and hard drug (e.g., cocaine) addiction was rife. Teenage gangs and juvenile criminals were common. More than 1,100 youthful offenders were arrested annually in the city. (From 1900 to 1920 the city had a legal red light district; the main problem was that the prostitutes fanned out into other areas as well.) Citizens were often very sickly. Cholera, smallpox, diphtheria, and respiratory diseases visited the community, sometimes in epidemical proportions. Employed persons lost up to sixty days a year because of sickness. Human waste wound up in the James River, the source of the drinking water supply; most homes had only outdoor privies. Trash heaps ringed the city. The board of health reported that for 1900 more than 20,000 dead animals and fowl, 5,200 barrels of rotten fruit and vegetables, and 8,700 barrels of offal were carted from the streets. The odor of horse manure permeated the air. In 1905, as many as 1,440 persons were homeless. Working conditions were appalling. With no workman's compensation, the many job-related injuries or deaths left families in abject poverty. Unemployment amounted to 20 percent of the workforce.

Two hangings in Richmond, from the time of the Cluverius execution

Public Executions in Richmond, Virginia

Chain-Gang in Richmond During Street Maintenance, 1868 (courtesy Library of Virginia).

in 1887 to 1899, drew wide attention. The executions occurred only three months apart. A local black man, Morris Hopkins, went to his death on April 24, 1895,[3] the first hanging since that of Cluverius in 1887. The hanging took place in the jail yard of Henrico County, at Seventeenth and Marshall streets, in the same vicinity of the Richmond jail. Because the walls of the county jail were much higher than those of the city jail, no one from the hillsides could see the hanging. Furthermore, only "representatives of the press and county officials" were admitted as witnesses. Rather pathetically, Hopkins, who eluded capture for four months, surrendered himself to the authorities and wound up being hanged.

Hopkins' crime had been an "atrocious one." He had been a longtime brick-maker at "the yard of Messrs Hooker & Phillips, in the West End, just beyond the corporate limits." On June 7, 1893, Hopkins fell into an argument with Henry Parsons, the manager of the plant, over money owed him. As a result, while Parsons' attention was diverted, Hopkins crept up behind him, and with "a heavy stick" knocked him down; then Hopkins "got upon the prostrate manager and stamped him." The "skull was very badly shattered, and concussion of the brain resulted." Parsons lingered

16. "Good-Bye, Boys"

on until June 27, when he died after failed surgery. A warrant was sworn out for the arrest of Hopkins, but he fled. The case was all but forgotten, when in November, Hopkins, accompanied by his father, went to the Henrico County jail and surrendered himself. The $100 reward offered for Hopkins' capture was ordered to be paid to his father, but it never was.

Hopkins did not come up for trial in the county court until April 12, 1894. Three days later, the jury, after being locked up for twenty-four hours, rendered a verdict of murder in the first degree. Hopkins was sentenced to hang, but a stay was granted to allow an appeal to the circuit court on a writ of error. The appeal failed, and the case went back to county court, where Hopkins was resentenced to die on April 3, 1895. The governor turned back another appeal, but granted a reprieve until April 24.

The night before the execution Hopkins spent mostly in prayer and singing, sleeping only a few hours. He arose at 5:30 A.M. He dressed himself "in a new black cheviot suit of neat fit, with a white shirt, turned down collar, and black satin bow." He then ate a breakfast of beefsteak, porksteak, onions, rolls, biscuits, and coffee. After breakfast he knelt in prayer. At 6:30 A.M. the prisoner was joined by the Rev. Archer Ferguson of Calvary Baptist Church (African American), Scott Burrell of the "colored" Young Men's Christian Association, and two "colored women" of the Young Men's Christian Association Auxiliary. The quintet prayed and sang. Hopkins sang alone "Jesus Is Mine," and "as he sung the title words he rolled his eyes upwards, seeming to be in a perfect elysium of bliss." Sheriff Simon Solomon then appeared and read the death warrant. The "right hand of fellowship was extended to Morris by his colored friends," who then took their leave. The prisoner shook hands with the *Dispatch* reporter, saying that he "hoped to meet him in glory." Deputy Voegler came to the door of the cell, and said, "Morris, are you ready?" "Yes, sir," was the reply.

As the prisoner entered the main corridor of the jail, he sang loudly, "Good-bye, boys," which was echoed from every cell. At the door of the jail, the handcuffs were adjusted, and Dr. Croxton took the prisoner's pulse, finding it normal. In the walk to the scaffold, 200 feet away, deputy E.L. Voegler led, and Sheriff Solomon followed. On the steps to the platform, Hopkins paused and grabbed the hand of the sheriff, expressing thanks for his kindnesses. He also said that he hoped the executioner would "meet him in glory."

On the platform with the condemned man were John and E.L. Voegler, who adjusted the noose, and the two preachers, Burrell and Ferguson. The latter two sang "I Need Thee Every Hour," joined by Hopkins, in a

Public Executions in Richmond, Virginia

loud voice. Ferguson prayed and followed this up with a "lengthy address," in the presence of the some 20–25 spectators. Hopkins stepped to the front of the platform, and said, "I have nothing to say except this: I have nothing in my heart against nobody, my soul is as pure as the angels in Heaven: my heart is as clear as can be. You all have heard of Dick Mosby [who testified against Hopkins in court], I reckon some of you know him. Well, Dick Mosby lied on me. I will soon be in Heaven, where I am going home to glory." Hopkins turned toward the deputy, and said, "So, Mr. Voegler, do your work like the law tole you."

Hopkins walked to the center of the platform onto the trap and stood under the rope. The preachers shook hands with him and walked down from the scaffold and exited the premises. As the Voegler brothers (E.L. and John), both Henrico deputy sheriffs, adjusted the noose and placed the black cap and hood over his head, the prisoner yelled out to Calvin Anderson, a "trusty colored prisoner," who had helped tend to him: "Farewell, Captain, they can't take my soul away. I am going to glory. Tell Dick Mosby, whatever you all do, to prepare to meet me in Heaven." Hopkins stood erect while his arms and legs were pinioned. It was now exactly 8:11 A.M.:

> Deputy Voegler pulled the string which signalled to the executioner below that all was ready, and in a moment the body shot through the trap with terrific force. It hung motionless for a while, the feet straightened out and the whole form became rigid. The legs then drew up, and thirteen distinct convulsions, most of which, however, were very slight, were counted. On one occasion the body bent almost double. A noticeable fact was that his hands never moved. There was not even a twitch of any of the fingers.
>
> The body remained suspended for exactly nine minutes before the doctors began examining it. At 21 minutes after 8 o'clock, the pulses in the radial artery ceased; the heart fluttered for two minutes longer. At precisely 23 minutes after 8 o'clock Morris was declared dead, and 4 minutes later his body was cut down by Calvin Anderson and Sam Clarke, two negro prisoners, and placed in a common pine coffin, which stood near the scaffold. The body, when the rope was cut, doubled up and fell all in a heap in the arms of the two men.... The lid was screwed down on the coffin and a handsome design, in the centre of which appeared in immortelles the letters "Y.M.C.A.," was placed thereon.
>
> After the crowd had dispersed, Drs. Chalkey and Leftwich held a postmortem examination, and ascertained that death was the result of strangulation. As is required by law an inquest was then held by Magistrate Lewis.

At 11:00 A.M. Hopkins' father arrived in a wagon to claim the body of his son. This was not easily done. In the meantime, Dr. W.P. Matthews,

16. "Good-Bye, Boys"

secretary of the state anatomical board, asked Sheriff Solomon to turn the body over to him (as provided by law) for use at the medical college of the University of Virginia. After consulting a judge, the sheriff complied with all the doctor's request. Hence "the aged father was left the funeral design which had been placed on the coffin" and drove back to his farm home.

A "pathetic incident" of this execution was the discovery of a little sister of Hopkins "crouched down behind the jail shortly after the hanging, crying bitterly." She had hoped to see her brother one more time before he died. Denied this as well as a view of the remains, "she refused to be pacified, and was driven off by her father, crying as though her heart would break."

The third white man to die on the gallows in Richmond since the Civil War was fifty-year-old Philip Norbourne Nicholas.[4] He may well have been innocent, as was claimed in the Phillips and Cluverius cases. A curious twist to the Nicholas crime was the resemblance of the cause of death to that in one of America's literary classics, *An American Tragedy*, by Theodore Dreiser. In both instances the victims are adrift from a boat, and, unable to swim, drown, with no assistance from the alleged perpetrator of the deed.

On the night of December 6, 1892, Nicholas, James Mills, and William Judson Wilkerson were at the home of the latter's mother. It was agreed that the three men the next morning would cross the river to the Chesterfield County side and grab honey from a bee-tree. The expedition "was suggested, planned, and carried out by Nicholas." Mills and Wilkerson consented reluctantly as neither could swim. The next morning at 9:00 A.M. the three men set out in a borrowed boat with two buckets for holding the honey, two axes, one hatchet, and protective netting. After landing, the men visited the bee-tree but decided not to cut it down and to return home. The small boat was ten feet long and two and a half feet wide. Nicholas sat in the rear, behind the other men, who faced front. About fifty yards from the Henrico (Richmond) shore, the boat quickly filled with water; Mills and Wilkerson were drowned, and Nicholas swam ashore. When the boat was pulled out of the water it was discovered that under the seat where Nicholas sat "there were three holes, freshly bored, with an inch-and-a-half auger." Corncobs, which had been cut to fit the holes, floated ashore.

Nicholas was immediately arrested, and at a coroner's jury a motive for the crime was established. Nicholas was having an affair with Mrs.

Public Executions in Richmond, Virginia

Mills, wife of one of the dead men, and had told her he would get rid of her husband and they would go away together. Nicholas was lodged in the Henrico County jail. Convicted in the Henrico circuit court, he was sentenced to be hanged in February 1895. On appeal, Virginia's supreme court found against Nicholas, and he was resentenced by the circuit court to be executed in July. In the interim the legislature had passed a law removing criminal jurisdiction from circuit courts, except on appeal from county courts. Defense attorneys, therefore, tried to get the resentencing overturned. An appeal again went before the supreme court, which ruled against Nicholas. With the governor refusing to intervene, recourse had vanished.

Philip Norbourne Nicholas was born in Buckingham County, near Scottsville on May 1, 1844. As a youth he served as a foreman of a gang of hands for railroads in Virginia and Georgia. For several years he worked at a stone quarry in West Virginia. In 1891 he moved to Henrico County, where he began employment at the Wickham farm. Nicholas, an unmarried man, lived in a room in the house of James Mills and his family, adjacent to the Wickham farm, near the Henrico-Goochland County line. According to a reporter's estimate, Nicholas was known as a "scheming man by his neighbors," few of whom trusted him or associated with him.

Besides the exchanges with the governor, two important statements came to light, published by the press, one by the condemned man on the eve of his execution and the other just after the execution, a bitter denouncement by relatives and a friend.[5] In the former, Nicholas' last statement, ten witnesses at Nicholas' trial are accused of flagrant perjury. The other document castigates the Virginia justice system:

> We feel that he [Phillip Norbourne Nicholas] has been the victim of injustice from the beginning to the end. Money and position is law in Virginia. If he had been a wealthy man he would have been brought from prison in a hurry, but being a poor man, he has been forced to die like a dog. There have been several murders committed — wilful murders — in and near Richmond in the last year or two, and those committing them have either been cleared at once, or sent to prison for a short time. But this poor man had enough after-discovered evidence in his possession to have cleared him, if he had been justly dealt with. He has been hurled into eternity on circumstantial evidence.... No man with common sense would have put on heavy boots and an overcoat, and taken two other men in a boat and drowned them in the river, when he was risking his own life thereby.... Poverty in Virginia is a great drawback as regards law....

16. "Good-Bye, Boys"

The day before his execution, Nicholas had long visits with two brothers. Two nuns of the Franciscan order came by. The Rev. Father Welbers in the afternoon said prayers in the cell. One of the reporters who visited asked Nicholas why he had switched from being a Baptist and embraced the Catholic Church. Nicholas said he did so after careful investigation of various faiths, and he accepted Catholicism because he thought it was the best religion.

Shortly after arising at 5:00 A.M. on Thursday, July 25, the day of his execution, Nicholas was visited by the two Franciscan nuns who had spent much time with him since he was sentenced to death. They stayed in prayer and meditation with him, leaving at 6:00 A.M. Father Welbers came by and began preparing an "improvised altar" from which he would say mass. A table was brought in and placed in the middle of the corridor opposite Nicholas' cell. The table was covered with a white cloth, on top of which were a large crucifix, four lighted candles, and two vases containing roses. Father Welbers celebrated mass at 6:30 A.M., assisted by two acolytes. Besides several prison officials, attendees were the two nuns; two reporters; John H. Hughes; William Alexander; W.F. Reddy; John Finnegan; and a Mr. Higgins. Besides the collects that were interspersed in the mass, Mr. Higgins recited special prayers from the missal. Reddy, of the Sacred Heart Church choir, and Finnegan, of the choir at St. Peter's Cathedral, sang "with deep feeling" the hymns "Nearer My God to Thee," "Rock of Ages," and "Jesus, Lover of My Soul." The condemned man received communion with great reverence. Bishop Augustine Van de Vyver appeared after the mass and administered the sacrament of confirmation to Nicholas. The bishop then gave "a brief but beautiful address" on "the goodness and the mercy of God," saying that communion had bound Nicholas to Jesus. At the conclusion of the service Nicholas returned to his cell and on his own engaged in further devotions. At 8:00 A.M. he ate a breakfast of fresh mackerel, veal cutlets, hot rolls, and coffee; later he drank whiskey punch. Until the time of his execution there were more religious ceremonies in the company of Father Welbers. Two brothers of Nicholas along with a few friends came by for a final farewell.

At 10:00 A.M. Sheriff Solomon went into Nicholas' cell and read the death warrant. Nicholas, in the center of the cell, attired in a black cheviot suit, "an immaculate shirt and turn-down collar, and a black silk stock tie," listened intently. Standing with him were Father Welbers, a "small company of newspaper-men and court officers." As the march to the gallows began, Deputy Voegler put a pair of handcuffs on the condemned

Public Executions in Richmond, Virginia

man. In the procession to the gallows, the sheriff and a *Dispatch* reporter led the way, followed by Nicholas and Father Welbers, and then Deputies Lew L. Fussell and Voegler and the twelve witnesses. Arriving at the jail yard, the procession halted, and "spectators filed in through the small gate." Nicholas, Father Welbers, and the officers then walked to the steps of the scaffold.

Sheriff Solomon shook hands with Nicholas and went into the basement of the courthouse, where he would pull the rope to the trap. The condemned man bent over and took a small crucifix from Father Welbers, kissed it, and, "gazing at it for a few moments, returned it." Nicholas then ascended the steps to the platform and walked onto the trap. Here he kicked off his shoes and "looked down upon the spectators without any show of emotion." The two deputies, Fussell and Voegler, quickly bound the arms and legs, adjusted the noose, and placed the "black cap" over the prisoner's head.

"The scene was most impressive and awe inspiring," wrote one reporter, "and not a soul moved for a moment." Father Welbers delivered a prayer:

> Depart, Christian soul out of this world, in the name of God; the Father Almighty, who created thee; in the name of Jesus Christ, the son of the living God, who suffered for thee; in the name of the Holy Ghost, who sanctified thee; in the name of all the angels and saints of God. May thy soul be this day in peace and thy abode in Holy Zion. Through Jesus Christ, our Lord. Amen.

Deputy Fussell pulled a cord signaling Sheriff Solomon to pull the rope connected to the trap. At exactly 10:06 A.M. the trap was sprung, and Nicholas' body shot down "as though released from a catapult." The rope stretched beyond the length planned, reaching nine feet due to its having been soaked from a steady rain:

> The first shock must have produced unconsciousness, for the body hung motionless for fully a minute. Then a twitching of the feet was noticeable, and in a few moments the legs drew up and convulsion after convulsion followed. There were thirteen altogether. Then the legs stiffened out, and the body again hung motionless. The doctors thereupon advanced and took the pulse. It was found that the heart, though weak, was beating very rapidly, and the pulse appeared to be strong. It gradually weakened until at 10:15 o'clock, nine minutes after the drop fell, it ceased at the radial artery. The heart continued to beat slowly, and it was not until 10:21 o'clock, exactly fifteen minutes after the body had been precipitated through the opening, that all signs of life disappeared.

16. "Good-Bye, Boys"

After the doctors announced death, the body was cut down. An autopsy found that death had been caused by strangulation and a dislocation of the fourth vertebra. The rope had cut deep into the neck. The tongue was swollen and hung from the mouth, and "around it was considerable foam." The face was purple, and the eyes dilated. The body was taken to James McDonough's funeral home on Eighteenth Street in a "neat coffin" that was engraved on top in silver plate: "Rest in Peace." The next morning at 9:00, Father Welbers conducted a funeral service. Interment was at the city's Catholic cemetery, Mount Calvary.

Once again an execution, supposedly private, had drawn a huge crowd. On the morning of the fatal event at the Henrico County jail, a "vast crowd of curiosity seekers" had jammed "the avenues to the jail." They appeared to gain "morbid satisfaction" that they were "at least in the neighborhood of death, even though they could not witness the grim details of the fearful reckoning." The windows of a warehouse on the west side of the jail, "which commanded a view of the scaffold, were crowded with eager on-lookers, and the high walls surrounding the prison yard and other points of vantage were not tenantless."

Nicholas' effects were given to Lew Fussell to donate to certain persons: his eyeglasses to a brother, a prayer book to a Mr. Gentry, and two small hymnbooks to two little children who had visited him in jail.

Thus was closed out another of Richmond's unusual murder mysteries. That the pace of hangings had not increased, considering a high crime rate and expanding population in central Virginia, attests not so much to opposition to the death penalty as to a barbaric tradition.

17

"YOU KNOWED I WON'T CRAZY"
1900–1907

"The ignorant negro met death like a hero," typically reported the *Richmond Dispatch* on the execution of William Woodson on December 13, 1900, the first of Richmond's last three hangings. By continuing to limit public viewing, the authorities succeeded in reducing the popularity of such macabre exercises. Yet the fact that media hype increased inversely as public access diminished became more and more evident. For example, during the last decade of the Richmond hangings, reportage on the deaths by noose of several victims in nearby communities reached a sensational level. A double lynching, on March 24, 1900, of Walter Cotton (who was black) and Brant O'Grady, a "white tramp," in Emporia, fifty miles south of Richmond, produced bold front-page headlines and expansive coverage in Richmond newspapers. The two men had killed two law officials who tried to arrest them.[1] Then Richmonders intently followed the murder case involving J. Samuel McCue, a former mayor of Charlottesville and Presbyterian elder convicted of bludgeoning to death his wife. The hanging on February 9, 1905, in Charlottesville received a front-page spread. Fifty Richmonders had been included in the jury pool for the trial.[2]

The execution of William Woodson was the third conducted within the state penitentiary compound. (The other two were Moses Johnson in 1845 and slave Clara Ann in 1862.)[3] The execution was witnessed by very few persons: officials, physicians, and four convicts. Woodson did not gain much sympathy. He had been "a bad negro nearly all of his life." Policemen had "to knock him down" to arrest him. He had done prison time in six states, as far away as the states of Washington and Pennsylvania. Usually arrested as a burglar or pickpocket, he had the nickname of "Bunkers."

17. "You Knowed I Won't Crazy"

In May 1900, Woodson attacked his cellmate, Ambrose Ferrebee, at Virginia's penitentiary while both men were working in the prison shoe factory. Woodson killed Ferrebee by bending the victim's head back and cutting his throat with a "keen-edged shoe-knife," severing the jugular vein. Woodson also attempted to kill a boy prisoner, who had been the source of the trouble, but he was prevented from doing so by being overpowered. Woodson was sentenced to death in the Richmond circuit court; an appeal did not win a new trial.

From his penitentiary cell a few days before his execution, William Woodson dictated a message to his mother:

> As a son to you I give you these few lines in the name of our Lord and Savior, Jesus Christ. Dear Mother, I must say, as a man who is now in Christ, and who shall trust in Him for the future, that I hope to meet you with our dear Lord in Heaven, where all trouble and trial are over. During all my years I never knew what the love of a mother was until I was in this trouble. Since then I have taken Christ as my helper, and have found out what love is. I realize that God loves all of us, and does not want any of us to be lost. All that any one can do is to give God his heart, and He will do the rest for him. When I was a sinner, I sinned as badly as one could sin, but I have given myself to Christ the best I know how. I am trusting in the Lord for all, and He is my strength. I will do as He wills me to do. I have done all I could for Christ, and the best we can do at all times is to put our trust and faith in Him always.
>
> I am sorry that I have put my mother and friends to so much trouble, but I trust that the good Lord has forgiven me for the deeds that I have done in the past.
>
> From one who has been well experienced in sin, but who has now made his peace with God.

In his enthusiasm over having undergone salvation, Woodson tried to convert his lawyer. Woodson told Roy Lewis, a counsel for the defense, that he should see the error of his ways and repent. To emphasize this need, Woodson said to Lewis: "Why, Mr. Lewis, you committed a grievous sin when you tried to make that jury believe I was crazy. You knowed I won't crazy."

Predawn December 13 brought a "stillness of death" to the prison, despite the fact that all 1,194 inmates were up and around, eating breakfast at 5:00. At this time, the superintendent, Major G.M. Helms, met in his office with the assistant superintendent, Captain Morgan, newspaper reporters, and several other prison officials. During the conference, Helms jumped to his feet and exclaimed, "Let's have it over with as quickly as possible." Helms and several officials went to Woodson's cell to pick up the prisoner, now attired in a cheap black suit. Woodson had been praying with two spiritual advisers, Reverends Preston Nash and John DuVal. The little party — a guard carrying a lantern going on ahead, followed by the prisoner supported on each side by the two ministers, and Major Helms and two officials walking behind — entered a "narrow paved court-yard." There stood the gallows, "its outlines dimly revealed by the light of two lanterns suspended at the ends of the horizontal timber from which the noose dangled." On the front of the scaffold was a small bicycle lamp.

Going up the twelve steps to the platform and placing himself on the trap, the "nervy darky never faltered once." All the while, Reverend Nash "kept pouring into the negro's ear the consolations of the Christian faith." His arms pinioned to his side and his legs bound together, Woodson declared he had nothing to say. "The black cap was slipped over Woodson's face, the noose placed about his neck, and drawn up tight. The clergyman turned away." "The east, seen over the prison wall, was growing gray." A "bell jingled; there was a grating sound; Woodson's body shot downward." There was no twitching of the arms or legs. The neck was broken. Although a heartbeat continued for eight minutes, it was estimated that death came in less than a minute. After thirteen minutes the body was cut down by four convicts— two white and two black — and put in a coffin. The horror seen upon the faces of the negroes was "almost pitiable." The body was turned over to the state anatomical board. The execution had gone "without a hitch," aided by the assistance of one experienced in such matters, Deputy Sheriff John Voegler of Henrico County.

Prison officials had finally learned measures on how to discourage the public from turning up at executions. Besides providing only limited room for spectators, advantages were found in not announcing the exact time of the event and holding it during nighttime.

A new site for the hanging of criminals from the state penitentiary at Richmond had its first and last use in the hanging of Jack Brown on January 2, 1903. The state farm (an auxiliary to the penitentiary and under the same superintendent), on a 986-acre tract in Goochland County, twenty-five miles from Richmond, opened in summer 1895. Most of the 250 prisoners were very old, infirm, or boys.[4] The choice of the execution site was due to the fact that the condemned man and the victim were inmates of the state farm; it was believed that the rural location would not attract many spectators.

Jack Brown, a black man from Norfolk, was serving fifteen years for

17. "You Knowed I Won't Crazy"

View of the Penitentiary, Richmond, Virginia (courtesy Library of Virginia).

housebreaking. He was convicted of killing another black convict, James H. Parker, from Isle of Wight County who was serving two years also for breaking into and entering a house, over a trivial argument.[5]

At 10:20 on the day of the hanging, Major G.M. Helms, superintendent of the penitentiary, and other penitentiary officials boarded the C. & O. train for the farm. Upon arrival they immediately proceeded with the execution, joined by A.G. Saunders, city sergeant of Manchester, who was in charge himself of a hanging to occur a week later. Besides these officials, the few others in attendance were Sheriff Crouch of Goochland County, Dr. Holman (the penitentiary physician), and Catholic priests J.B. O'Reily and de Moynck. Father O'Reily the day before had administered to Brown the Catholic sacrament of baptism.

Father de Moynck accompanied the condemned man toward and onto the gallows. The priest administered the last rites, and Brown kissed a crucifix handed to him just before the black cap was placed over his head. Brown said farewell to the attendants. The trap was sprung, the neck was broken, and, and after six minutes Dr. Holman pronounced life extinct. The body was interred on the state farm grounds.

The little village across the James River, called Manchester (incorporated into Richmond in 1910 and sometimes irreverently dubbed "dogtown" or "skinner town," for catfish skinners), had its only hanging within the town limits on January 9, 1903.[6] Ernest Davis, a young black man, went to his death on gallows erected in the Manchester jail yard.[7] The

Public Executions in Richmond, Virginia

same rope that hanged Jack Brown the week before was used. It had to be cut from Brown's neck, having been imbedded into the flesh" from Brown's "heavy fall" through the trap. Many "Negro women and children" in addition to men and boys from Richmond and Manchester were around the jail when the execution took place.

Ernest Davis' end came as a result of a quarrel on August 7, 1902, over two black women — Kate Hull and Rosa Hayes. In the fight that resulted, John Henry Stokes was stabbed in the heart by Davis with a knife that Sidney Hilton had given him. Davis, Hilton, and two other accessories, Marcellus Hatcher and Wyatt Callias, left Stokes dying in a pool of blood at Seventeenth and Hull streets. The perpetrators of the crime were soon apprehended. Upon arrest Davis exclaimed, "You think I killed that negro, but I didn't." Davis, nevertheless, was sentenced to die and Hilton to eighteen years; Hatcher and Callias were acquitted. Not long before his execution, Davis admitted to stabbing Stokes at the urging of the others.

Davis had been convicted in the October term of the corporate court of Manchester. His counsel, Joseph R. Pollard, a black lawyer from Richmond, tried to get a new trial from the court of appeals, but this was denied. Governor Montague did grant a respite from December 12 to January 9.

This last Richmond gallows drama followed a mode similar to those of the past. The clergy and religion played a prominent part. On the day before the hanging the Manchester jail witnessed a prayer and song session, with the prisoner moved to tears. Reverend Asa Driscoll, Reverend R.M. Chandler, and several friends of the condemned man were there for the devotions. "Negro prisoners" in the jail joined in the singing of "Nearer My God to Thee" and other hymns.

Before dawn on the day of day of the hanging, Davis ate a breakfast of stewed oysters, bread, and coffee. Friends and clergymen were allowed to visit him up until time to be taken to the gallows. The ministers were Anthony Binga of the "colored" First Baptist Church in Manchester, Richard Ferguson of Richmond, H.E. Jeffress, and F.W. Williams. Just before the walk to the gallows, Davis joined with his visitors in singing "Farewell" and several other hymns. All the "colored" prisoners in the jail participated in singing "Farewell."

At 6:45 A.M. city sergeant J.G. Saunders read the death warrant to Davis, and then Saunders, several guards, and Reverends Binga and Ferguson led Davis to the gallows. On the scaffold Saunders asked Davis if he had anything to say. The answer was "yes." Davis held up his head, and

17. "You Knowed I Won't Crazy"

said, "I am glad that God is with me, and hope that this may be a lesson for all. Let it be a warning. I trust in God and have been forgiven. God has promised to save me. I hope that you will meet me around God's Throne. That is all I have to say. Good-by."

Davis wore a blue serge suit and a black necktie. "Shackles and ropes" were placed around his hands and feet and the black cap over his head. Deputy city sergeant Herbert Fergusson pulled the rope releasing the trap door. From a drop of six feet, Davis died of strangulation. It was considered that the pangs of death were not as gruesome as they could have been: Davis' "legs moved backward and forward, his muscles relaxed, and his body was soon apparently limp and lifeless." In fifteen minutes Davis was pronounced dead, and five minutes later the body was lowered into a coffin. When the black cap was removed it was found that Davis' tongue "protruded from his mouth and saliva covered his face. The rope had cut a hole across the neck and somewhat disfigured it."

Thus Richmond's last hanging had achieved a goal of reformers—a

Children at the Virginia penitentiary (near a hanging site) (courtesy Library of Virginia).

less adverse effect of an execution upon society — by making it completely private. Not all death penalty abolitionists favored this development, because by making executions more palatable to the public there would be less outcry against the practice. Virginia had officially abolished public hangings in 1869, the same time that Canada did the same and one year after Great Britain did so.[8] Ironically, whereas public executions had been justified chiefly as a measure to preserve order, the shift to a private system was in accord with the same reason.

Private executions diminished their redemptive meaning. No longer could clergymen publicly counsel condemned criminals and reach out from the gallows exhorting spectators to avoid fatally sinful paths. Nor could the unfolding drama on the scaffold show a penitent criminal about to be launched into eternity who declared his anticipation of soon being joined with God in glory. Moreover, paying the ultimate price of forfeiting life in public had demonstrated the viability of state and religion functioning together to bring about public submission to authority. As one author notes, "Lest the drama of penitence be lost on the multitude assembled to witness the execution spectacle, ministers clarified the relationship of the criminal to the populace-at-large."[9]

The requirement of only a dozen or so witnesses at an execution held within isolated prison walls and the prohibition on reporting details of the event meant lost opportunities to impress upon the public the necessity of imposing civil-religious order. With the change, proponents of the death penalty lost one of the most potent justifications for the abolition of capital punishment — the demonstration of its horror.

It may be noted that, while executions seemed to be headed toward a more humane route (even a few states already had opted for abolition), by 1904 in Virginia the number of capital crimes had increased to eight (including the addition of capital crimes previously so only under the slave code): murder, treason, arson, rape, attempted rape, armed robbery, burglary, and kidnapping.[10]

During the interim between Richmond's last hanging on January 9, 1903, and the first death by electrocution at the state penitentiary on October 13, 1908, quite a few hangings took place statewide, fifteen in 1907 alone, and six in 1908 through October.[11] Interestingly, one local community (Bedford County) persisted in conducting a hanging (of Joel Payne, a black man), on April 9, 1909, after the new execution law became operative.[12]

Epilogue

"A Striking Innovation"
1908

Corrections officials eagerly awaited the introductory use of the electric chair at the state penitentiary on October 13, 1908, "marking the advent of a striking innovation upon the method of executing criminals in Virginia."[1] The more enlightened segment of the state's citizens had long favored restraining public view of the barbarous and often bungled hangings. The move from outdoors to inside jail compounds diminished opportunities for stirring up morbidity and raucous behavior among spectator crowds. There was also a movement to make executions more humane. With awareness of the Edison-Westinghouse demonstrations causing death to animals by electricity and the successful use of the electric chair in New York, New Jersey, Massachusetts, and Ohio, Virginians were ready for the new form of capital punishment.

The Virginia legislature mandated the two changes in early 1908. In January a delegate from Henrico County, C.W. Throckmorton, introduced a bill requiring all executions in the state to be conducted at the state penitentiary. Delegate Williams of Southampton County offered an amendment that called for the installation of an electric chair at the penitentiary as the only means for executing criminals, thus negating hanging as a death penalty.

Certain public figures opposed the suggested changes. Major E.F. Morgan, superintendent of the penitentiary, claimed that the prison's guard force of fifty-one men could not spare anyone to go into the localities to fetch condemned prisoners to Richmond or to "perform the duties" of an execution. Senators Early, Folkes, and Keezel considered that no compelling need had been demonstrated. No other southern state had yet opted

Epilogue

A Front View of the Penitentiary at Richmond (courtesy Library of Virginia).

for the electric chair. Moreover, it was best to retain local executions, to be a "warning to certain classes in the neighborhood wherein the crime was committed." Strong advocates of the proposed changes were Dr. Charles V. Carrington, physician at the penitentiary, and speaker of the house of delegates Byrd. Proponents of the measure argued cost effectiveness, saying it would save localities from having to pay the full charge of guarding death row prisoners and building scaffolds. It was estimated that executions had cost local governments roughly $250 per event, although in some instances lower amounts had been expended, even as little as ten dollars.[2]

"An ACT to establish a permanent place in the state penitentiary at Richmond, Va., for the execution of felons upon whom the death penalty is to be imposed, to change the mode of execution so that the death sentence shall be by electricity" was passed on March 16, 1908, and went into effect on July 1. It provided a "death chamber" at the penitentiary equipped with an electric chair for the execution of all felons under sentence of death. Fifteen to thirty days before an execution, the superintendent was required to have the condemned person brought to the penitentiary and to appoint one or more guards over such prisoner. The superintendent

Epilogue

had full authority in conducting an execution. Witnesses would be limited to the superintendent or his assistants, the penitentiary surgeon or his assistant, twelve "respectable citizens," and, if desired, "counsel for the convict" and a "minister of the gospel." One thousand dollars per execution was voted to defray expenses. Section 10 of the law pointedly stated: "No newspaper or person shall print or publish the details of the execution of criminals under this act. Only the fact that the criminal was executed shall be printed or published."[3] Immediately, at the cost of $7,000, an electric chair was installed in the basement of a new cell building.[4]

Richmond's press applauded. Because of this "most progressive step along humanitarian lines," the "gallows with its ghastly accessories" was abolished from Virginia soil."[5] The abolition of the "barbaric method of executing felons by local hanging by the establishment of an electric chair at the penitentiary is one of the best deeds ever wrought by a Virginia Legislature."[6] Looking in hindsight a century and a half later, corrections official Paul W. Keve noted this: "There was a new mannerliness in the executions which, in great contrast with the previous bawdy spectacles, now were private, quiet, well-disciplined rituals. It seemed that the business of executing had become more civilized, if such can be said about so macabre a practice. Fairness in the application of such punishment was a consideration for later times."[7] At last executions in Virginia could be implemented in a placid situation (in a small room amid the quietude of a dozen witnesses) and supposedly in an efficient and reasonably humane fashion. The first mandated death by electrocution lived up to these expectations, if not always in subsequent electrocutions.

Typically, as to be expected, the first victim of the killer-chair, Henry Smith, was a young black man, who gave his age as nineteen but was probably twenty-two years old. Similar to those who followed, he was very poor. In only rare exceptions, such as John Price Posey and Thomas J. Cluverius, have the Richmond victims of state homicide been other than the cast-offs of society. Henry Smith would be the first of forty-eight persons put to death by the electric chair for rape or attempted rape. Incidentally, no white person in Virginia has been executed for rape. Although the press was prohibited by law from describing an actual execution, it was not restrained from informing the public of the many related details.[8]

Smith, described as being 5'8" and weighing 150 pounds, with a "broad flat nose, thick lips and thick neck," had previously been an inmate of the penitentiary, serving a one-year term for grand larceny in the city of Portsmouth. He was released on January 18, 1907. As to his capital

Epilogue

offense of August 11, 1907, in Portsmouth, Smith climbed onto the roof of the home of 76-year-old Mrs. Albert Powell and gained entrance through the second story window. Smith "assaulted [raped]" Mrs. Powell, "beat her into insensibility," and robbed the place. He managed to evade capture for several days. He had stolen only fifteen dollars. Smith was apprehended upon identification given by J. Robert Pope, a "negro boy" who had been delivering groceries at the time. "I heard the voice of a woman," Pope testified, "as if she was praying for mercy and soon after Mrs. Powell called to me from an upstairs window to catch that negro. Running to the rear of the house I saw a man leave the kitchen door."

All in a day and a half, September 7–8, 1908, Smith had a trial, which ended in a hung jury, was retried, convicted, and sentenced to death. This time the jury deliberated only fifteen minutes. In September Smith was brought to the penitentiary in Richmond and lodged in a "detention cell" (solitary confinement), forbidden to see anyone other than prison officials and clergy.

On execution day, October 13, 1908, Smith had the company of the Rev. W.H. Dean of the Leigh Street Methodist Church and S.C. Burrell of the Colored Young Men's Christian Association. Besides prayers, Smith joined the clergymen in singing hymns, the sounds of which could be heard beyond the prison walls. The condemned man entered the "death chamber" at 7:20 A.M. Ten minutes later he was pronounced dead. Thus the first death penalty by electrocution was proclaimed a success.

Only seventeen days after Smith's execution, another black boy, age seventeen, went to his death in Virginia's electric chair.[9] His offense was attempted rape. Winston Green was electrocuted at 7:30 A.M. on October 30, 1908. Green, in September, had "attempted to assault a white girl" in Chesterfield County and had been prevented from doing so by the screams from his intended victim. Green was arrested a few hours after the incident. Less than two weeks after the crime, on September 26, he was sentenced by the Chesterfield County court to Virginia's electric chair. It seems that Green must have been in or near the range of mental retardation because he had sought to drag the victim from a carriage in which she was riding with two companions.

Green was taken to a detention cell at the penitentiary about twenty days before his execution. He was attended by two "colored ministers." Putting Green to death proceeded even more smoothly than the electrocution little more than two weeks before. Superintendent Morgan, who again had charge of the execution, was "besieged on all sides by applicants

Epilogue

for permits" to witness the execution. He held his own, however, in denying any increased access.

Sadly, among the early electrocutions were those of teenagers. John Eccles and Henry Sitlington, both seventeen years old, went to the electric chair in 1910. Virginia Christian, age seventeen, was put to death in 1912, one of 123 women executed in Virginia between 1632 and 2010 (only one other has been electrocuted — Teresa Lewis, on September 23, 2010). Percy Ellis, age sixteen, went to the chair in 1916. All the above mentioned (except Lewis) were black.[10]

The pending execution of an illiterate, nineteen-year-old mountaineer (which occurred on July 10, 1925) brought a wave of petitions and entreaties on behalf of clemency. Rodney Hoke had been convicted of murdering "old man Brown," a peddler who had strolled into Hoke's "neighborhood" along Ogley's Creek in Alleghany County. In Hoke's defense it was claimed the lad had been put up to the deed by others and that he was uneducated, very poor, had a "lawless" father, and had been "muddled" with drink at the time of the murder.[11] A review panel found Hoke absolutely without any remorse,[12] and the penalty was carried out.

As was to be expected, idle curiosity led persons to speculate on how awful was the ordeal of dying by the electric chair. On March 5, 1916, the *Times-Dispatch* printed a full-page analysis of "how it feels to die in the electric chair." This piece was based on a near death experience of Henry Tenious, who had stepped on a live wire on an elevator in Cleveland, Ohio. Henry "uttered a heartbreaking cry, and fell lifeless to the floor." Although declared dead he was eventually revived. During his relapse, Henry heard extremely loud sounds, his mind went blank, he suffered horrible pain, and he had a sensation of "burning up."[13]

Were not the context so grim, a comment in the annual report of Richmond's health department for 1910 would seem a bit humorous. In discussing the city's mortality rate for 1909, it was noted that there would have been 134 fewer deaths if the number of nonresident decedents had not increased. Of the nonresidents, seventeen were criminals electrocuted at the penitentiary. "In all of these cases except one the criminals were not residents of Richmond, and did not commit in Richmond the crime for which they were executed."[14] Thus the inclusion in the city's census of persons who went to the electric chair (listed as required by federal regulations) had raised Richmond's mortality rate.

Epilogue

"Burn, Baby, Burn"
post-1908

The story of the public's response in Richmond to executions post-1908 is one of ups and downs, varying from the simply matter-of-fact to high curiosity and emotional outlet for those cases involving drama and media hype. No executions occurred in Richmond at the penitentiary from 1962 to 1982 because of extended legal complications and the Supreme Court-imposed moratorium from 1972 to 1976. Once the executions started up again, an almost state of battle existed on both sides of the street in front of the penitentiary's entrance between anti- and pro-capital punishment demonstrators. All returned to relative quietude when the execution chamber was moved to rural Southside Virginia at the Greensville Correctional Center in Jarratt. The last execution at the penitentiary was that of Buddy Earl Justus on December 13, 1990, and the first at the Greensville facility was Albert Clozza on July 24, 1991. Since January 1, 1995, condemned criminals have had the choice of the mode of execution — lethal injection or electric chair (to date only four have opted for the latter).[15]

The most bizarre behavior of the public to a post–1908 execution undoubtedly was when two members of the Tri-State Gang went to the chair on February 2, 1935. The two John Dillinger–styled gangsters, Robert Mais (age 29) and Walter Legenza (age 42), had allegedly shot to death Ewell M. Huband, a Federal Reserve mail truck driver, in a hold-up near Broad Street Station on March 8, 1934. Arrested and imprisoned, the two escaped from the Richmond jail, aided by a pistol that was concealed in a can of baked chicken. Recaptured in New York, they were brought back to Richmond for trial and were condemned to death. Highlighting the case in the public's eye was that it paralleled the infamous Lindbergh kidnapping-murder case in New Jersey, which ended with the conviction (February 13, 1935) and execution (April 3, 1936) of Bruno Hauptmann. The exploits of the Tri-State Gang were made into a movie, *Highway 301*.[16]

On execution day, Mais died at 7:48 A.M. and Legenza at 8:06. Legenza,[17] with two broken legs in casts, had to be lifted onto the chair. The execution had some semblance to the mass public display of bygone days. Members of two juries were present, and newspaper men swarmed into the front office of the prison. Outside, at the intersection of Belvidere and Spring streets, a small crowd gathered, mostly from the underclass residents of adjacent Oregon Hill.

Epilogue

The bodies of the gangsters were turned over to two funeral homes for public view: Mais to the Frank A. Bliley Funeral Home and Legenza to the Phaup Funeral Home. "Throngs of curious Richmonders—men, women and children—crowded past the biers of the executed gangsters." Managers of the two funeral homes said that they had never seen "such hordes of visitors," estimated at 3.000 persons, who filed past the two biers during the afternoon and evening of the day of the execution. "Many women wept silently as they passed." Others "approached within a few feet of the body, and then hurriedly turned away." Children under sixteen years old were barred from the viewing unless accompanied by an adult; at Bliley's several hundred came in the company of their parents. At Phaup Funeral Home groups of twenty to thirty at a time were admitted to the room where Legenza's body lay. "An attendant obligingly lifted the covers to show the scars on the dead man's legs where the electric charge had seared the flesh."

Despite this display of public morbidity, the executions at the penitentiary did not draw large crowds to the walls of the facility. One would have thought that the execution of the Martinsville Seven on February 2 and 5, 1951, would have stirred up a protesting mob, but there was only a ripple of commotion. The victims had been sentenced for the alleged rape of a white woman. Before the early morning execution of three of the men on February 2, a white man, George Thomas Hailey, went to the chair. Even though there were no physical demonstrations, thousands of petitions and other pleas had gone to the Virginia government for clemency on behalf of the Martinsville Seven.[18]

During the post moratorium period of 1982–1990, while executions were still held in Richmond, a ritual confrontation developed for executions (now held at nighttime), with two opposing groups (anti- and pro-capital punishment) facing off at each other at the intersection of Belvidere Street (the penitentiary bordering this street) and, perpendicularly, Spring Street. The "antis" were allowed to post themselves at the entrance of the prison, and the raucous locals from the poor neighborhood (Oregon Hill) staked out their turf across the street.

Probably the closest that a modern execution day resembled the open air "carnivals of death" of the nineteenth century was the execution of Linwood Briley on October 12, 1984, and that of his brother, James, on April 18, 1985. The two, along with a third brother, Anthony, and a sixteen-year-old neighbor, Duncan Meekins, had been convicted in a series of murders, including that of a popular disc jockey, John Gallaher. Linwood

Epilogue

and James were among the seven escapees from the Mecklenburg Correctional Center on May 31, 1984. The two Briley brothers were captured several weeks later in Philadelphia. Interestingly, like many of his predecessors, Linwood Briley, as execution neared, made known that he expected to receive salvation; on the day before he faced death, he said, "Tomorrow — U, me, his, GOD still lives on."

Outside the penitentiary, at Belvidere and Spring streets, on October 12, 1984, several hundred people gathered. One hundred twenty opponents to the death penalty marched six blocks from the Catholic cathedral to the prison where they lit candles, sang, and prayed. Some of them held signs, such as "No State Murder" and "Choose Life." Across the street a pro-death penalty rally formed, mostly from the poor residents of the adjacent neighborhood of Oregon Hill. The city's chief of police had ordered thirty-five uniformed officers and a half-dozen detectives to maintain order and closed off Spring Street. Near the execution time the pro-capital punishment crowd began chanting and yelling, while the anti-death penalty protesters became silent. The pros carried signs, including "Fry Em," "Kill the Negro," "Burn, Briley, Burn," "Burn, Baby, Burn," and "Have Mercy on Linwood — Reduce Voltage to 220." Amid the waving of Confederate flags and setting off of firecrackers, someone in the pro-death group sang a refrain from a popular rock song: "Na na na na, Na na na na, Hey, Hey, Hey Good-bye."[19]

At 7:45 A.M. on April 18, 1985, before the scheduled execution of James Briley at 11:00 P.M., a riot broke out in the penitentiary when a group of convicts jumped a guard as part of a plan to take hostages in order to prevent Briley's execution. The attackers had sharpened pieces of metal, and the guards had clubs. It took nearly an hour to bring the prison under control; nine guards and one convict were injured. The execution went off as scheduled, and, surprisingly, only a small group of protesters to the death penalty gathered outside the penitentiary.[20]

Subsequent executions at the penitentiary (until they were moved to the Greensville Correctional Center in 1991) went smoothly, although there were usually the two small groups of opposing demonstrators. Signs were again in evidence, most usually "Burn, Baby, Burn." For Morris Odell Mason's execution on June 25, 1985, the displays included "Fry Like Bacon, Koon" and "Burn Damn You."[21]

An irony was that most persons who went to the electric chair were black and the neighborhood bordering the penitentiary was all poor whites who exuded racial hatred. As late as recent times a black person entered

Epilogue

the neighborhood at his own risk. Only a generation ago several black men driving through Richmond (on Belvidere, an intra-urban extension of U.S. Routes 1 and 301) went a block westward where they alighted at a tavern on the corner of Pine and China streets and were subsequently brutally assaulted. An unconfirmed rumor among old-timers was that a black man was lynched, which affair went unreported.

Whatever may be said of Oregon Hill's past and its legends, today the area is placid and is being redeveloped into an upscale area. Even the penitentiary is now gone. Long gone, too, are the public and semipublic hangings. Whereas Virginia (and Richmond) had retained public executions and jail yard hangings longer than most other areas in the United States, it was not until August 14, 1936, at Owensboro, Kentucky, that the hanging of twenty-two-year-old Rainey Bethea for assaulting and murdering a seventy-year-old white woman became America's final public execution.

The death penalty has become all but an anachronism as it is implemented in Virginia and throughout the United States. In 2009 only fifty-two of the 3,279 persons on death row were executed; forty-six were executed in 2010. Ninety-five countries have abolished capital punishment; more than half of the world's executions occur in China.[22] Sixteen states in the United States have abolished the death penalty, with ten more on the verge of doing so.[23]

Throughout the history of inflicting the death penalty in Virginia there have been two consistencies. Most of those executed have come from a low socioeconomic status. Furthermore, while in proportion to the growth of population the actual incidence of executions over time diminished, there has been a steady, if slow, trend of the number of capital offenses increasing. In 1796 Virginia, there were only two offenses that could result in the death penalty (for whites); today there are fifteen.[24]

One might conclude that at long last we are relieved of the barbarous public executions of the past. This is a perilous assumption. Americans have just as much blood lust as in the past. The pervasive violence and killings depicted in the media and especially in almost all that is produced on television, movies, and video games should dispel any notions to the contrary. History can repeat itself, and it is more likely to do so in the context of a lowered moral plane. A case in point is the execution of John Allen Muhammed, one of the two "Washington beltway" killers, in November 2009. Although all video coverage of the execution was prohibited, every detail leading up to it was reported by the news networks.

Epilogue

CNN counted down the hours and minutes leading up to Muhammed's death. It is a fair guess to state that a sizeable segment of the American public favors the broadcast of executions.

In a commentary regarding Muhammed's execution, John M. Crisp, an English professor at Del Mar College, argued in a featured article the desirability of bringing back public executions. He mentions that people naturally crave public displays of killing. The Mexicans and Spaniards have the "brutally honest ritual" of the bullfight, and yet have abolished capital punishment and only Americans have capital punishment. Although Crisp himself is morally opposed to capital punishment, he believes "given the public consensus in its favor" it is not "likely to be abolished in our country any time soon." He, therefore, recommends bringing executions back into public view, like the death penalty in countries such as Iran and North Korea. He concludes:

> Those who argue that public executions would brutalize our sensibilities haven't seen the "Saw" series of movies—all my students have—or watched ultimate cage fighting on TV. By those standards, lethal injection is tame.
>
> Too tame, perhaps. A public hanging would be less humane, but much more telegenic.
>
> We've entrusted the state with the authority to kill very bad people. Some would argue that we have the right to watch. I'd say that it's an obligation.[25]

The position that the death penalty is fixed in the American way of life and that a majority of Americans are not apt to question the scheme of things overlooks how a forceful leader can effect change. Coming to mind are presidential decisions affecting slavery and segregation. More pertinent, one is reminded of two heroic native–American leaders. Tecumseh (the great Shawnee chief), at age fifteen in 1783, after having witnessed the burning at the stake of a white captive, denounced his comrades for their cowardly action and pledged that he would not stand by to let such horror happen again. Thus ended at least one form of Shawnee cruelty. A generation later in mid America, a young man who later became a Pawnee chief interrupted the Morning Star ceremony that involved the brutal murder-sacrifice of a captive maiden. Flinging himself upon the death platform, Petalasharo freed the girl and rode away with her. From that time on the people of the tribe were grateful that the awful practice had ended, and there were no more human sacrifices.

All of this is relevant to our own time. Governor George Ryan of

Epilogue

Illinois, for example, single-handedly commuted the death penalty for some one hundred fifty inmates to life in prison without parole. In March 2011, Governor Patrick J. Quinn, following suit, signed into law the termination of the death penalty in Illinois.[26]

Outright abolition is the best guarantee to prevent Virginia (and Richmond) from returning to its grisly past of public executions.

APPENDICES

Consisting of A. Profile of an Executioner — John Caphart; B. The Last Days of Spencer Kellogg, in His Own Words, September 1863); C. "Sleepless Sentinel at Castle Thunder"; D. Sentencing of James Jeter Phillips by Judge George L. Christian of the Henrico Circuit Court, July 10, 1868; E. The Prosecutor, Colonel W.R. Aylett, States the Case Against Thomas J. Cluverius, 1885; F. "An ACT *to establish a permanent place in the State penitentiary ... [and] to change the mode of execution," March 16, 1908; G. Richmond Executions*

A. Profile of an Executioner — John Caphart

The following account is included in David D. Ryan, ed., *A Yankee Spy in Richmond: The Civil War Diary of "Crazy Bet Van Lew"* (Mechanicsville, PA: Stackpole Books, 1996), 98–99.

Old Caphart

His age was not far from 70. His hair long & white, his beard long, heavy & grey, all stained with tobacco juice. His head deep buried in his old greasy high crowned, broad brimmed felt hat. His tall figure, his stoop, his forward shoulders, tottering giant. His profanity, his infidelity, of wh[ich] he excitingly boasted. His general antipathy. His fine speaking voice. His heavy club, an unfailing companion. His cursing every thing that was Yankee & every thing and every body that told ... sympathy for a suffering Northern man. His often expressed wish that he might have the powers to consign every man, woman & child equally.... This man, striking in appearance, could be seen treading our streets. The sight of him made humanity sick & strong men to shutter as he passed. He was one of the Castle Thunder officials & detectives. His iniquity gained him the sobriquet of "Anti-Christ," as he seemed to possess no single characteristic of that good & benevolent Being. This name "Anti-Christ" was so

Appendix A

common that one ignorant person thought it was his proper name, so one day a negro woman who had never heard him called by any other name & innocently thinking it was right, when in company with a dark friend & wishing to display a great deal of her African politeness, said with much animation, "Good evening, Mr. Anti-Christ, how do you do this evening?"

This was the first time a negro had ever called the old fellow by this name & it was too much for his ill nature to tolerate; so up went the old club & out belched the usual oath, blow & curse coming together, blow after blow his wrath boiled over. "G__d__ your blk Niggers that I'll Anti-Christ You!" "Oh please Mr. Anti-Christ, don't beat me; what have I done Mr. Anti-Christ?" & for awhile nothing w[ould] be heard but "Mr. Anti-Christ" blows and entreaties. The result was Mr. Anti-Christ was terribly insulted by "a Nigger" & "a Nigger" was terribly beaten by Mr. Anti-Christ. But the Negro not being advised of her mistake as to the name of the venerable detective went off wondering what made old Mr. Anti-Christ beat her so.

The old man having nothing to support himself & family upon but his sal[ary] of $75 Confed[erate] money per month, soon found himself in danger of starvation & for a while was assisted from the purses of his brother detectives—their salaries were better than his only from the fact that their families were smaller & less required of their support.... This class were capable of great corruption & extortion.

Caphart was a sort of refugee from Norfolk, where he had once acted as a detective & had nothing to live upon but his monthly pay & this rapidly depreciating. From sheer exhaustion, produced by insufficient food, his strength gradually failed & he became [word illegible]—still the long white hair & tobacco stained beard, the greasy old broad brimmed hat, the familiar club, the large grey eyes and brazen stare of the old detective were seen at the C[our]t office, for he still lived to see others suffer & their pains were his pleasure. The night dark & rainy in mid winter 64 and 65, the old detective left his seat at the stove of the office for the last time. That night a little stranger unfortunate in having to call him grandfather, opened his eyes upon the world. The old man was lying upon his bed, heard the wail of the newly born. Word was brought to him that he had a grandson. [He] raised himself. "Oh well, I must go up street in the morning & get him a p[ai]r of boots." He fell back upon the bed & was no more. It was his delight to recount the numerous executions at wh[ich] he had officiated, & he had enjoyed his heaven here in seeing the violent deaths of the unfortunate victims of law & the still more unfortunate who p[ai]d.

Appendix B

B. The Last Days of Spencer Kellogg Brown in His Own Words, September 1863

The following is an excerpt of a letter from Spencer Kellogg Brown to his father, and is included in George G. Smith, *Spencer Kellogg Brown and His Life in Kansas and Death as a Spy* (New York: D. Appleton, 1903), 365–369.

Last month brought the anniversary of my birthday, announcing me of age. I wrote you a long letter then, which I hope you have received. Since the day of my trial I have not yet heard my sentence, but I know my time on earth is short. I try to await with patience the result, hoping in the mercy of my Saviour.

On Sunday I spoke a few words to my fellow-prisoners, who were gathered together to worship God. It seemed to move them much as I first made known then the death I was expecting, and many besides myself were in tears. May God bless it for good. On Saturday, before trial, I wrote to my wife, in my Bible (which I wish to go to her — my Prayer-Book Kitty will keep), and to Kitty. Both will be brought to you by Mr. J.H. Sherman, a fellow-prisoner, as soon as he can do it. Yesterday (Monday) I saw a minister, Mr. Scandlin, who is going this morning North, on a flag-of-truce boat, and by him sent you a telegram to write immediately — perhaps I may be able to hear from you.

Also, I sent by him some word to you, by a letter he will write you; and some trinkets; and a ring my wife gave me, to go to her again; if she be not found, for Kitty or Mother to keep. Mr. Sherman will bring other trinkets made in prison. Also, the disposition I wish to be made of my pay — I will say, shortly, it is to be drawn, and invested for my wife in United States bonds, of which the principal, during her life, is to remain untouched; the interest will be turned over to her. After her death the principal will revert to Freddy. I have given Mr. Sherman both written and verbal directions about it. I would be much pleased if they might be followed as nearly as practicable. You can also hear, by writing to him, any particulars concerning myself or trial.

Later. Sunday passed in comfort and hope in the mercy of God; in prayer, and such meditation as one could enjoy in a room where there were more than sixty persons; and religious conversation with some of the many good brethren confined with me. I look past the gloom of the dark valley, and find cheer in the hope of the better world. I thank God often that He has put me in prison, for here He has been pleased to teach me of Himself, as I do trust.

Appendix B

While I remember, I will tell you of a certain Dr. Wm. C. Crane, Episcopal clergyman of Jackson, Mississippi, with whom I left a letter and some considerable papers for you. I made mention of certain debts owing to some of the officers of the Essex — some ten or fifteen dollars, in all. Settle them, if you can, when the pay is drawn.

But I come back again. To-day (Tuesday) I am in expectation of hearing the sentence of death read to me, and of closer confinement, in a cell. But my Father in heaven, by His great mercy, inspires me with continued peace of mind, and I rest in His mercy. Yesterday evening was an hour of great depression to me. I had heard some one of my fellow-prisoners describe the interest shown in his case by the United States Commissioner of Exchange, and I could not help feeling, "How far are my friends from comforting me now!" All were interested in his story, and I walked by myself up and down the room, which we cannot leave, and thought of my loneliness. Oh! my Father, "God's loving-kindness is better than life," and I would rather die here by this ignominious death, than be that man outside as yet of the mercy of God. I thank Him often, dear Father, that I have been brought to prison to learn Him and His mercy.

And now, Father, I know no better way of cheering you than Christ took—"In my Father's house are many mansions"—let us hope to meet there. I would say to you as I did to Kitty: think of me as living, and waiting for you. Hoping ever in God's mercy, love Him better for His kindness unto me. Think of the many dangers in which He as preserved me safely, and at the last taught me the better way; then hope for the rest of the children. It should greatly cheer and comfort you that God has taught, we trust, Kitty and myself, the two oldest ones, of Himself, and you should be the more trustful in Him, and the more comforted in your troubles, by this. One thing remember, dear Father: "Precious in the sight of the Lord is the death of his saints." So do not forget it was infinite wisdom, guided by infinite mercy, that took me from the world so early. I had hoped, indeed, to live to comfort and help you; but God will choose His own means of supporting those whose bread and water He has promised "shall be sure." Do not, then, at any time, let your mind dwell upon the fearfulness of the manner of my death; but turn from it to the wonderful goodness of the Lord, who, when in the bitterness of my agony, more than a year since, I called upon Him to spare me until I could know that I was a Christian, was pleased to hear me, and granted me the whole year that is past — wonderful instance of His goodness in answering prayer.

Cheer your souls then, my parents, with the thought of the marvelous

Appendix C

goodness of God, and think often of paradise, where your son hopes to wait for you. Remember that "the mercy of the Lord endureth for ever." So keep on praying for Rocky and the rest.

And now, dear Father, I pray God will bless you, and take care of you, and provide for you in your old age. I had hoped to do it; but now "the Lord will provide." God has everywhere raised up friends for me in prison; surely for you, in a less difficult place, He can do the same. At Jackson, when I was in the deepest confiencement [sic], He caused me to be continually visited by His ministers, and comforted, cheered, and strengthened, very often. While I was travelling in irons, helpless, He remembered me, and I wanted neither help in my helplessness nor comfort in my heart. At Atlanta He raised me up friends in a wonderful manner. Travelling from there here very heavily ironed, He provided for me constant care. Since, I have had books in abundance, preaching almost every Sabbath, and kind brethren always near.

Although the rations are small, I have rarely gone hungry, and most of the time, as now, have had money with me. Have always had plenty of clothes—am one of the best provided for in the room. Yet when I was taken I had but one suit. So good has God been to me, and I have learned to trust in Him, and can say from experience, "His promises are sure." Remember all this was where I could scarcely help myself at all, and you will see how great has been His goodness.

C. "Sleepless Sentinel at Castle Thunder"

Nero, an enormous dog, accompanied his master Captain George W. Alexander, Superintendent of Castle Thunder prison, to hangings.

Captain Alexander's Dog

Well do the people of Richmond of that day remember him in his tight-fitting suit of black trousers, buckled at the knees; his black stockings and black loose shirt, relieved only by a white collar, with his long, black whiskers flowing in the wind, riding at full gallop on his black horse along our streets, with his large, magnificent black dog Nero following at his heels.

A short history of this dog will not be out of place or uninteresting. Since the war I have seen many accounts published in our papers about him, all of which, in some particulars, were incorrect. I heard during the war from the Hon. James Lyons and Mayor Joseph Mayo the history of Nero, and I will give it as it was related to me by them.

Appendix C

Some time in 1859 or 1860 he was brought to Richmond, a puppy, by the captain of a Bavarian vessel which landed at Rocketts. The captain gave the puppy to Mr. John Allen, of the firm of Ginter & Allen. Mr. Allen gave him to Mr. James Lyons. Mr. Lyons allowed Joe Mayo, the Mayor of the city, to take him and keep him in the city jail, as a sort of guard, because he was too large and ferocious-looking to be permitted to go at large. When Captain Alexander came to Richmond, he saw Nero in the city jail and was greatly struck at his size and beauty. He persuaded Mr. Mayo, with Mr. Lyon's consent, to allow him to take Nero to Castle Thunder, and there he remained until the close of the war. He was of the breed known as the Bavarian boar hound — dogs used for hunting the wild boar in Bavaria and in the interminable forests of Germany. The wild boar is one of the strongest and most courageous of animals, and does not fear even the terrible tiger. In India sportsmen have come across boars and tigers dead, the latter bearing the marks of the boar's terrible tusks. When aroused and brought to bay the eyes of the wild boar look savage and glow like red-hot charcoal. Their strength is sufficient to rush beneath a horse's belly and bear him and the rider on his back sheer off his legs, and sometimes their tusks are seven inches long.

Nero a Noble Specimen

It was to hunt such game as this that Nero's noble progenitors were used, and truly he was a noble specimen of his lordly race. He weighed 182 pounds, and was well able to enter the combat with such a foe. Visitors at the Castle were amazed at him, and their spontaneous exclamations at sight of him would be: "Goodness! What a splendid dog!" He was permitted to run about the Castle as he pleased, and was a great favorite with the prisoners. Ordinarily he was good natured, playful, and docile, but when angered or provoked he was terrible looking, and dangerous. I have seen Captain Alexander whip him with a horsewhip, at the same time have a cocked revolver in his other hand, which occasionally he would fire over his head, and then he appeared the very impersonation of ferocity subdued by the will of man. After the city fell into the hands of the Federal troops and Castle Thunder was vacated, Nero took up his abode with Mr. Stephen Childrey, who had been commissary of the prison, and while there had generally had him fed. Some time in the summer of 1865 some Yankees took the dog and carried him through the Northern States and exhibited him as a show to the people. Flaming advertisements were posted about him. He was said to be the dog which was kept at Libby Prison to eat Yankee

Appendix C

prisoners, and his qualities, disposition, and immense size were set forth in grandiloquent style. This, of course, attracted public attention, and much money was realized from his exhibition. Mr. Childrey, who accompanied him on this northern tour, returned home six months thereafter and he told me that his share of the profits was $3,000.

Fond of the Drama

Captain Alexander, when in Richmond, was very fond of theatrical performances. He wrote several plays, which were acted at the Richmond Theatre. One of these, "The Virginia Cavalier," was a great favorite with the people during the war, and it ran for the unprecedented time of 100 nights, consecutively, at the Theatre. In one of the scenes Captain Alexander appeared for a short time, mounted on his black horse, with Nero barking at his side, and rode across the stage at a rapid gait, and this spectacle always aroused among the spectators the most vociferous applause.
— *Richmond Times Dispatch*, March 3, 1895

That Big Black Dog Again

We announced, some days since, that Hero [Nero], the famous Russian bloodhound, that did the duty of a sleepless sentinel at Castle Thunder post, had evacuated with the Confederate Government and struck the Trans-Mississippi trail. From a personal dog paragraph in a Northern paper, we perceive that Hero has arrived in the vicinity of Washington, and was quite a hero indeed. Mr. Munn, sutler of the 140th New York regiment, captured him in Richmond, and sent him North, a prisoner of war.

Hero is a dog about seven feet in length from tip to top, weighing nearly two hundred pounds. He is a splendid cross between a Russian bloodhound and a bull-dog, and combines the faithfulness of the one with the ferocity of the other. We have seen him seize little dogs that came around his heels, shake them and cast them twenty feet from him. The stoutest man he would bring to the ground by one gripe [*sic*] on the throat, and it was always a difficult matter to get him off if he had once tasted or smelled blood.

His dogship belonged originally to Joseph Mayo, late Mayor, and by him was loaned to Capt. G.W. Alexander, at one time Commandant of the Castle post.

Hero too, had a theatrical turn, and used to perform a dog's part in the play of the "Virginia Cavalier," at the New Theatre. Abandoning the stage, Hero returned to his post as sentinel at the Castle, and remained

Appendix D

through the successive reigns of the several commandants up to the evening of Monday, April 3, 1865.

Hero was a "rebel" dog during all the days of the rebellion, but we learn he has taken a fancy to his captors, and is trying to be a good, loyal, Union dog.

Hero in Richmond, was an official, stern-looking dog, and he was as well known as any of the crabbed officials themselves, and was respected accordingly. His old acquaintances will be glad to hear that his dogship has the prospect of an engagement for exhibition. Some menagerie or Barnum will get him.

—*Daily Richmond Whig*, May 19, 1865

"The Guard at Castle Thunder"

A huge Russian blood-hound, which for four years acted as the guard at Castle Thunder has just been brought to this city by Mr. Sidney Munn, who is now staying at the Astor House. This hound is probably one of the finest specimens of the canine tribe that has been seen in this city. Jet black, standing over three feet in height, with a huge but well-proportioned head and body, and thews and sinews that might belong to a small bullock he presents a very formidable appearance, and was doubtless an efficient guard to the rebel prison. His weight is said to be about 180 pounds. He was imported when quite young for the purpose of being trained to fight boars, in which amusement he became quite proficient. His owner states that within a year or two he had fought three pitched battles with full grown boars, and came off victorious in each. He formerly belonged to Capt. ALEXANDER, who repeatedly refused $700 in gold for him, and matched him in a bear fight for $12,000. The animal is said to possess an amiable temper when not provoked. His appetite is good, six or seven pounds of meat forming an ordinary meal. He is certainly one of the greatest curiosities that has yet been imported from Richmond.

—*New York Times*, May 24, 1865

D. Sentencing of James Jeter Phillips by Judge George L. Christian of the Henrico Circuit Court, July 10, 1868

The following is found in "Drinker's Farm Tragedy" (Richmond: V.L. Fore, 1868), in *Virginia Trooper*, May 1954, pp. 31–34.

Appendix D

The Clerk of the Court: "James Jeter Phillips, stand up." As he arose calmly and deliberately, every eye was bent upon him.

The Clerk: "You have been indicted, tried and found guilty of murder in the first degree. Have you anything to say why sentence of death should not now be pronounced against you?"

The Prisoner: "Nothing, sir; no more than that I am innocent before Almighty God and man."

Judge Christian then said: "James Jeter Phillips, you have been arraigned before the bar of this court to answer an indictment found against you by the grand jury of Henrico county, charging you with the wilful, deliberate, and malicious murder of your wife. To that indictment you pleaded 'not guilty,' and a jury of your country has been called to decide the solemn issues between you and the Commonwealth. In order that you might have a perfectly fair and impartial trial, a jury has been brought from a distant county, composed of men without bias or prejudice against you. That jury, after a calm and deliberate consideration of your case, in a trial of unprecedented length, after having heard all that could be urged in your behalf by the able and eloquent counsel who have stood by you in your extremity with so much zeal and fidelity — that jury has pronounced you guilty of murder — guilty of murder in the first degree — guilty of the wilful and malicious murder of your own wife. Against the crime of murder the law denounces the penalty of death. The wilful and malicious destruction of the life of any human being in the peace of God, and under the protection of the law, is a crime [at] which humanity shudders— a crime which, everywhere, under all forms of society, is regarded with the deepest abhorrence, and punished with the extremest penalty; but when the victim of such a crime is a weak, defenceless woman, carried or enticed into a lonely wood, where no cry for help could be heard, and there stricken down, beaten, and the life crushed from the feeble form by that hand which should only have been raised to shield and guard it from harm; when the woman was the wife of your bosom, who had a right to cling to you, and did cling to you, for protection and safety — whom had sworn at God's Holy altar to love, cherish and protect: When all this is considered, your crime becomes one so dreadful, so shocking to humanity, that a whole community stands aghast with horror at its cold-blooded cruelty and atrocity.

"I do not say this for the purpose of harrowing your feelings (God knows I would not add a single pang to the agonies of this dreadful hour), but I say this for the purpose of impressing you, if possible, with the enormity of the crime which you have committed against God and the laws of your

Appendix E

country. I say it, too, for the purpose of holding up your unhappy fate as a warning to others. There may be in this vast crowd some who have yielded to temptation — who have taken the first step in crime. To such your doom comes as a solemn warning that crimes, however secret, will surely be revealed; that no secrecy, nor darkness, nor careful concealment, can escape the scrutiny of that Omniscient Eye that penetrates every veil, nor that Omnipotent Hand of retributive justice which shall sooner or later surely bring the transgressor to judgment and punishment.

"But I must now proceed to perform the solemn and painful duty of pronouncing upon you the dread sentence of the law. Oh, it is a sad and mournful task! to have to speak to one so young, to one whose early training and character gave the promise of a useful and happy life — to be compelled to speak to such a one that word which is to consign him, in the midst of life, in the full flush and strength of his manhood, to a violent and ignominious death. It fills my heart with unspeakable grief; and I should not be adequate to the dreadful task but for the reflection that it is not I, but the law, that pronounces your doom; that I am but its humble minister; that it but speaks through me that stern voice of retributive justice which shall surely call to judgment him who stains his heart with crime and his hands with blood.

"It but remains for me to pronounce upon you the sentence of the law; which sentence is, that you, James Jeter Phillips, shall be taken hence to the jail of this county, and there kept in solitary confinement until the 6th day of November next, on which day, between the hours of 10 in the morning and 6 in the evening, you shall be taken to the usual place of execution and there hanged by the neck until you are dead. I can only commend you to the mercy of heaven, and solemnly, warn you, on this the last time that I shall ever meet you on this earth, that you devote the brief remnant of your mortal life in preparing to meet the awful doom which awaits you as the penalty of your dreadful crime. The penalty is death, and may the All-Merciful and Infinite God have mercy on your soul. Mr. Sheriff, you will take charge of the prisoner."

E. The Prosecutor, Colonel W.R. Aylett, States the Case Against Thomas J. Cluverius, 1885

This excerpt is taken from George A. Booker, *The Virginia Tragedy: Trial and Conviction of Thomas J. Cluverius*, March 13, 1885 (Richmond: Johns and Goolsby, 1885), 105–123.

Appendix E

Colonel Aylett then took up and read the instructions of the court, the first four of which had been tendered by the prosecution and the other two by the defence. He read them slowly, commenting as he proceeded. The presumption of innocence, he admitted, stands over and hovers about the accused until the evidence breaks down the presumption. A reasonable doubt is not fanciful or whimsical doubt. It is a doubt you can give a good a reason for. It is such a doubt as would stagger you in your own affairs— a doubt for which a good reason can be given. Nor do we claim, said he, that a mere preponderance of testimony will justify a conviction. You must look for the evidence that will remove "all reasonable doubt." If you can't tell whether it was a case of murder or suicide, then you are to give him the benefit of the doubt; but if the evidence drives the doubt from your minds and places the crime on him, why, then, you must find him guilty. A moral certainty is not like a mathematical certainty; it is not like two and two make four, or the demonstration of a proposition in Euclid, but is a certainty satisfactory to your minds and conscience. Doubts may still be there, because all human affairs are matters of doubt. So Colonel Aylett went on explaining the legal phases of the instructions, doing it clearly and tersely, and therefore interestingly. Occasionally he fitted his explanation to the case in hand. His enunciation was strong and sonorous, his carriage commanding, his periods well turned and trimmed, and his style pleasing and effective. Continuing his remarks, Colonel Aylett said:

"Guilt, guilt, dark and bloody guilt, gentlemen of the jury, must be your verdict unless you can find a reasonable hypothesis for the innocence of the prisoner." The case rests on circumstantial evidence, and in support of this sort of evidence he cited the case of Vanderpool, out West, and remarked that out of eleven hundred cases reported in which men were hung on circumstantial evidence, there had only been found one case that an innocent person had been made way with. Families might strike for its members and for family blood, and the world should be charitable; but when you see the finger of evidence pointing to the person, and to him alone, there was but one conclusion, and that was that he was guilty. People trust every day to circumstantial evidence.

The rain that fell during the night was not seen by those who slept during its fall, and waked in the morning to find the streets and gutters clean; but still we knew that the rain had fallen. In fact, said the Colonel, we act in life more on circumstantial than we do on direct testimony. In every day matters and in our intercourse with the world we are guided by it to a certain extent.

Appendix E

The Chief Heads

There were two heads under which this case ought to be considered. The first was, "Has there been a murder?" The second, "Who was the murderer?" Taking up the murder theory, the speaker went on to tell of the finding of the body in the reservoir by Mr. Lysander W. Rose, to whom he alluded as "that good old Virginia gentleman," making his daily visits around the reservoir. Next he referred to our faithful and learned coroner, who came out and viewed the body on that bleak March day, as it lay there cold, stiff and stark on the granite walk; and how, after a partial inquest, the body was sent to the Alms-house for further investigation. Yes, gentlemen of the jury, the poor woman was found there, the watch-key was found, and the tracks were found leading from the hole in the fence to the reservoir. When all these things was [sic] found out the suicide theory perished. In fact, said the speaker, it never had any vitality. The track seen was that of a man, and he had a woman in charge, and he ought to account for her. If that man was the prisoner, has he ever accounted for the woman? Colonel Aylett reviewed what had been said by witnesses about a desperate struggle between a man and a woman on the walkway, and pictured the scene. The news of her death spread, and the world throbbed with sympathy for the poor unfortunate. No case in the annals of time has ever racked and thrilled the people to a greater extent.

They arose and put into use measures which had culminated in the arrest of the prisoner at the bar. Thus came the revelations of the January visit, the Belle Isle visit, and other matters, and the finger of evidence pointed to Thomas J. Cluverius as the man. The suicide theory started perhaps with the remark to Conductor Wright on the Chesapeake and Ohio train, that she wished the train would run off and kill her. Was this remarkable? Even in chaste and holy love this feeling prevailed with women in her delicate condition, and was it possible that a woman as timid as she was, would ever have gone to a locality so lonely, and jumped into a place like the reservoir, tearing the sleeve of her jersey in so doing. I am arguing to bearded men, said Colonel Aylett; men of brains; and he then told of the lack of water in the stomach or lungs in order to disprove suicide, and in this connection asked if it was probable that she would have disposed of her satchel, hat and cloak, in the manner she did if suicide had been contemplated. The instincts of humanity makes a woman love life when in the condition of Fannie Madison. She was a murdered woman and her death was a violent one, and without parallel in the whole country. Decoyed

Appendix E

from Bath, used for vile purposes, and then murdered. Who did it? What did he do? Where is the finger ring she wore? Possibly this contained language that would have pointed out who did the deed. There was a hand of Providence in this matter and it pointed to the prisoner. He evidently thought that the body would be thrown in the reservoir at a point just above the waste pipe, and he hoped doubtless that she would never rise to the surface, but be drawn into the pipes. He couldn't afford to take her through the streets with the lamps lighted. A murderer hasn't time for reflection. God only sees the man who commits so dark a deed, and the murderer forgets that there is a God.

The prisoner possessed himself of her person and her good name, and she withheld nothing from him. He might have known where Dunstan lived through her, and have put the shawl on his fence to divert attention from himself and to Dunstan. Did she put the clothes-bag in the river? Hardly. He took the bag to see what was in it, and it was possible that he left it in some convenient place the day before, and afterwards (the next morning) took it and threw it in the river. As sure as you are born he went where he left this evidence the morning he left the city and deposited the evidence of his crime in James River. [At this point the prisoner smiled derisively.]

The prisoner heard the same barking of dogs that Aaron Watkins heard, and when he heard them he fled. I feel as I were insulting your intelligence to dwell on this part of the testimony, said Colonel Aylett, and I leave it.

When a murder is committed, who is to be benefited? Think of this. When a man's throat is cut on the highway, what is it for, if not gold or silver? When a woman, soon to be a mother, is murdered, who is to be benefited, if it is not the man who is the father of the child? And now, gentleman, who was the father of that child? I say the prisoner at the bar was that father, and that he committed a double murder — that of his offspring and the woman he had deceived. Again, the most damnable thing in this entire matter is the fact that it has never been shown that the prisoner [had] ever done one kind thing for the poor dead woman. He was engaged to Miss Bray, and he had to put poor Lillian out of the way. Now for the motive. Can you imagine a case that motive does not more thickly crowd? Ah! gentlemen, had his crime ever been known, would not his old aunt have hissed him from her home? Would he not have been sent out from his place as assistant superintendent of the Sunday-school at Olivet church, and have been driven from his place as a lawyer at the bar? Disaster, financial

Appendix E

and professional ruin, dark and hideous, would have bursted upon him wherever he turned.

Colonel Aylett paid counsel for the defence a high compliment, saying that under the depressing influence of the trial they had done their work faithfully and efficiently, and continuing, said: The prisoner advised her to "marry that fellow," and at the time she was in correspondence with that honest man, Mr. Cary Madison. Yet the prisoner wanted this poor soiled dove to throw herself anywhere. To escape the grave she perhaps wrote to the boy Emmet Williams. All these letters, harmless as they were, had been preserved, but his cruel, heartless letters had been destroyed except one, and along with that came the lowest and dirtiest thing that ever befouled the English language — that so-called poetry On the Delaware. He ought to be hung for ever sending such a thing to a virtuous woman — a composition so foul that the boys had to be sent out of the court room before it could be read to the jury.

I watched the jury, and I can say here that while it was being read they looked like they were in the presence of a corpse, so utterly horrid and atrocious was the language.

The court resumed its session at 4 o'clock, when Colonel Aylett resumed his remarks. He said he had dropped his argument at a point where the motive for murder was being discussed. Seduction was prominent, and he wanted to show that the boy carried her to Walker's for this purpose. The presence of Rose Hillyard was not to be discussed. Lillian was proved to be twenty-one years of age on the 27th of July; and shortly after, having been with Cluverius at Burlington, she left her parental home and went to her uncle's. No calamity could ever have befallen her if she had remained in her parental home. Do you recall, gentlemen of the jury, that Walker recited the fact that she went to Cluverius for advice? Superior mind, education and villainy gave him mastery over her. What he is is not shown by evidence, but by his letters and that poem. Where is Biggs? They have not dared to put him on the stand. At an early period both were guilty and they carried in their bosom a common secret, the degradation of which both knew. The most damning proof was the time when Miss Bray declared off the engagement in July; he then played the other string to his bow. Then he went back to his old love. If I could have seen his eye moisten with a tear for his poor dead playmate and cousin, I might have believed him guiltless. You have seen efforts made to blacken her grave and make her name a hissing and a by-word. Do you not know it was a base and guilty falsehood made to shelter him from the coming doom? He

Appendix E

came to Richmond and put up at the Davis' House. She registered at the Exchange as Miss Merton — the name he gave at college. Claggett Jones recognized her at the Exchange as Miss Madison. What was she doing there? Mr. Archer recognized him, Henrietta Wimbish recognized him. They denied the mustache, but we think we have knocked the black out of the mustache. It was not what men don't see, but what they do see. Men have sworn that they had not seen a mustache, but there were three or four others who had sworn that they had seen him with a mustache. Two of his college mates had sworn to his wearing a mustache. He had seen him pinching and twisting and patting his lips as if he had a mustache. No one could deny this. Cary Madison's and Emmett Williams' letters are chaste and virtuous, but all of his were gone. Why are all of his gone except the letter advising her to marry and that abominable piece of poetry that makes the blood boil whenever it is thought of? If she was in trouble with her father and mother, ought he have taken advantage of it? What man of honor would have polluted and defiled her, instead of seeking to rescue her? She went to Bath to holier and purer atmosphere, and yet he followed her, and we find him here on the 5th of January with her. He told Mr. Cuthbert that he hadn't seen her since September, 1884. Was not this a falsehood, and didn't he have a reason for it? Prisoner denies this. It was for a guilty purpose, and for his protection. John Wren had rendered signal service, and it afforded Colonel Aylett great pleasure to speak of it. When he came into the hotel he commenced to play a part in keeping with his whole crime. It made no difference about the old man. We have the young one. He was skilled and trained in his duplicity, and kept up the part. He inspired the Curtis letter, and he was trying to play off a Harry Curtis. What did Tyler know about this letter, which to each was well known? Tyler saw them together in the parlor, and saw her light burning at 12 o'clock, and it was the last light she ever saw on earth. Dillard recognized him as the man who sent in the note. Tyler saw them together, Tucker saw them get on the street car; a negro could recognize men quicker than most people — their minds were unemployed and better calculated to recall faces. A key of a strange and old make is found there by John Williams, a small boy, who stood his cross examination better than any witness I most ever saw. He carried it to John Wren, and it has been identified. Joel said he thought the prisoner was the man whom he had seen with the key; that the key was the same; that he mended it for Cluverius. He wanted the key opened, and the defence objected. Read Calvert Harris' order on Joel for the watch to be delivered to the prisoner. Didn't this identify him? He got

Appendix E

the old negro's money under false pretences. He was high in the church, assistant superintendent of the Sunday school, and a model of Christian men. There is a character for you. Is there any signing of the magistrate here? said the Colonel, showing the order for the watch. This deserves to be framed with the poetry "On the Delaware," and yet misguided men have come here and sworn to his good character. Walker had identified the key to the best of his ability because the prisoner had offered to swap. He had identified the key himself by the attempted destruction of its identity. Captain Epps charged Mr. Robins to look for the watch chain, but there was nothing to it. Oliver saw it, too. When they reached Richmond the pendent was gone. How lame and impotent was his brother's tale that he brought it along, thinking it would be important. He had furnished the Commonwealth with evidence to hang his brother. The falsehood told by the prisoner furnishes the Commonwealth with another of the many misstatements with which the case bristles. His own guilty action had identified the key. The Tunstall key neither fitted nor wound the watch of the prisoner's, and the one found did. Did he ask for what he was arrested? The coolness of that family was something past understanding. None of them asked for what he had been arrested. Their behavior was wonderful. It was a time for screams and palpitation of the heart, and yet no one was startled.

This was a moral young man, who drank whenever an opportunity offered, and smoked when he could, and who had the nerve to pray (and he ought to have prayed). He entered upon the trial laughing, smiling. When his cousin's clothes were laid out, and Mrs. Dickerson was on the stand, his eyes were dry, when hardly any one else's in the court-room was. The two letters, dated the 14th of March — one to his aunt and one his grandmother, were referred to. He made her write these letters under some develish [sic] pretext. He wanted to show that she would be alive on the 14th, while he would be in King William. What a skilful and diabolically-conceived plan was this, that his own hand should free him from suspicion. The paper and envelopes found on the prisoner when arrested, correspond with the letter and paper of the letters written by Lillian. The reason he wanted company on his visit to Richmond was to identify him as being away when the manufactured testimony showed Lillian alive.

Colonel Aylett alluded to the change of clothing when the prisoner was arrested. He said even if it was testified to by the brother — he wouldn't say proven — that they changed clothing, it was a mighty bad time to change clothes. He changed his slouch hat for a derby hat, and the excuse

Appendix E

was that it had a hole in it. Where is the hat that their own witness (Mr. Jones) saw at King & Queen Courthouse on Monday with a hat-mark in it. Again, why did he write a postal card at Little Plymouth on the 16th and date it at Tappahannock? His guilty soul was restless and was beating at its doors to make proclamation of its guilt. That is the only way to account for his writing to Mr. Walker, to whom he had never written before.

He told Mr. Robins that he was well known here and could explain where he was, but has never done it. He said that he could prove where he was and would get detectives from abroad to clear him; and intimated that some one like him had personated him, yet he had never accounted for his whereabouts between 8 and 12 o'clock the 13th of March. Oh! oh, the danger that hovers over him from his failure to account for those fatal hours between 8 and 12:00 P.M. Oh, the terrible peril he is in from his failure to keep his promise to account for himself at that time. Of all the men in the world he is the one man who can do it. And yet with all the anxiety of friends and with all the fears that must hang over him, and all the fidelity and ability of counsel no one word is vouchsafed to you where he was between those fatal hours. There is but one supposition and hypothesis, gentlemen, consistent with all the other facts, dangerous facts, in this cause — that he was out at that reservoir there in his guilty work of killing that woman. Every other fact in the cause make loud proclamation of it and there is no escape from the inexorable destiny that chains him there, at that place, and within that time. What other effort is it that he makes to account for himself? Why, Bagby is put upon the stand. Bagby says he saw him at the Dime Museum at the afternoon performance, and that it commenced about 2 o'clock, and wound up at 4 or a little past 4, and that although he sat within five seats of him, he did not observe him afterwards, and he thinks if he had remained there he would have observed him. That is all that accounts for him there. But that does not bring him to safe ground, gentlemen of the jury. He can account for himself in January on some night as being present at the Moody meeting; he can account for himself on Thursday night as being at Geo. R. Bagby's for supper; but this night of all nights he vouchsafes to you nothing — nothing to save him from his doom. It is true while coming up with the officers of justice, he told one of them he was at the Dime Museum, but you will hardly credit that statement without proof from somebody else, unless you have greater faith in the truth of his statements than this case authorizes you to have. Of all the facts that damage him in this cause, the failure to prove where

Appendix E

he was then, is the darkest, the deadliest fact. How does he meet this terrible accusation? He brings men here to prove his good character. Gentlemen, how can that save him in the face of these facts before you? In doubtful cases very often parties are reinforced by proof of good character. But is this a doubtful case? Is there a case where good character can turn the scales? Of what value is good character when an offence is as clearly made out as this is by the circumstances? Why, gentlemen, could not Judas Iscariot, before his fall, have proven by the eleven disciples that he had a first-class character? Do you not suppose that before his sin had found him out, all save the Son of God would have proved for Judas that he was a man of first-class character, and that the disciples would have put their sign manual to it? Do you not suppose that Benedict Arnold, before he betrayed the American cause, could have obtained proof of his good character from the Father of his Country down? Did not John W. Webster, hung for the murder of Harkman, a professor in the Harvard University, standing high and lofty before the world as a man of science and of letters, and of irreproachable character, murder his creditor in his office and burn him up in his furnace? Did ever a man prove a better character than his? Did not Eugene Avam, a man whose name shown brilliantly at the top of the ladder of fame and of letters in Europe, honored by the world worshiping at his shrine, prove a good character?

But the tempter came, and he fell, and twenty years after the death of his victim, when his victim's bones, rotten and fleshless, were dug from the ground, Eugene Avam died in the face of the best character that was ever proved by man. Has it been so long ago that the case of Colt has passed from the memory of some of the older gentlemen among you? John C. Colt, the son of Samuel Colt, the brother of the pistol manufacturer, knocked down with a hatchet and dismembered and salted up the remains of his victim and shipped him to a southern port. His sin found him out, and he anticipated his doom by suicide in the tombs. Did he not prove a good character? It will not do, gentlemen of the jury — it will not do. And when I looked at the prisoner during this trial and watched his demeanor, his calmness, his smiles when he ought not to have smiled, his defiant bearing, I was reminded, gentlemen, of another piece of acting, in Scriptures, which reveals the difference between the innocent and the guilty. Do you recollect when the Lord said to one of his disciples, "One of you shall betray me," that they began to be exceedingly sorrowful, and one after another, the innocent, trembling and whispering, said, " Lord, is it I? Is it I? Is it I?"— the pure and spotless and innocent ones, trembling and

Appendix E

shaking, and cowed. But at last the guilty one with brazen front and defiant air, said, "Lord, is it I?" and He said, "Thou hast said it."

Gentlemen of the jury, it seems to me that I have covered, or nearly covered, all of the material points that it is necessary to present to you, or that I should be expected to present to you by my friends on the other side. My esteemed associate suggested another fact — that he not only does not account for himself that night, but that he does not account for himself at any other hour in the day, when the Commonwealth says he was at another place. He does not account for himself when we proved that he was at Belle Isle; he does not account for himself when we proved that he was at the American Hotel; he does not account for himself when we got him on the street cars; he does not account for himself when we got him at the house of prostitution. Settle these matters, gentlemen, if you can, consistently with his innocence.

We stand here as the representatives of public justice. We stand here as the representatives of the people, of the State, of the Commonwealth. In some States the style of these prosecutions is, "The People against the Prisoner"; in others, "The State against the Prisoner." Here we have it, "The Commonwealth against the Prisoner." We stand here, gentlemen of the jury, as the representatives of the law, which shelters our homes and protects our lives, which hovers over our cradles and follows us to our graves, and protects our remains after they are interred in mother earth. We stand here as the representatives of our mothers, of our wives, of our daughters and our sisters. We ask at your hands a verdict that shall make woman safe in this land from the seducers and the murderers. We say that if his victim had been a strong and guarded man we could feel as if, perhaps, some degree of mercy might be meted out to him. But she was a lone and loving and trusting woman — the mother of his child. Great God, gentlemen, in all the annals of crime has such a crime ever been committed? Will they talk to you about mercy? Mercy! Has he not lived too long? Turn him loose for his progeny to vex and plague mankind? Does not that show what blood flow in his veins? [Holding aloft a woodcut sketch.] Standing here for the men and women of the Commonwealth of Virginia, for our beloved women, I demand his life as forfeited to the law — his life for her life! There is not a home in Virginia that did not feel insecure after that body came up on the surface. The whole State seemed pregnant with danger; and if he escapes, who is safe? Gentlemen, it is your duty to destroy him. Stand up to your duty like men. I have seen too many good and brave men shed their blood in these trenches around Richmond — the best and

Appendix E

noblest of their race — to falter in my duty in asking for his life at your hands. Guard the households, and guard the daughters of the Virginians! This case has become historic. I saw a few days ago [in the *Dispatch*] a picture that has perpetuated your faces. Your memories and your deeds will be perpetuated by a becoming record made up by him [the stenographer] whose facile pen records every word as it drops from my lips. The great reading, listening and watching world has seen and heard the facts on which you are called upon to find your verdict, and they are as intelligent as you, and they will try you, and they will try me, and they will try all the actors in the scene. Yesterday evening, sick, tired and wearied out by the labors of the court-room, and the heat of the atmosphere, I went out to Hollywood; that lovely spot, that silent city of the voiceless dead. There are many there, gentlemen, that are dear to me, at whose tombs I like to stand, and think, and feel moved, perhaps, by that strange emotion that often makes us seek companionship with the dead and those long gone from us. As I stood there, and as I wandered on by that stone monument, placed there by the women of Virginia before they had stopped even the shot holes in their houses, to commemorate the valor and the virtues of the men of Virginia, I saw, clustered around and about these humble graves that mark the soldiers' last repose, many of whom were friends and comrades; they were not those who fell where their manly bosoms met the storm of war, not those pierced by bullets and torn by shells; but they were those whose young lives ebbed out in the hospitals of Richmond, soothed by the gentle ministering hands of the women of Richmond, lingering long enough perhaps to carry on their cheeks to the other world a kiss of a mother, wife or sister, bedewed with their tears. As I stood there, gentlemen, thinking of what I was to say here to day, and looking towards the reservoir — that scene of crime — and thought of those screams that came by there, and that went down the valley and were heard by that colored man, the thought came into me that if there was any duty above all others that twelve men owed to the female sex of Virginia, and to the people of Virginia, it was to vindicate the law in this case and protect the women of Virginia. Gentlemen, I am done. I thank you for the kind attention that you have vouchsafed me in taking leave of you and of this case, so far as this case is concerned. I thank you, gentlemen, sincerely for the kind attention you have given me. I thank his Honor for his courtesy and his fairness, and his ability in his rulings. I thank my friends upon the other side that they have borne, perhaps, so well with my imperfections; and I thank all the citizens of Richmond — the police, the detectives, and

Appendix F

the gallant citizens of Richmond—for the aid they have vouchsafed to us in this great trial. Falter not, gentlemen of the jury, falter not in your duty—show the mercy to him which he showed to his poor victim. The evidence which is here is complete and satisfactory. It could be no more satisfactory unless one more witness could come. If Lillian Madison could burst the bonds of death that hold her and stagger into this court room with her winding sheet, and with her wounded lips and brow, and fall down and point to him as the man, it could hardly be plainer. Farewell poor Lillie, thou art sleeping in the lone and silent grave, still you are remembered by all the tender mothers of Richmond and every where else.

F. "An act to establish a permanent place in the State penitentiary at Richmond, Virginia, for the execution of felons upon whom the death penalty is to be imposed, to change the mode of execution so that the death sentence shall be by electricity," March 16, 1908

1. Be it enacted by the general assembly of Virginia, That the superintendent of the State penitentiary, at Richmond, is hereby authorized and directed to provide a permanent death chamber within the confines of said penitentiary, and which said death chamber shall have all the necessary appliances for the proper execution of felons by electrocution. In said death chamber shall be executed all felons upon whom the death penalty has been imposed.

2. Each execution shall be conducted by the said superintendent or some assistant or assistants designated by him.

3. The clerk of the court in which is pronounced the sentence of death against any convict shall, as soon as may be, after such sentence, deliver a certified copy thereof to the superintendent of the penitentiary at Richmond. Not more than thirty nor less than fifteen days before the time fixed, in the judgment of the court, for the execution of said sentence, the superintendent of the penitentiary shall cause to be conveyed to the said penitentiary such condemned felon in the manner now prescribed by law for the conveyance of felons sentenced to confinement in the penitentiary, and the superintendent, in his discretion, may appoint more than one guard to convey the condemned felon, and the expenses

Appendix F

of such guard or guards shall be paid in the manner and under the requirements now prescribed by law for the conveyance of convicts to the penitentiary.

4. The said superintendent or the assistants appointed by him shall proceed, unless a suspension of execution be ordered, at the time named in said sentence to cause the said felon under sentence of death to be electrocuted until he is dead. At the execution there shall be present the superintendent, or his assistants, the surgeon of the penitentiary or his assistant and twelve respectable citizens. The counsel for the convict and a minister of the gospel may be present.

5. The superintend[ent] shall certify the fact of the execution of the condemned felon to the clerk of the court by which such sentence was pronounced, who shall file such certificate with the papers of the case and enter the same upon the records of the case.

6. Should the condemned felon, while in the custody of the superintendent of the penitentiary, be granted a reprieve by the governor, or obtain a writ of error from the Supreme court of appeals, or should the execution of the sentence be stayed by any competent judicial proceeding, notice of such reprieve or such writ of error or stay of execution shall be served upon the superintendent of the penitentiary, as well as upon the condemned felon, and the said superintendent shall yield obedience to the same. In any subsequent proceeding the mandate of the court having regard to the condemned felon, shall be served upon the superintendent of the penitentiary as well as the said felon. Should the said felon be resentenced by the court, then the proceedings shall be as hereinabove provided under the original sentence.

7. Should a new trial be granted such condemned felon after he has been conveyed to the penitentiary, then he shall be conveyed back to the place of trial by such guard or guards as the superintendent may direct, their expenses to be paid as is now provided by law for the conveyance of convicts to the penitentiary.

8. Nothing in this act shall be so construed as to change or alter the manner of execution of the sentence of death when imposed on account of crimes committed before this act goes into effect.

9. The sum of one thousand dollars, or so much thereof as may be necessary, is hereby appropriated out of the funds in the State treasury, not already appropriated, for the purpose of carrying out the provisions of section one of this act.

10. No newspaper or person shall print or publish the details of the

Appendix G

execution of criminals under this act. Only the fact that the criminal was executed shall be printed or published.

11. Upon application of the relatives of the person executed, the body after execution shall be returned to their address and at their cost.

12. All acts or parts of acts inconsistent with this act are hereby repealed.

G. Richmond Executions

Executions, 1782–1903

(abbrev.: B — Black; W — White; H — Hispanic; F — Female)

Name	Race	Date of Execution	Offense
John Chapman	W	January 25, 1782	horse stealing
James Robinson	W	January 25, 1782	burglary
Maurice Wheeler	W	November 29, 1782	murder
John Raines	W	December 5, 1783	horse stealing
Michael Newman	W	December 5, 1783	robbery
Stephen Yancey	W	December 3, 1784	murder
Matthew Womble	W	January 28, 1785	murder
John Tyler	W	January 28, 1785	murder
Presley Hunt	W	July 29, 1785	burglary
John Burton	W	July 29, 1785	burglary
— Richards	W	July 29, 1785	burglary
Reuben Jones	W	July 29, 1785	murder
Tobey	B	August 4, 1786	burglary
Thomas Macauley	B	August 4, 1786	rape
James Goss	W	Dec. 1786 or Jan. 1787	horse stealing
Elisha Lassetter	W	January 26, 1787	murder
Isaac Reade	W	January 26, 1787	murder
Richard Downs	W	July 27, 1787	burglary
Joseph Taylor	W	January 27, 1787	horse stealing
— Dick	B	January 27, 1787	murder
James Phillips	W	December 2, 1787	burglary
William Wilson	W	December 2, 1787	horse stealing
George Abbott	W	June 8, 1787	murder
John Price Posey	W	January 25, 1788	arson
James M'Connell Fox	W	January 25, 1788	murder
John Candy (alias Edmund Watkins)	W	June 9, 1788	burglary
William Armstrong	W	June 9, 1788	robbery
John Coody	W	June 9, 1788	murder
Archibald Carroll (Irishman)	W	August 3, 1788	murder

Appendix G

Name	Race	Date of Execution	Offense
Harry	B	January 11, 1793	administering poison
William (Billy) Harris	B	August 20, 1796	burglary
Jacob	B	December 1, 1797	burglary
Tom	B	February 2, 1799	burglary
Guy	B	February 2, 1799	burglary
Mayor Bob	B	February 9, 1799	stabbing with intent to kill
*Solomon	B	Sept.–Oct. 1800	insurrection
Peter	B	"	"
Tom	B	"	"
Gabriel	B	"	"
Martin	B	"	"
Frank	B	"	"
Will	B	"	"
John	B	"	"
Isaac (1)	B	"	"
Isham	B	"	"
Michael (1)	B	"	"
Ned	B	"	"
Billy	B	"	"
Charles	B	"	"
Jupiter	B	"	"
Sam	B	"	"
Sawney	B	"	"
Gilbert	B	"	"
William	B	"	"
Isaac (2)	B	"	"
Laddis	B	"	"
Sam, alias Sam Graham	B	"	"
George	B	"	"
Dick	B	"	"
Michael (2)	B	"	"
Sam, alias Sam Bird	B	"	"
Arthur	B	July 18, 1802	"
Billy Scott	B	March 3, 1805	rape
Bob	B	May 1805	burglary
Archer	B	October 1815	horse stealing/burglary
Jordan	B	March 24, 1820	murder
James	B	November 3, 1820	horse stealing
Jose Casares	H	August 17, 1827	murder

*The names (Solomon through Sam [Bird]) of the Gabriel conspirators (see Chapter 3) executed are taken from Philip J. Schwarz, *Twice Condemned: Slaves and the Criminal Laws of Virginia, 1705–1865* (Baton Rouge: Louisiana State University Press, 1988), 324–327.

Appendix G

Name	Race	Date of Execution	Offense
Jose Morando	H	August 17, 1827	murder
Felix Barbeito	H	August 17, 1827	murder
Robert Gibson	W	October 27, 1818	murder
Daniel	B	July 30, 1830	murder
Frank	B	December 1, 1837	murder
Jack	B	May 6, 1842	burglary
Washington	B	May 6, 1842	burglary
Moses Johnson	B	December 19, 1845	murder
Henry Moses	B	March 24, 1846	murder
Giles (1)	B	September 6, 1846	murder
Giles (2)	B	December 10, 1847	murder
King	B	May 12, 1848	murder
Edward Clements	W	April 23, 1852	murder
Thomas Reed	W	April 23, 1852	murder
Jane Williams	BF	September 10, 1852	murder
John Williams	B	October 22, 1852	accessory to murder
Washington	B	December 12, 1854	arson
William D. Totty	W	November 16, 1860	murder
Jordan	B	March 24, 1862	—
Timothy Webster	W	April 29, 1862	espionage
Clara Ann	BF	May 23, 1862	murder
John Richardson (alias Louis Napoleon)	W	August 22, 1862	counterfeiting
Margaret Butt	BF	January 9, 1863	murder
Alfonzo C. Webster	W	April 10, 1863	espionage
(unnamed)	—	May 29, 1864	—
Michael Bucton	B	February 6, 1863	murder
Henry	B	October 8, 1864	arson & assault
Ben	B	October 21, 1864	burglary
William	B	October 21, 1864	burglary

Civil War Military Executions

[All by firing squad, except where noted with †(hanging); Offense: All, except two, desertion; Race unknown; presumably most were white.]

— Griffin	September 23, 1861
John Squires	July 6, 1862
Martin Hogan	August 12, 1862
Patrick McGowan	October 4, 1862
John Kelleher	October 4, 1862
John F. Parke	November 3, 1862
William Thompson	January 5, 1863
Michael Kearns	January —, 1863
John Mulligan	January 20, 1863

Appendix G

Name	Race	Date of Execution	Offense
David Kennedy		January 23, 1863	
Ten N.C. Soldiers (execution at Richmond rescheduled to camp near Montpelier)		September 5, 1863	
Spencer Kellogg		September 25, 1863	
Capt. Spencer Deaton†		February 19, 1864	
Michael Brander†		December 23, 1864	
Thomas Jones†		February 18, 1865	
William Cooper		March 27, 1865	
Frederick W. Brand		March 27, 1865	
Isaac Chaney	W	July 16, 1866	murder
Albert Tyler	B	May 29, 1869	murder
James Jeter Phillips	W	July 22, 1870	murder
Charles Henry Lee	B	August 3, 1883	murder
Barbara Miller	BF	September 14, 1883	murder
Thomas J. Cluverius	W	January 14, 1887	murder
Morris Hopkins	B	April 24, 1895	murder
Philip Norbourne Nicholas	W	July 25, 1895	murder
William Woodson	B	December 13, 1900	murder
Jack Brown	B	January 2, 1903	murder
Ernest Davis	B	January 9, 1903	murder

(Note: There were undoubtedly more executions at Richmond or on its periphery that were not brought to the attention of the public.)

Other Executions with a Richmond Connection

Name	Race	Date of Execution	Offense
John S. Wormley (Chesterfield County)	W	June 24, 1853	murder
Alexander Gardner (New Kent County)		February 11, 1870	murder
Thomas McGiffin (Greensville County)		July 21, 1871	murder
Richard Green (Prince George County)		July 28, 1871	murder
William Henry Johnson (Prince George County)		July 28, 1871	murder
Hillary Page (Chesterfield County)		September 1, 1876	arson

Chapter Notes

Abbreviations (All except the *New York Times* are Richmond newspapers)

APA-CT	Auditor of Public Accounts: Condemned blacks executed or transported, 1781–1865, LV.
CSP	William P. Palmer et al., eds., *Calendar of Virginia State Papers*, 11 vols. (Richmond: 1875–1893).
DD	*Daily Dispatch*
DRE	*Daily Richmond Enquirer*
DRW	*Daily Richmond Whig*
LV	Library of Virginia
NYT	*New York Times*
RE	*Richmond Enquirer*
RNL	*Richmond News Leader*
RT-D	*Richmond Times-Dispatch*
VGAA	*Virginia Gazette or the American Advertiser*
VGWA	*Virginia Gazette and Weekly Advertiser*
VHS	Virginia Historical Society
VIC	*Virginia Independent Chronicle*

Preface

1. Otto Bettmann, *The Good Old Days: They Were Terrible* (New York: Random House, 1974), xi–xiii.

Chapter 1

1. *RE*, July 19, 1839; Isaac Weld, *Travels Through the States of North America and the Provinces of Upper and Lower Canada, 1795, 1796, and 1797* (1807; repr., New York: August M. Kelly, 1970), 182–83, 190; William A. Christian, *Richmond: Past and Present* (1912; repr., Spartanburg, SC: Reprint Company, 1973. orig. pub. 1912), passim.
2. APA-CT, October 29, 1847 and March 6, 1848; *RT-D*, June 6, 2010; Paul W. Keve, *The History of Corrections in Virginia* (Charlottesville: University Press of Virginia, 1986), 61; Veronica A. Davis, *Here I Lay My Burdens Down: A History of the Black Cemeteries of Richmond, Virginia* (Richmond: Dietz Press, 2003), 11; T. Tyler Potterfield, *Nonesuch Place: A History of the Richmond Landscape* (Charleston, SC: History Press, 2009), 82.
3. E.g., *DD*, August 24, 1863.
4. APA-CT, February 6, 1837, April 4, 1842, October 29, 1847, March 6, 1848.
5. Ibid., June 2, 1851.
6. Keve, *Corrections*, 6.
7. Samuel J.T. Moore, Jr., *Moore's Complete Civil War Guide to Richmond* (Richmond: S.J.T. Moore, Jr., 1973), 86; Arch F. Blakey, *General John H. Winder, C.S.A.* (Gainesville: Uni-

Notes — Chapter 2

versity of Florida Press, 1990), 157; Frances H. Casstevens, *George W. Alexander and Castle Thunder* (Jefferson, NC: McFarland, 2004), 39.

8. Casstevens, *Alexander and Castle Thunder*, 41.

9. Ibid., *RE*, January 23, 1823.

10. Moore, *Complete Guide*, 67; Earle Lutz, *A Richmond Album* (Richmond: Garrett & Massie, 1937), 68.

11. For problems in the administration of the penitentiary in the nineteenth century, see William Gaines, "The 'Penitentiary House,'" *Virginia Cavalcade* 6 (Summer, 1956): 11–17.

12. Weld, *Travels*, 188 and 191; Christian, *Richmond*, 23.

13. Lutz, *Richmond Album*, 118.

14. *RE*, October 14, 1825; "Act concerning district courts," January 19, 1807, in Samuel Shepherd, comp., *The Statutes at Large of Virginia* (1835; repr., New York: AMS Press, 1970), 3: 305; Eugene L. Schwaab, ed., *Travels in the Old South* (Lexington: University Press of Kentucky, 1973), 1: 99–100; William H. Gaines, Jr., "Courthouses of Henrico and Chesterfield," *Virginia Cavalcade* 1 (Winter 1960), 33–34; Kathryn Preyer, "Crime, the Criminal Law and Reform in Post-Revolutionary Virginia," *Law and History Review* 1 (1983): 76n.

15. Herbert A. Johnson, ed., *The Papers of John Marshall*, vol. 1 (Chapel Hill: University of North Carolina Press, 1974), 171n.

16. Marianne P. Sheldon, "Richmond, Virginia: The Town and Henrico County to 1820" (PhD diss., University of Michigan, 1975), 447.

17. Daniel J. Flanigan, "Criminal Procedure in Slave Trials in the Antebellum South," *Journal of Southern History* 40 (1974): 550.

18. E.g., Hustings Court Order Book #6, February 4, 1805; John J. Reardon, *Edmund Randolph: A Biography* (New York: Macmillan, 1974), 161, 171; "An Act establishing district courts...," December 22, 1783; William W. Hening, comp., *The Statutes at Large ... Virginia*, vol. 12 (Richmond: 1823), 532–33. 544, 546, 730, and 737; Charles Cullen, *St. George Tucker and Law in Virginia, 1772–1804* (New York: Garland, 1987), 81, 85; Johnson, ed., *Papers of Marshall*, 1: 291–92 and n.

19. Reardon, *Randolph*, 360, 480n.; Shepherd, comp., *Statutes at Large*, 3: 358, 360–61, Dec. 1807.

20. Shepherd, comp., *Statutes at Large*, 2: 5–10, December 15, 1796; Sheldon, "Richmond," 317; Caleb P. Patterson, *The Constitutional Principles of Thomas Jefferson* (Austin: University of Texas Press, 1953), 21–22.

21. Sheldon, "Richmond," 441–42, 447.

22. APA-CT, passim.

23. Ibid., February 3, 1829, and June 16, 1852.

24. Ibid., May 5 and 20, 1834, and October 22, 1852.

25. Philip J. Schwarz, *Twice Condemned: Slaves and the Criminal Laws of Virginia, 1705–1865* (Baton Rouge: Louisiana State University Press, 1988), 299n.

26. APA-CF, June 2 and 25, 1851, October 6, 1851, January 12, 1852, and February 13, 1865.

27. Ibid., passim.

28. Ibid., e.g., March 13, 1848, July 7, 1851, and December 11, 1860.

29. E.g., April 4, 1852, June 11 and 25 and December 6, 1860.

Chapter 2

1. *VGAA*, January 26, 1782; *VGWA*, January 26, 1782.

2. While Gen. Anthony Wayne and his Pennsylvania Continentals were in the vicinity of Richmond, a soldier was hanged for marauding on July 22, 1781, another for killing an officer, on August 12, 1781, and still another on November 4, 1781 (Harry M. Ward and Harold E. Greer, Jr., *Richmond during the Revolution, 1775–1783* [original manuscript copy, in custody of the authors], 250–59); E. Lee Shepard, ed., *Marching to Victory: Capt. Benjamin Bartholomew's Diary of the Yorktown Campaign, May 1781 to March 1782* (Richmond: VHS, 2002), 14, 16, 27.

3. *VGAA*, November 30, 1782.

4. Thomas Jefferson, *Notes on the State of Virginia*, ed. David Waldstreicher (Boston: Bedford/St. Martin's, 2002), 189.

5. Christian, *Richmond*, 31.

6. *VGAA*, July 19 and December 6, 1783; *VGWA*, December 6, 1783.

Notes—Chapter 3

7. Sheldon, "Richmond," 448.
8. *VGAA*, August 6, 1786; Johnson, ed., *Papers of Marshall*, 1: 169, 171n.
9. *VGAA*, December 4, 1784, and January 29, 1785.
10. *VGWA*, July 30, 1785.
11. John Marshall to Edmund Randolph, December 24, 1786, Johnson, ed., *Papers of Marshall*, 1: 193n.
12. *VIC*, January 31. 1787; *VGWA*, February 1, 1787.
13. *VIC*, August 1, 1787; *VGWA*, August 2, 1787.
14. *VIC*, June 13, 1787; *VGWA*, December 6, 1787.
15. John T. Posey, *General Thomas Posey: Son of the American Revolution* (East Lansing: Michigan State University Press, 1992), 279–81.
16. Ibid., 281, 284–85.
17. Posey, *Posey*, 287; Council of State Opinion, February 20, 1783, Johnson, ed., *Papers of Marshall*, 1: 96–97; General Court item, October 3, 1784, *CSP*, 3: 616; Hutchinson and Rachal (and Robert Rutland), eds., Papers of Madison, 6: 347n and 10 (1977): 155n.; Washington to John Price Posey, August 7, 1782, John C. Fitzpatrick, ed., *Writings of George Washington*, 39 vols. (Washington, D.C. GPO, 1931–44), 24: 485–87.
18. Posey, *Posey*, 287; John Price Posey to Washington, January 27, 1787, W.W. Abbot and Dorothy Twohig, eds., *Papers of George Washington*, Confederation Series, vol. 4 (Charlottesville: University Press of Virginia, 1995): 545–47 and n.
19. William Clayton to the governor of Virginia, July 20, 1787, *CSP*, 4:321.
20. *VIC*, July 18, 1787; *VGWA*, July 19, 1787; Posey, *Posey*, 289; Edmund Berkley and Dorothy Berkeley, *John Clayton: Pioneer of American Botany* (Chapel Hill: University of North Carolina Press, 1963), 172.
21. *VIC*, August 22, 1787; Posey, *Posey*, 289–90; Malcolm H. Harris, *Old New Kent County* (West Point, VA: no publisher, 1977), 1: 97.
22. *VGWA*, October 18, 1787.
23. Charles T. Cullen, *St. George Tucker and Law in Virginia, 1772–1804* (New York: Garland, 1987), 61–62.
24. Quoted in Ibid., 62; Posey, *Posey*, 291.
25. Posey, *Posey*, 289–91.
26. Quoted in Ibid., 291.
27. *VGWA*, January 31, 1788.
28. Ibid., November 1, 1787.
29. Posey, *Posey*, 291; Harris, *New Kent County*, 99.
30. *VGWA*, May 1 and June 1, 1788.
31. Ibid., June 19 and August 7, 1788.
32. APA-CT, January 11, 1793.
33. Edward C. Carter, ed., *The Virginia Journals of Benjamin Henry Latrobe* (New Haven: Yale University Press, 1977), 1: 191–92; Virginius Dabney, *Richmond: The Story of a City* (Garden City, NY: Doubleday, 1976), 67.
34. AP-CT, February 9, 1799.

Chapter 3

1. James Monroe to the mayor of Petersburg, August 30, 1800 (1900; repr., Stanilaus M. Hamilton, ed., *The Writings of James Monroe*, vol. 3 (New York: Arno Press, 1969) 3: 201.
2. Douglas R, Egerton, *Gabriel's Rebellion: The Virginia Slave Conspiracies of 1800 and 1802* (Chapel Hill: University of North Carolina Press, 1993), 19–28; Philip J. Schwarz, "Gabriel's Challenge: Slaves and Crime in Late Eighteenth-Century Virginia," *Virginia Magazine of History and Biography* 90 (1982): 283–309; Gerald W. Mullin, *Flight and Rebellion: Slave Resistance in Eighteenth-Century Virginia* (New York: Oxford University Press, 1972), 144, 147–49.
3. Mullin, *Flight and Rebellion*, 149–51.
4. Ibid., 152.
5. Egerton, *Gabriel's Rebellion*, 46–47; Nicholas Halasz, *The Rattling Chains: Slave Unrest and Revolt in the Antebellum South* (New York: David-McKay, 1966), 86–88.
6. Monroe to Col. David Lambert, September 2 and to Speaker of the General Assembly, December 5, 1800 (Hamilton, ed., *Writings of Monroe*, 3: 203–6 and 241 resp.).

Notes — Chapter 4

7. General Orders, September 15, 1800 (Hamilton, ed., *Writings of Monroe*, 217).
8. Monroe to Commanders of 12th and 38th Regiments and to Col. Thomas Newton, October 3, 1800, (Hamilton, ed., *Writings of Monroe*, 212 and 213 resp.).
9. Egerton, *Gabriel's Rebellion*, 80.
10. Ibid., 81–82; Julian P. Boyd, ed., *Papers of Thomas Jefferson*, vol. 32 (Princeton: Princeton University Press, 2005), 175n.
11. APA-CT, September 18, 1800; *Virginia Argus*, September 16, 1800; Egerton, *Gabriel's Rebellion*, 84–86.
12. Egerton, *Gabriel's Rebellion*, 85–88.
13. Monroe to Jefferson, September 15, 1800 (Hamilton, ed., *Writings of Monroe*, 3: 208–9).
14. James Callendar to Jefferson, c. September 18, 1800 (Boyd, ed., *Papers of Jefferson*, 32: 174–75).
15. Monroe to William Prentis, October 11, 1800 (Hamilton, ed., *Writings of Monroe*, 3: 215; Egerton, *Gabriel's Rebellion*, 93–94).
16. Monroe to John Drayton, October 21, 1800 (Hamilton, ed., *Writings of Monroe*. 3: 217; Egerton, *Gabriel's Rebellion*. 110–11).
17. Egerton, *Gabriel's Rebellion*, 104–8.
18. Ibid., 108.
19. Ibid., 108–10.
20. *Virginia Argus*, October 14, 1800; Monroe to John Drayton, October 21, 1800 (Hamilton, ed., *Writings of Monroe*, 3: 216).
21. Schwarz, *Twice Condemned*, 325–26; Egerton, *Gabriel's Rebellion*. 112–13.
22. Egerton, *Gabriel's Rebellion*, 134–37, 145; Joseph C, Carroll, *Slave Insurrections in the United States, 1800–1865* (Boston: Chapman & Grimes, 1938), 60, 231; Peter M. Bergman, *The Chronological History of the Negro in America* (New York: Harper & Row, 1969), 85.
23. Julian C. Pollard, *Richmond's Story* (Richmond: Richmond Public Schools, 1954), 76.
24. Robert Sutcliff, *Travels in Some Parts of North America in the Years 1804–1805 and 1806* (York, Eng.: C. Peacock, 1811), September 24, 1804, p. 50.

Chapter 4

1. *RE*, "The Penitentiary," May 20, 1817.
2. Philip J. Schwarz, *Slave Laws in Virginia* (Athens: University of Georgia Press, 1996), 14.
3. APA-CT, June 10, 1816.
4. Ibid., March 7, 1801.
5. Ibid., March–May 21, 1805.
6. Ibid., February 16 and March 24, 1820.
7. *RE*, September 29 and October 30, 1818.
8. *Richmond Daily Compiler*, October 29, 1818.
9. Ibid., November 2, 1818.
10. "An Act to empower the governor to transport slaves condemned...," January 15, 1801 (Shepherd, comp., *Statutes of Virginia*, 2: 279); Boyd, ed., *Papers of Jefferson*, 32: 145n.; Schwarz, "Transportation of Slaves from Virginia, 1801–1865," *Slavery & Abolition* 7 (1980): 216–17.
11. Schwarz, "Transportation of Slaves," 239.
12. Ibid., 219.
13. A selective list (APA-CT): March 20, 1806; April 29, May 10, and July 17, 1811; June 10 and July 16, 1816; February 14, July 21, August 4, and September 3, 1829; December 2, 1835; February 11, 1836; October 3 and November 10, 1837; December 18, 1840; January 29, August 10 and 23, and December 4, 1841; January 11–12 and August 20, 1842; May 20 and June 30, 1843; October 14 and November 29, 1844; August 8 and September 16,1845; November 8 and 22, 1849; March 9. 1852; February 12, 1861; October 12, 1863; July 13 and August 16, 1864; and February 15, 1865.
14. Ibid., July 17 and 29, 1840; October 6, 1851; January 12, 1852; and February 13, 1865.
15. Ibid., May 5 and 20, 1834 and September 16 and November 15, 1852.
16. Ibid., February 6 and March 23, 1837 and November 15 and December 4, 1852.
17. Ibid., April 15 and 21, 1826, October 14, 1840, and January 4, 1841.

Notes—Chapters 5, 6

18. Hustings Court Order Book (Richmond), February 4, 1807.
19. APA-CT, February 3 and 12, 1829.
20. Ibid., September 11, 1815.
21. Ibid., March 29, 1816; Herbert Aptheker, *American Negro Slave Revolts* (1943; repr., New York: International Publishers, 1983), 255–56.
22. APA-CT, October 13, 1823.
23. *RE*, December 21, 1816.
24. Ibid., August 17, 1816.
25. Ibid., February 17, 1820.
26. Ibid., November 6, 1818.

Chapter 5

1. E.g., execution of four pirates in Boston, February 18, 1819 (*RE*, February 27, 1819); five pirates hanged in Savannah on April 28, 1820 (*RE*, April 11, 1820); three pirates executed in Boston, June 15, 1820 (*RE*, June 23, 1820); seventeen pirates to be executed in Jamaica (*RE*, September 28, 1824); and sixteen pirates confined in Boston awaiting trial (*RE*, September 9, 1834).
2. Ibid., January 10, 1825.
3. *A Brief Sketch of the Occurrences on Board the Brig* Crawford *on Her Voyage from Matanzas to New York; Together with an Account of the Trial of the Three Spaniards, Jose Hilario Casares, Felix Barbeito, and Jose Morando, in the Circuit Court of Richmond, before Chief Justice Marshall, for Piracy and Murder, Committed on Board the Said Brig; with Other Circumstances Calculated to Illustrate Those Transactions* (Richmond: Samuel Shepherd, 1827), hereafter referred to as *BS*.
4. *RE*, July 10, 1827; Charles F. Hobson, ed., *Papers of John Marshall*, vol. 11 (Chapel Hill: University of North Carolina Press, 2002), 28–29 and n.
5. *BS*, 6.
6. Ibid., 5–8, 19–20; *RE*, July 13, 1827; Hobson, ed., *Papers of Marshall*, 11: 31n, 33n.; Wirt Armistead Cate, "History of Richmond" (Valentine Richmond History Center), 1: 331.
7. *BS*, 5, 19–20, 26–27, 48–51.
8. Tardy' s biography and role in the *Crawford* affair is printed in "Awful Account of the Cruel and Ferocious Pirate, Alexander Tardy," in Henry K. Brooke, *Highwaymen and Pirates' Own Book* (Philadelphia: John B. Perry, 1848), 60–72.
9. *BS*, 26–28, 31.
10. Ibid., 33–34. In 1789, six pirates who commandeered a ship flying the French flag were captured on Virginia's Eastern Shore and sent back to France for trial (John Kearnes to Gov. Beverly Randolph, August 10, 1789, *CSP*, 5: 17–18).
11. *BS*, 40–41; *RE*, July 20, 1827; Hobson, ed., *Papers of Marshall*, 11: 29n. and 33; Cate, "Richmond," 1: 330.
12. The account of the execution is taken from *RE*, August 21, 1827.
13. James H. Bailey, *A History of the Diocese of Richmond* (Richmond: Diocese of Richmond, 1956), 60–61. Hore's chapel was located on land donated by Joseph Gallego, a native of Spain, who established Gallego Mills (Henry B. Bailey II, *History of St. Peter's Church, Richmond, Virginia* (Richmond: Lewis, 1959), 12.
14. Emma G. Trigg. "Ballad of the Spanish Pirates," in *The Spanish Pirates and Other Poems* (Verona, VA: McClure, 1973), 13.
15. Ibid., 14–15.
16. *RE*, August 31, 1827.

Chapter 6

1. APA-CT, August 3, 1840; March 15 and December 13, 1843; May 4, 1846; and March 12, 1848.
2. Schwarz, "Transportation of Slaves," 228.
3. E.g., APA-CT, November 26 and December 20, 1859; July 2, 1860; January 2, 1860; January 2, 1860; October 12, 1863.
4. E.g., *DD*, July 15, 1857.

Notes — Chapters 7, 8

5. *DRW,* May 25 and August 2, 1830. Daniel's master was Robert G Scott.
6. Ibid., June 12 and 21, 1830.
7. Ibid., July 30–31 and August 2, 1830.
8. Ibid., November 17 and 30 and December 1, 1830.
9. APA-CT, October 26 and December 2, 1837.
10. *RE,* October 3, 1845.
11. Ibid., December 23, 1845, gives the complete account.
12. Richard M. Lee, *General Lee's City* (McLean, VA: EPM, 1987), 15.
13. Maurice Duke and Daniel P. Jordan, eds., *A Richmond Reader* (Chapel Hill: University of North Carolina Press, 1983), 86.
14. APA-CT, January 20 and March 27, 1846.
15. Ibid., December 4, 1847.
16. *DRE,* December 11, 1847.
17. APA-CT, misc. reel 2554, 111–12.
18. *DRW,* July 12 and 19, 1830.
19. *RE,* November 15 and 18, 1831.
20. *DRW,* July 7, 1830.
21. *RE,* August 4, 1835.
22. *DRW,* March 1, 1830.
23. *DRW,* July 1, 1841.
24. Ibid., July 1, 1841.

Chapter 7

1. Except where noted, this chapter condenses *Particulars of the Dreadful Tragedy in Richmond on the Morning of the 19th July, 1852, Being a Full Account of the Awful Murder of the Winston Family* (Richmond: John D. Hammersley, 1852). Newspaper accounts that are only slightly different from this narrative include these: *DD,* July 20–22 and 26, August 13, September 8, 11, 15 and October 23 and 27, 1852; *RE,* September 13–14 and 17, 1852; *Richmond Republican,* July 21, September 10–11, 13, and 15 and October 23, 1852. See also APA-CT, September 14, 1852.
2. George B. Taylor, *Virginia Baptist Ministers,* 4th Series (Lynchburg, VA: J.P. Bell, 1913). 348–50, 355; Jeremiah B. Jeter, *The Recollections of a Long Life* (Richmond: Religious Herald, 1891), 204, 209–11, 351; Lee, *General Lee's City,* 65.
3. *Richmond Republican,* September 10, 1852.
4. Ibid., September 11, 1852.
5. *DD,* September 11, 1852.
6. Ibid.; *RE,* September 14, 1852.
7. *Richmond Republican,* September 11, 1852.
8. *RE,* September 17, 1852.
9. *Richmond Republican,* September 15, 1852.
10. Ibid., October 13, 1852. Lucy Randolph, who was scheduled to be executed along with John Williams for the murder of her baby, had her sentence commuted by the governor (*DD,* October 15 and 22 and November 12, 1852).

Chapter 8

1. Frederick L. Olmstead, *The Cotton Kingdom: A Traveller's Observation on Cotton and Slavery in the American Slave States* (New York: Alfred A. Knopf, 1953), 38–39.
2. William A. Link, "The Jordan Hatcher Case: Politics and a 'Spirit of Insubordination' in Antebellum Virginia," *Journal of Southern History* 64 (1998): 617.
3. Ibid., 621–22.
4. Ibid., 622–26; *RE,* April 26–27, 1852; Midori Takagi, *Rearing Wolves to Our Own Destruction: Slavery in Richmond, Virginia, 1782–1865* (Chapel Hill: University of North Carolina Press, 1999), 112. Quote in Harrison M. Ethridge, "The Jordan Hatcher Affair of 1852," *Virginia Magazine of History and Biography* 84 (1976): 450, 463.
5. Link, "Hatcher Case," 626.
6. *DD,* May 7, 1852; Cate, "Richmond," 1: 426; Link, "Hatcher Case," 628–29.
7. Link, "Hatcher Case," 632–33.

Notes—Chapter 9

8. Ibid., 635, 646; Ethridge, "Hatcher Affair," 463.
9. *DD*, January 15 and April 10 and 23, 1852.
10. *Richmond Republican*, April 23, 1852.
11. *DD*, April 24, 1852; *RE*, April 27, 1852; James H. Bailey, *History of St. Peter's Church, Richmond, Virginia* (Richmond: Lewis, 1959), 22.
12. *DD*, April 24, 1852.
13. *Richmond Republican*, April 26, 1852.
14. APA-CT, December 12, 1854.
15. *RE*, November 1 and 4, 1853.
16. *DRE*, April 30, 1855.
17. *Richmond Republican*, January 1, 1852.
18. *DD*, November 3–5, 1856.
19. Ibid., April 20, 1855.
20. Ibid., April 11, 1855.
21. *RE*, April 11, 1854.
22. *DD*, August 20 and September 28, 1851.
23. *DRE*, February 15, 1855, and February 14, 1856; APA-CT September 11, November 26 and December 16, 1859, June 11 and July 2, 1860, and January 8, 1862.
24. *DRE*, September 6, 1854.
25. *DD*, June 11 and 22 and October 17, 1857.
26. *DRE*, August 3–4 and October 9 and 18, 1858.
27. Ibid., December 10, 1856; *DD*, September 11, 1856.
28. *DRE*, December 6, 1854.
29. *DD*, July 30, 1856.
30. Ibid., April 25 and May 1, 1856.
31. *DRE*, February 19, 1858.
32. Ibid., June 27, 1853; Francis E. Lutz, *Chesterfield: An Old Virginia County*, vol. 1 (Richmond: William Byrd Press, 1954), 116–17, 215–16.

Chapter 9

1. "Military Crimes Subject to the Death Penalty," in Jack A. Bunch, *Military Justice in the Confederate State Armies* (Shippensburg, PA: White Mane Books, 2000), 47.
2. Casstevens, *Alexander and Castle Thunder*, 39, 62; Ernest B. Furguson, *Ashes of Glory: Richmond at War* (New York: Vintage, 1996), 44; "The Old Camp Lee," *Southern Historical Society Papers* 26 (1898): 242–45.
3. B. Jones, *Under the Stars and Bars: A History of the Surry Light Artillery; Recollections of a Private Soldier* (Dayton, OH: Morningside Bookshop, 1975), 127. 335; Emory M. Thomas, *The Confederate State of Richmond* (Austin: University of Texas Press, 1971).
4. Kenneth Radley, *Rebel Watchdog: The Confederate States Army Provost Guard* (Baton Rouge: Louisiana State University Press, 1989), 154; Mark A. Weitz, *More Damning Than Slaughter: Desertion in the Confederate Army* (Lincoln: University of Nebraska Press, 2005), 94–95, 156–57.
5. William M. Robinson, *Justice in Grey: A History of the Judicial System of the Confederate, States of America* (Cambridge: Harvard University Press, 1941), 362–63; Bunch, *Military Justice*, 148.
6. Casstevens, *Alexander and Castle Thunder*, 37, 48.
7. Ibid., 47–48, 221, 223; Elizabeth R. Varon, *Southern Lady, Yankee Spy: The True Story of Elizabeth Van Lew* (New York: Oxford University Press, 2003), 83–84; Stanley Kimmel, *Mr. Davis's Richmond* (Bramhall House, 1958), 142.
8. Bruce Catton, *Glory Road* (Garden City, NY: Doubleday, 1952), 233–34; James A. Harrold, "Surgeons of the Confederacy," *Confederate Veteran* 40 (1932): 173–174.
9. *DRE*, September 24, 1861; Bunch, *Military Justice*, 97.
10. *DD*, June 13, 16, and 26, 1862.
11. Ibid., August 1, 6, 16, and 18, 1862; *DRE*, August 1, 13, and 16, 1862.
12. "The Late Military Execution," *DD*, August 27, 1862.
13. Ibid., October 6, 1862; *Daily Richmond Examiner*, October 6, 1862.
14. *DD*, October 21, 1862.

15. Ibid., October 31, 1862; *Daily Richmond Examiner,* October 27, 1862.
16. *DD,* January 21 and 24, 1863.
17. Ibid., February 6, 1863.
18. Ibid., January 31, 1863.
19. *DD,* June 8 and 20, 1863.
20. Ibid., February 6, 21 and 23, 1863.
21. *DRE,* September 9, 1863; John O. Casler, *Four Years in the Stonewall Brigade* (1893; repr., Dayton, OH: Morningside Bookshop, 1971), 189–90; Jayne E. Blair, *Tragedy at Montpelier: The Untold Story of the Confederate Deserters from North Carolina* (Bowie, MD: Heritage Books, 2003), 72–97; McHenry Howard, *Recollections of a Maryland Confederate Soldier and Staff-Officer* (1914; repr., Dayton, OH: Morningside Bookstore, 1975), 225–27.
22. Blair, *Tragedy at Montpelier* 111–12.
23. *DRE,* January 7, 1864.
24. Ibid., February 20, 1864; Casstevens, *Alexander and Castle Thunder,* 1–4.
25. *DD,* February 19, 1864.
26. *DD,* February 20, 1864.
27. Ibid.
28. *DRE,* February 20, 1864; *Daily Richmond Examiner,* February 20, 1864; Varon, *Southern Lady,* 84; David D. Ryan, ed., *A Yankee Spy in Richmond: The Civil War Diary of "Crazy Bet" Van Lew* (Mechanicsburg, PA: Stackpole, 1996), 65–66; Casstevens, *Alexander and Castle Thunder,* 237; Sandra V. Parker, *Richmond's Civil War Prisons* (Lynchburg, VA: H.E. Howard, 1990), 19.
29. *DD,* March 24, 1864.
30. Ibid., December 22, 1864.
31. *DD,* March 20, 1865.
32. Robert I. Alotta, *Civil War Justice: Union Army Executions Under Lincoln* (Shippensburg, PA: White Mane, 1989), 153.
33. Ibid., 155.
34. Ibid., 158.
35. Ibid.
36. Ibid., 162.
37. Ibid., 163.

Chapter 10

1. Harnett T. Kane, *Spies for the Blue and Gray* (Garden City, NY: Hanover House, 1954), 87.
2. Alan Axelrod, *The War Between the Spies* (New York: Atlantic Monthly Press, 1992), 12–19; William G. Beymer, *Famous Scouts and Spies of the Civil War* (San Diego: Musty Attic Archives, 1993), 65.
3. William G. Beymer, *On Hazardous Servicer Scouts and Spies of the North and South* (New York: Harper & Brothers, 1912), 264.
4. Furgurson, *Ashes of Glory,* 126–27; Beymer, *On Hazardous Service,* 273–74.
5. Donald E. Markle, *Spies and Spymasters of the Civil War* (New York: Hippocrene Books, 1994), 145–46; Axelrod, *War Between the Spies,* 139–42; Richard P. Weinert, "Federal Spies in Richmond," *Civil War Times Illustrated* (February 1965), 29–30.
6. *DD,* April 5, 1862; Kane, *Spies,* 105–6; Beymer, *On Hazardous Service,* 284–85.
7. *DD,* April 22, 1862; Kane, *Spies,* 105; Beymer, *On Hazardous Service,* 286–87.
8. Beymer, *On Hazardous Service,* 286; Kane, *Spies,* 106.
9. Alan Pinkerton, *The Spy of the Rebellion: A True History of the United States Army During the Late Rebellion* (Hartford: M.A. Winter, 1885), 555–57.
10. Victor Vifquain, *The 1862 Plot to Kidnap Jefferson Davis,* ed. Jeffrey H. Smith and Phillip T. Tucker (Mechanicsburg, PA: Stackpole, 1998), 78.
11. Furgurson, *Ashes of Glory,* 126; Varon, *Southern Lady,* 75.
12. Clifford Dowdy, *Lee* (Boston: Little, Brown, 1965), 192.
13. Pinkerton, *Spy of the Rebellion,* 556.
14. *DD,* April 30, 1862; *DRE,* April 30, 1862.
15. Pinkerton, *Spy of the Rebellion,* 559.

Notes—Chapter 11

16. *DD*, April 30, 1862; Beymer, *Famous Scouts and Spies,* 71.
17. Pinkerton, *Spy of the Rebellion,* 559.
18. *Daily Richmond Examiner,* April 13, 1863; Casstevens, *Alexander and Castle Thunder,* 235; Pinkerton, *Spy of the Rebellion,* 559.
19. *DRE,* March 30, 1863; *Daily Richmond Examiner,* April 1 and 20, 1863; Casstevens, *Alexander and Castle Thunder,* 235–36.
20. *DD,* April 10 and 11, 1863; *Daily Richmond Examiner,* April 13, 1863; Furguson, *Ashes of Glory,* 126–27.
21. Kane, *Spies,* 214–17, 220–21, 225–27. Spencer Kellogg chronicles his spying as recorded in *Spencer Kellogg Brown: His Life in Kansas and His Death as a Spy,* edited by George G. Smith, which includes his diary and many letters (New York: D. Appleton, 1903); Philip van Dorn, *Secret Missions of the Civil War* (New York: Rand McNally, 1959), 108ff.
22. Casstevens, *Alexander and Castle Thunder,* 187, 228.
23. Smith, ed., *Kellogg,* 350–51.
24. Ibid., 378–79; *DD,* September 26, 1863; Casstevens, *Alexander and Castle Thunder,* 68; Stern, *Secret Missions,* 119–20; Kane, *Spies,* 228–29.
25. *DD,* September 26, 1863.
26. Quote in Kane, *Spies,* 229.
27. Smith, ed., *Kellogg,* 380.
28. Jones, *Under the Stars and Bars,* 129.
29. Smith, ed., *Kellogg,* 379.
30. Varon, *Southern Lady,* 101.

Chapter 11

1. Sallie B. Putnam, *Richmond During the War* (New York: G.W. Carleton, 1867), 151.
2. Blakey, *Winder,* 138–141, 146; Radley, *Rebel Watchdog,* 180–84; Mark E. Neely, Jr., "Habeas Corpus," in Richard N. Current, ed., *The Encyclopedia of the Confederacy* (New York: Simon & Schuster, 1993), 727.
3. *DD,* September 10 and November 17, 1860; Duke and Jordan, eds., *Richmond Reader,* 107.
4. *DD,* November 5, 1860.
5. Ibid., November 17, 1860.
6. Ibid.. November 30, 1860.
7. Ibid., November 17, 1860.
8. *RE,* November 16, 1860.
9. *DD,* May 24, 1862.
10. Ibid., April 7 and 26, 1862.
11. John F. Morgan, "Counterfeiting," in Current, ed., *Encyclopedia of the Confederacy,* vol. 1 (1993), 421.
12. *DD,* August 23, 1862.
13. Ibid., April 7, 1862.
14. Ibid., April 7 and 26 and May 6 and 8, 1862, and July 24 and August 8, 1863.
15. Ibid., May 8–9 and August 21, 1862.
16. Ibid., August 22–23, 1862.
17. *DRE,* August 23, 1862.
18. Ibid.
19. Kerry Segrave, *Women and Capital Punishment in America, 1840–1899* (Jefferson, NC: McFarland, 2008), 76–77.
20. *DD,* January 8 and 10, 1863; *DRE,* January 3, 1863.
21. *DD,* January 10, 1863.
22. Ibid., *Richmond Whig,* January 10, 1863.
23. *DD,* January 31 and February 6–7, 1863.
24. Ibid., May 30, 1863.
25. Ibid., September 3, 1864; *DRE,* October 8, 1864.
26. Takagi, *Rearing Wolves,* 132.
27. *DD,* July 16 and 19, August 29, September 23–24, and October 22, 1864; *DRE,* October 22, 1864; Execution Warrant certified, October 21, 1864, APA-CT.
28. *DD,* October 22, 1864; *DRE,* October 22, 1864.

Notes — Chapters 12, 13

29. *DD*, May 19, 1863; Thomas M. Boaz, *Libby Prison and Beyond: A Union Staff Officer in the East* (Shippsburg, PA: Burd Street Press, 1999), 98–99.

Chapter 12

1. *DD*, July 17, 1866.
2. *DD*, July 17, 1866; *DRE*, July 17, 1866.
3. Michael Chesson, *Richmond After the War, 1865–90* (Richmond: Virginia State Library, 1981), 79.
4. *DRE*, July 21, 1866.
5. *DD*, January 1, 1869.
6. Christian, *Richmond*, 304.
7. Herbert T. Ezekiel, *The Recollections of a Virginia Newspaper Man* (Richmond: H.T. Ezekiel, 1920), 18–19.
8. *DD*, March 1 and May 29, 1869; *DRE*, February 25, 1869.

Chapter 13

1. John D. Bessler, *Death in the Dark: Midnight Executions in America* (Boston: Northeastern University Press, 1997), 32–33, 41; Christopher S, Kudlac, *Public Executions: The Death Penalty and the Media* (Westport, CT: Praeger, 2007); Raymond Paternoster, *Capital Punishment in America* (New York: Lexington Books, 1991), 7.
2. *DD*, August 13, 1870.
3. Ibid., January 13, 1880.
4. Ibid., January 5 and February 12, 1870.
5. Ibid., December 31, 1869 and January 7, 1870; *RDW*, January 7, March 11, and April 14, 18, and 20, 1870.
6. G. Watson James, "The Jeter Phillips Murder Case, or the Drinker's Farm Tragedy" (Richmond, 1954), 4–5; James Evans, "Toll House, Williamsburg at Darbytown Road, March 30, 1936"; Christian, *Richmond*, 294–95.
7. James, "Phillips Murder Case," 8–9; *DD*, July 23, 1870.
8. Christian, *Richmond*, 295; George A. Booker, *The Virginia Tragedy: Trial and Conviction of Thomas J. Cluverius for the Murder of Lillian Madison, March 13, 1885* (Richmond: Johns & Goolsby, 1885), 158–59.
9. Christian, *Richmond*, 294, 297.
10. *DD*, November 23, 1867 and July 1–2, 4–6, 8–11, 1868; *DRE*, July 10–11, 1868; John A. Cutchins, *Memories of Old Richmond, 1881–1944* (Verona, VA: McClure, 1973), 29, 120.
11. Christian, *Richmond*, 297.
12. *DRE*, November 5 and December 18, 1868; *DD*, November 5 and 23, 1869, and July 23, 1870; James, "Phillips Murder Case," 35–37; Ezekiel, *Recollections*, 20.
13. *DD*, July 21, 1870.
14. Ibid., July 23, 1870.
15. Ibid., July 25, 1870.
16. Ibid., July 23, 1870.
17. Ibid.
18. Booker, *Virginia Tragedy* (includes quote), 162–64.
19. *DD*, July 23, 1870.
20. Ibid., January 1, 1870.
21. Ibid., July 27, 1871; *DRE*, July 8 and 29, 1871.
22. *DRE*, July 28–29, 1871.
23. Ibid., July 29, 1871.
24. Ibid., May 2 and June 1, 1871.
25. Ibid., July 8, 1871.
26. Ibid., July 19 and 21, 1871.
27. *DD*, July 22, 1871.
28. Ibid., January 1, 1874, and January 1, 1875.
29. Ibid., September 18, 1876.
30. Ibid., September 2, 1876.

Notes—Chapters 14, 15, 16, 17

Chapter 14

1. *DD*, August 4, 1883.
2. The following narrative regarding Charles Henry Lee's execution is based on the reportage in *DD*.
3. Ibid., September 15, 1883.
4. The narrative concerning Barbara Miller's execution is based on reportage in *DD*, August 4 and September 14–15, 1883.

Chapter 15

1. This chapter is primarily based on the accounts published in *DD*, January 14–15, 1887; Booker, *Virginia Tragedy;* and G. Watson James, *The Famous Cluverius-Lillian Madison Murder Case* (Richmond: Department of State Police, 1953); also comment from Christian, *Richmond*, 390–91, and Beth Brown, *Wicked Richmond* (Charleston, SC: History Press, 2010).
2. Christian, *Richmond*, 394.
3. Thomas J. Cluverius, *My Life, Trial and Conviction*, 2nd ed. (Richmond: S.J. Dudley, 1887).
4. Brown, *Wicked Richmond*, 67–68.
5. Christian, *Richmond*, 391–92.
6. From the *Virginia Trooper*, November 1952, in James, *Famous Cluverius-Madison Murder Case*, 16–17.
7. Leigh, Phillip, *Lillian's Marriage and Murder: Cluverius Did Not Kill Her; The Sequel Told* (Richmond: Patrick Keenan Printer, 1887).
8. *DD*, January 1, 1888, concerning February 14, 1887.

Chapter 16

1. Christian, *Richmond*, 469.
2. The following statistics are from Jerry Lazarus, "The Good Old Days Were...," *RT-D*, February 11, 1979, based chiefly on the city's annual Board of Health Reports (copies in LV). For facts about Manchester (now part of the city), see *RT-D*, April 12, 2000.
3. This account is based on *DD*, April 24–25, 1895.
4. The Nicholas case and execution are fully covered in *DD*, July 25–26, 1895.
5. The signees of the document were William H. Nicholas, John D. Nicholas, R.F. Lane, Otho L. Nicholas, Mrs. Clara L. Nicholas, and Mrs. Adelaide S. Nicholas.

Chapter 17

1. *Richmond News*, March 24, 1900.
2. *RT-D*, February 10, 1905.
3. This account of the Woodson case and execution is based on *DD*, December 14, 1900.
4. Keve, *Corrections*, 93–94.
5. This account of Jack Brown's case and execution is from the *Times* of January 3, 1903; *DD*, January 2–3, 1903, 1903; and *Richmond News*, January 2, 1903.
6. *DD*, January 9, 1903, recalled that "four negroes were hung outside the corporate limits of Manchester about one hundred years ago for the murder of Mrs. Betty Morrisette." The author has found no extant corroborating evidence for this assertion.
7. This account of the Davis case and execution is based on *DD*, January 9 and 10.
8. Bessler, *Death in the Dark*, 33, 36–37.
9. Louis P. Masur, *Rites of Execution: Capital Punishment and the Transformation of American Culture, 1776–1865* (New York: Oxford University Press, 1989), 43.
10. K.M.M. and A.J.J., "Capital Punishment in Virginia," *Virginia Law Review* 58 (1972): 99, 106–10. Three offenses that could result in capital penalties that were added later in the twentieth century were (1) to enter a bank armed with intent to commit robbery; (2) to possess a machine gun in any crime of violence; and (3) to possess or use a sawed-off shotgun in any crime of violence.

Notes — Epilogue

11. The Espy File, copy LV; *RT-D*, October 18–19, November 23 and 29–30, and December 13–14, 1907, and March 18 and 28, April 11, and September 12 and 19, 1908.
12. William J. Bowers, *Legal Homicide: Death as Punishment in America, 1864–1982* (1974; repr., Boston: Northeastern University Press, 1984), 514, 519.

Epilogue

1. *RT-D*, October 13, 1905.
2. *RNL*, January 25 and March 5, 1908.
3. "An Act ... for the execution of felons...," March 16, 1908, in *Acts and Joint Resolutions passed by the General Assembly...*, 1908 session (Richmond: Davis Bottom, 1908), 684–86.
4. Keve, *Corrections*, 147.
5. "Gallows Gone from Virginia," *RT-D*, March 6, 1908.
6. Ibid., March 13, 1908.
7. Keve, *Corrections*, 148.
8. The Smith story is based on *RNL*, October 10 and 13, 1908; "The Martinsville Seven," *RT-D*, February 6, 2011.
9. *RNL*, October 30, 1908.
10. Ibid., March 15, 19, 6; *RT-D*, July 30 and September 23, 2010; *Norfolk Virginian-Pilot*, September 5, 1993; Bowers, *Legal Homicide*, 514–15,
11. *RNL*, April 18 and July 8–10, 1925; *RT-D*, July 11, 1925.
12. The author recalls a conversation, about 1975, with Arthur W. James (1890–1985), who served in the review of Hoke's sentence and decided against clemency, saying that the boy, though winsome, was entirely cold blooded. James was Virginia's commissioner of Public Welfare, 1932–38 and 1946–50, and also the U.S. consultant to the Japanese welfare system. An article on James appears in *RT-D*, February 2, 1951.
13. Ibid., March 5, 1916.
14. *Annual Report of the Health Department of the City of Richmond for the Year Ending December 31, 1909* (Richmond: Clyde W. Saunders), 1910, 8–9.
15. Laura LaFay, "Electrocution in Virginia: The Science, Ritual and History of Putting People to Death," *Norfolk Virginian-Pilot*, September 5, 1993; Execution Database — Death Penalty Information Center, August 1, 2006 (copy LV); *RT-D*, August 8, 2004; Bowers, *Legal Homicide*, 518–19.
16. Harry M. Ward, *Richmond: An Illustrated History* (Northbridge, CA: Windsor, 1985), 245, 247.
17. The Mais-Legenza case and executions account is based on coverage in *RT-D*, February 3, 1935, and *RNL*, February 2, 1935.
18. *RNL*, February 2 and 5, 1951; *RT-D*, February 2, 1951, and February 6, 2011.
19. *RNL*, October 13, 1984.
20. Ibid., April 18, 1985.
21. Ibid., June 26, 1985.
22. "China Leads in Executions," *NYT*, March 31, 2010; John Schwartz, "Death Penalty Down in U.S., Figures Show," *NYT*, December 21, 2010.
23. Joe Bargmann et al., "Debating the Cost of Capital Punishment," *Parade*, January 31, 2010.
24. Kudiac, *Public Executions*, 25; "Virginian Likely to Escape Death Penalty," *RT-D*, January 4, 2010.
25. John M. Crisp, "Bring Back Public Executions," *RT-D*, November 18, 2009.
26. *NYT*, April 13, 2011.

BIBLIOGRAPHY

Newspapers

Daily Richmond Enquirer, 1844–1873
Daily Richmond Whig, 1828–1886
New York Times, 1886–1903
Norfolk Virginian-Pilot, 1993
Richmond Daily Compiler, 1811–1847
Richmond Daily Dispatch, 1852–1903
Richmond Daily Examiner, 1861–1867
Richmond Enquirer, 1804–1872
Richmond News, 1899–1903
Richmond News Leader, 1903–1992
Richmond Republican, 1852–1853
Richmond Sentinel, 1863–1866
Richmond Standard, 1878–1882
Richmond Times-Dispatch, 1903–2011
Richmond Virginia Gazette and Weekly Advertiser, 1782–1809
Richmond Virginia Gazette or the American Advertiser, 1781–1786
Richmond Virginia Independent Chronicle, 1783–1789
Richmond Whig, 1863
(Richmond) Virginia Argus, 1793–1803

Primary Sources

Abbot, W.W., and Dorothy Twohig, eds. *Papers of George Washington*. Confederation Series, vol. 4. Charlottesville: University Press of Virginia, 1995.
Acts and Joint Resolutions Passed by the General Assembly of the State of Virginia, Session 1908. Richmond: Davis Bottom, 1908.
Annual Report for the City of Richmond for the Year Ending December 31, 1909. Richmond: Clyde W. Saunders, 1910.
Auditor of Public Accounts—Condemned Blacks Executed or Transported. Library of Virginia.
Brief Sketch of the Occurrence on Board the Brig Crawford ... *An Account of the Trial of the Three Spaniards*.... Richmond: Samuel Shepherd, 1827.
Brockenbrough, William, comp. *Virginia Cases, or Decisions of the General Court of Virginia, Chiefly on the Criminal Law ... 1815–1821*. Richmond: Peter Cotton, 1826.

Bibliography

Carter, Edward C., ed. *The Virginia Journals of Benjamin Henry Latrobe.* 3 vols. New Haven: Yale University Press, 1977.
Casler, John O. *Four Years in the Stonewall Brigade.* 1893. Reprint, Columbia: University of South Carolina Press, 2005.
Chesson, Michael B., and Leslie Roberts, Jr., eds. *Exile in Richmond: The Confederate Journal of Henri Garidel.* Charlottesville: University Press of Virginia, 2001.
Cluverius, Thomas J. *My Life, Trial and Conviction.* 2d ed. Richmond: S.J. Dudley, 1887.
Denny, Robert E., ed. *Civil War Prisons and Escapes: A Day-by-Day Chronicle.* New York: Sterling, 1993.
Drinker's Farm Tragedy: Trial and Conviction of James Jeter Phillips for the Murder of His Wife. Richmond: V.L. Fore, 1868.
Duke, Maurice, and Daniel P. Jordan, eds. *A Richmond Reader.* Chapel Hill: University of North Carolina Press, 1982.
Fitzpatrick, John C., ed. *Writings of George Washington.* 39 vols. Washington, D.C.: GPO, 1931–44.
Hamilton, Stanilaus M., ed. *Writings of James Monroe.* Vol. 3. 1900. Reprint, New York: Arno, 1969.
Harwell, Richard B., ed. *The Confederate Reader.* Secaucus, NJ: Blue and Grey Press, 1957.
Hening, William W., comp. *The Statutes at Large ... Virginia.* Vol. 12. Richmond: 1823.
Hobson, Charles F., ed. *Papers of John Marshall.* Vol. 11. Chapel Hill: University of North Carolina Press, 2002.
Howard, McHenry. *Recollections of a Maryland Confederate Soldier and Staff Officer.* Dayton, OH: Morningside Bookshop, 1975.
Hutchinson, William T., and William M.E. Racha;, eds. *The Papers of James Madison.* Vol. 6. Chicago: University of Chicago, 1969.
Jefferson, Thomas. *Notes on the State of Virginia.* Edited by David Waldstreicher. Boston: Bedford/St. Martin's, 2002.
Johnson, Herbert A., ed. *Papers of John Marshall.* Vol. 1. Chapel Hill: University of North Carolina Press, 1974.
Jones, B. *Under the Stars and Bars: A History of the Surry Light Artillery; Recollections of a Private Soldier.* Edited by Lee A. Wallace, Jr. Dayton, OH: Morningside Bookshop, 1975.
Minutes of the Seventy-Sixth Annual Session of the Baptist General Association. Richmond: Dispatch Printing House, 1899.
Oberg, Barbara B., ed. *The Papers of Thomas Jefferson.* Vol. 32. Princeton: Princeton University Press, 2005.
Olmsted, Frederick L. *The Cotton Kingdom: A Traveller's Observations on Cotton and Slavery in the American Slave States.* 1861. Reprint, New York: Alfred A. Knopf, 1953.
Palmer, William P., comp. *Calendar of Virginia State Papers.* 11 vols. Richmond: 1875–93.
Particulars of the Dreadful Tragedy in Richmond in the Morning of the 19th July, 1852 ... Trials of the Murderers ... and Execution Upon the Gallows, Richmond. John D. Hammersley, 1852.
Putnam, Sallie B. *Richmond During the War.* New York: G.W. Carleton, 1867.
Richmond, Virginia, Hustings Court Books. Library of Virginia.

Bibliography

Rutland, Robert A., ed. *Papers of James Madison*. Vol. 10. Chicago: University of Chicago Press, 1977.
Ryan, David D., ed. *A Yankee Spy in Richmond: The Civil War Diary of "Crazy Bet" Van Lew*. Mechanicsburg, PA: Stackpole, 1996.
Schwaab, Eugene L. *Travels in the Old South*. 2 vols. Lexington: University Press of Kentucky, 1973.
Shepherd, E. Lee, ed. *March to Victory: Capt. Benjamin Bartholomew's Diary of the Yorktown Campaign, May 1781 to March 1782*. Richmond: Virginia Historical Society, 2002.
Shepherd, Samuel, comp. *The Statutes at Large of Virginia*. 3 vols. 1835. Reprint, New York: Arno Press, 1970.
Smith, George G., ed. *Spencer Kellogg Brown: His Life in Kansas and His Death as a Spy,1842–1863, as Disclosed in His Diary*. New York: D. Appleton, 1903.
Sutcliff, Robert. *Travels in Some Parts of North America in the Years 1804, 1805, and 1806*. York, England: C. Peacock, 1811.
Weld, Isaac, *Travels Through the States of North America and the Provinces of Upper and Lower Canada, 1795, 1796, and 1797*. 1807. Reprint, New York: August M. Kelly, 1970.

Secondary Sources

Allen, Howard W., and Jerome M. Clubb. *Race, Class and the Death Penalty: Capital Punishment in American History*. Albany: State University of New York Press, 2008.
Alotta, Robert I. *Civil War Justice: Union Army Executions Under Lincoln*. Shippensburg, PA: White Mane, 1989.
Aptheker, Herbert. *American Negro Slave Revolts*. 1943. Reprint, New York: International, 1983.
Axelrod, Alan. *The War Between the Spies*. New York: Atlantic Monthly Press, 1992.
Ayers, Edward L. *Vengeance and Justice: Crime and Punishment in the Nineteenth-Century American South*. New York: Oxford University Press, 1984.
Bailey, James H. *History of St. Peter's Church, Richmond, Virginia: 125 Years, 1834–1959*. Richmond: Lewis, 1959.
_____. *A History of the Diocese of Richmond*. Richmond: Diocese of Richmond, 1956.
Ballagh, James C. *History of Slavery in Virginia*. Baltimore: Johns Hopkins University Press, 1902.
Bargmann, Joe, et al. "Debating the Cost of Capital Punishment." *Parade*, January 31, 2010.
Bergman, Peter M. *The Chronological History of the Negro in America*. New York: Harper & Row, 1969.
Berkeley, Edmund, and Dorothy Berkeley. *John Beckley: Zealous Partisan in a Nation Divided*. Philadelphia: American Philosophical Society, 1973.
_____. *John Clayton: Pioneer of American Botany*. Chapel Hill: University of North Carolina Press, 1963.
Bessler, John D. *Death in the Dark: Midnight Executions in America*. Boston: Northeastern University Press, 1997.
Bettmann, Otto. *The Good Old Days: They Were Terrible*. New York: Random House, 1974.
Beymer, William G. *Famous Scouts and Spies of the Civil War*. Abridged ed. of 1912 ed. San Diego: Musty Attic Archives, 1993.

Bibliography

———. *On Hazardous Service: Scouts and Spies of the North and South*. New York: Harper & Brothers, 1912.
Blair, Jayne E. *Tragedy at Montpelier: The Untold Story of the Confederate Deserters from North Carolina*. Bowie, MD: Heritage Books, 2003.
Blakey, Arch F. *General John H. Winder, C.S.A.* Gainesville: University of Florida Press, 1990.
Booker, George A. *The Virginia Tragedy: Trial and Conviction of Thomas J. Cluverius for the Murder of Lillian Madison, March 13, 1885*. Richmond: Johns & Goolsby, 1885. (This book also includes the Jeter Phillips case.)
Bowers, William J. *Legal Homicide: Death as Punishment in America, 1864–1982*. 1974. Reprint, Boston: Northeastern University Press, 1984.
Brooke, Henry K. *Highwaymen and Pirates' Own Book*. Philadelphia: John B. Perry, 1848.
Brown, Beth. *Wicked Richmond*. Charleston, SC: History Press, 2010.
Bunch, Jack A. *Military Justice in the Confederate State Armies*. Shippensburg, PA: White Mane, 2000.
Carmichel, Peter S. "'So Far from God and So Close to Stonewall Jackson': The Execution of Three Shenandoah Valley Soldiers." *Virginia Magazine of History and Biography* 111 (2003): 33–66.
Carroll, Joseph C. *Slave Insurrections in the United States, 1800–1865*. Boston: Chapman & Grimes, 1938.
Casstevens, Frances H. *George W. Alexander and Castle Thunder*. Jefferson, NC: McFarland, 2004.
———. *"Out of the Mouth of Hell": Civil War Prisons and Escapes*. Jefferson, NC: McFarland, 2005.
Catton, Bruce. *Glory Road*. Garden City, NY: Doubleday, 1952.
Chesson, Michael. *Richmond After the War, 1865–1890*. Richmond: Virginia State Library, 1981.
Christian, William A. *Richmond: Her Past and Present*. 1912. Reprint, Spartanburg, SC: Reprint Company, 1973.
Crisp, John M. "Bring Back Public Executions." *Richmond Times-Dispatch*, November 18, 2009.
Cullen, Charles T. *St. George Tucker and Law in Virginia, 1772–1804*. New York: Garland, 1987.
Current, Richard C., ed. *Encyclopedia of the Confederacy*. 5 vols. New York: Simon & Shuster, 1993.
Cutchins, John A. *Memories of Old Richmond (1881–1944)*. Verona, VA: McClure, 1973.
Dabney, Virginius. *Richmond: The Story of a City*. Garden City, NY: Doubleday, 1976.
Davis, Veronica A. *Here I Lay My Burdens Down: A History of the Black Cemeteries of Richmond, Virginia*. Richmond: Dietz, 2003.
Dowdy, Clifford. *Lee*. Boston: Little, Brown, 1965.
Durey, Michael. *"With the Hammer of Truth": James Thomson Callender and America's Early National Heroes*. Charlottesville: University Press of Virginia, 1990.
Eckenrode, H.J. "Negroes in Richmond in 1864." *Virginia Magazine of History and Biography* 46 (1938): 193–200.
Egerton, Douglas R. *Gabriel's Rebellion: The Virginia Slave Conspiracies of 1800 and 1802*. Chapel Hill: University of North Carolina Press, 1993.
Ethridge, Harrison M. "The Jordan Hatcher Affair of 1852." *Virginia Magazine of History and Biography* 84 (1976): 446–63.

Bibliography

Ezekiel, Herbert T. *The Recollections of a Virginia Newspaper Man.* Richmond: Herbert T. Ezekiel, 1920.
Flanigan, Daniel J. "Criminal Procedure in Slave Trials in the Antebellum South." *Journal of Southern History* 40 (1974): 537–64.
Furgurson, Ernest B. *Ashes of Glory: Richmond at War.* New York: Vintage, 1996.
Gaines, William H., Jr. "Courthouses of Henrico and Chesterfield." *Virginia Cavalcade* (Winter 1968), 31–37.
_____. "The Penitentiary House." *Virginia Cavalcade* (Summer 1956), 11–17.
Hackley, Woodford B. *"Faces on the Wall": Brief Sketches of the Men and Women Whose Portraits and Busts Are at the University of Richmond.* Richmond: Virginia Baptist Historical Society, n.d.
Halasz, Nicholas. *The Rattling Chains: Slave Unrest and Revolt in the Antebellum South.* New York: David McKay, 1966.
Harris, Malcolm H. *Old New Kent Bounty.* 2 vols. West Point, VA: no publ., 1977.
Harrold, James A. "Surgeons of the Confederacy." *Confederate Veteran* 40 (1932): 172–74.
Heidler, David S., and Jeanne T. Heidler. *Encyclopedia of the American Civil War.* 5 vols. Santa Barbara: ABC-Clio, 2000.
Henley, Bernard. "Colonel George W. Alexander: The Terror of Castle Thunder." *Richmond Literature and History Quarterly* (Fall 1980): 48–50.
James, George W. *The Famous Cluverius-Lillian Madison Murder Case.* Richmond: Virginia Department of State Police, 1953.
Jeter, Jeremiah B. *The Recollections of a Long Life.* Richmond: Religious Herald, 1891.
"John Kerr." *Encyclopedia of Southern Baptists.* Vol. 2. Nashville: Broadman, 1958.
Johnston, Hugo J. *Race Relations in Virginia and Miscegenation in the South, 1776–1860.* Amherst: University of Massachusetts Press, 1970.
Jordan, Winthrop D. *White Over Black: American Attitudes Toward the Negro, 1550–1812.* Chapel Hill: University of North Carolina Press, 1968.
Kane, Harnett. *Spies for the Blue and Gray.* Garden City, NY: Hanover House, 1954.
Keve, Paul W. *The History of Corrections in Virginia.* Charlottesville: University Press of Virginia, 1986.
Kimball, Gregg D. *American City, Southern Place: A Cultural History of Antebellum Richmond.* Athens: University of Georgia Press, 2000.
Kimmel, Stanley. *Mr. Davis's Richmond.* New York: Bramhall House, 1958.
K.M.M. and A.J.S. "Capital Punishment in Virginia." *Virginia Law Review* 58 (1972): 97–142.
Knight, Ryland. "Robert Ryland." In Taylor, James B. *Virginia Baptist Ministers.* Philadelphia: J.B. Lippincott, 1859.
Koestler, Arthur. *Reflections on Hanging.* New York: Macmillan, 1957.
Kudlac, Christopher S. *Public Executions: The Death Penalty and the Media.* Westport, CT: Praeger, 2007.
LaFay, Laura. "Electrocution in Virginia: The Science, Ritual and History of Putting People to Death." *Norfolk Virginian-Pilot,* September 5, 1993.
Larkin, Jack. *The Reshaping of Everyday Life, 1790–1840.* New York: Harper & Row, 1988.
Lazarus, Jerry. "The Good Old Days Were..." *Richmond Times-Dispatch,* Section B, February 11, 1979.
Lee, Richard M. *General Lee's City.* McLean, VA: EPM, 1987.

Bibliography

Leigh, Phillip. *Lillian's Marriage and Murder: Cluverius Did Not Kill Her: The Sequel Told.* Richmond: Patrick Keenan, 1887.
Link, William A. "The Jordan Hatcher Case: Politics and 'A Spirit Insubordination' in Antebellum Virginia." *Journal of Southern History* 64 (1998): 615–48.
Lowery, Charles D. *James Barbour: A Jeffersonian Republican.* Tuscaloosa: University of Alabama Press, 1984.
Lutz, Francis E. *Chesterfield: An Old Virginia County.* 2 vols. Richmond: William Byrd Press, 1954.
_____. *A Richmond Album.* Richmond: Garrett & Massie, 1937.
Markle, Donald E. *Spies and Spymasters of the Civil War.* New York: Hippocrene, 1994.
Moore, Samuel J.T., Jr. *Moore's Complete Civil War Guide to Richmond.* Richmond: Samuel J.T. Moore, Jr., 1973.
Masur, Louis P. *Rites of Execution: Capital Punishment and the Transformation of American Culture, 1776–1865.* New York: Oxford University Press, 1989.
Mordecai, Samuel. *Richmond in By-Gone Days.* 1856. Reprint, Richmond: Dietz, 1946.
Mullin, Gerald W. *Flight and Rebellion: Slave Resistance in Eighteenth-Century Virginia.* New York: Oxford University Press, 1972.
Neely, Mark E., Jr. "Habeas Corpus." In *Encyclopedia of the Confederacy.* Edited by Richard Current. Vol. 2. New York: Simon & Schuster, 1993.
New York Times. "China Leads in Executions," March 31, 2010.
"The Old Camp Lee." *Southern Historical Papers* 26 (1898): 241–46.
Parker, Sandra V. *Richmond's Civil War Prisons.* Lynchburg: H. & E. Howard, 1990.
Paternoster, Raymond. *Capital Punishment in America.* New York: Lexington Books, 1991.
Patterson, Caleb P. *The Constitutional Principles of Thomas Jefferson.* Austin: University of Texas Press, 1953.
Pinkerton, Allan. *The Spy of the Rebellion: A True History of the United States Army During the Late Rebellion.* Hartford: M.A. Winter, 1885.
Pollard, Julia C. *Richmond's Story.* Richmond: Richmond Public Schools, 1954.
Posey, John T. *General Thomas Posey: Son of the American Revolution.* East Lansing: Michigan State University Press, 1992.
Potterfield, T. Tyler. *Nonsuch Place: A History of the Richmond Landscape.* Charleston, SC: History Press, 2009.
Preyer, Kathryn. "Crime, the Criminal Law and Reform in Post-Revolutionary Virginia." *Law and History Review* 1 (1983): 53–85.
Radley, Kenneth. *Rebel Watchdog: The Confederate States Army Provost Guard.* Baton Rouge: Louisiana State University Press, 1989.
Reardon, John J. *Edmund Randolph: A Biography.* New York: Macmillan, 1974.
Richmond Times-Dispatch. "Gallows Gone from Virginia," March 6, 1908.
_____. "The Martinsville Seven," February 6, 2011.
_____. "Virginian Likely to Escape Death Penalty," January 4, 2010.
Robinson, William M. *Justice in Grey: A History of the Judicial System of the Confederate States of America.* 1941. Reprint. Holmes Beach, FL: W.W. Gaunt, 1991.
Ryland, Robert. "Reminiscences of the First African Baptist Church, Richmond." *American Baptist Memorial,* nos. 1–4 (September–December 1855).
Saunders, Robert M. "Crime and Punishment in Early National America: Richmond, Virginia, 1784–1820." *Virginia Magazine of History and Biography* 86 (1978): 33–44.

Bibliography

Schwartz, John. "Death Penalty Down in U.S., Figures Show." *New York Times*, December 21, 2010.
Schwarz, Philip J. "Gabriel's Challenge; Slaves and Crime in Late Eighteenth-Century Virginia." *Virginia Magazine of History and Biography* 90 (1982): 283-309.
_____. *Slave Laws in Virginia*. Athens: University of Georgia Press, 1996.
_____. "The Transportation of Slaves from Virginia, 1801-1865." *Slavery and Abolition* 7 (1986): 215-40.
_____. *Twice Condemned: Slaves and the Criminal Laws of Virginia, 1705-1865*. Baton Rouge: Louisiana State University Press, 1988.
Segrave, Kerry. *Women and Capital Punishment in America, 1840-1899*. Jefferson, NC: McFarland, 2008.
Selcer, Richard. "George E. Pickett." In *Encyclopedia of the Confederacy*. Edited by Richard Current. New York: Simon & Schuster, 1993, 1208-9.
Sheldon, Marianne B. "Black-White Relations in Richmond, Virginia, 1782-1820." *Journal of Southern History* 45 (1979): 27-44.
Shields, John C. "Old Camp Lee." *Southern Historical Society Papers* 26 (1898): 241-46.
Speer, Lonnie R. *Portals to Hell*. Mechanicsburg, PA: Stackpole, 1997.
Stanard, Mary N. *Richmond: Its People and Its Story*. Philadelphia: J.B. Lippincott, 1923.
Stern, Philip van Doren. *Secret Missions of the Civil War*. New York: Rand McNally, 1959.
Takagi, Midori. *Rearing Wolves to Our Own Destruction: Slavery in Richmond, Virginia, 1782-1865*. Charlottesville: University Press of Virginia, 1999.
Taylor, George B. *Virginia Baptist Ministers*. 3d-4th Series. Lynchburg: J.P. Bell, 1912-13.
Taylor, James B. *Virginia Baptist Ministers*. 2nd series. Philadelphia: J.B. Lippincott, 1859.
Teeters, N.K. "Public Executions in Pennsylvania, 1682-1834." *Journal of the Lancaster Historical Society* 64 (1960): 148-64.
_____, and Jack H. Hedblom. *Hang by the Neck: The Legal Use of Scaffold and Noose, Gibbet, Stake and Firing Squad from Colonial Times to the Present*. Springfield, IL: Charles C. Thomas, 1967.
Thomas, Emory M. *The Confederate State of Richmond*. Austin: University of Texas Press, 1971.
Trigg, Emma G. *The Spanish Pirates and Other Poems*. Verona, VA: McClure, 1973.
Varon, Elizabeth R. *Southern Lady, Yankee Spy: The True Story of Elizabeth Van Lew*. New York: Oxford University Press, 2003.
Vifquain, Victor. *The 1862 Plot to Kidnap Jefferson Davis*. Edited by Jeffrey Smith and Phillip T. Tucker. Mechanicsburg, PA: Stackpole, 1998.
Wade, Richard C. *Slavery in the Cities: The South, 1820-1860*. New York: Oxford University Press, 1964.
Walthall, Ernest T. *Hidden Things Brought to Life*. Richmond: 1908.
Ward, Harry M. *Richmond: An Illustrated History*. Northridge, CA: Windsor, 1985.
_____, and Harold E. Greer, Jr. *Richmond During the Revolution, 1775-1783*. Charlottesville: University Press of Virginia, 1977.
Weinert, Richard P. "Federal Spies in Richmond." *Civil War Times Illustrated* (February 1965), 28-33.
Weitz, Mark A. *More Damning Than Slaughter: Desertion in the Confederate Army*. Lincoln: University of Nebraska Press, 2005.

Bibliography

White, Blanche S. *First Baptist Church, Richmond, 1780–1955.* Richmond: Whittet & Shepperson, 1955.

Theses and Typescripts

Cate, Wirt A. "History of Richmond." 3 vols. Richmond Valentine Richmond History Center, n.d.

Cei, Louis B. "Law Enforcement in Richmond: A History of Police-Community Relations, 1737–1974." Ph.D. diss., Florida State University, 1975.

Duggan, Richard M. "The Military Occupation of Richmond, 1865–1870." Master's thesis, University of Richmond, 1965.

Ernst, William H. "Leaders and Social Change: Urbanization Process in Richmond, 1840–1880." PhD diss., University of Virginia, 1978.

"The Espy File: Executions by State" (Chronologically). Library of Virginia.

Evans, James A. "Tollhouse Report: Williamsburg at Darbytown Road, March 30, 1936." Survey Report, March 30, 1936.

"Executions Database." Death Penalty Information Center. Washington, D.C. Library of Virginia search, August 1, 2006.

Hunter, Adelaide M. "Punishment of Crime in Virginia, 1775–1820." Master's thesis, Duke University, 1947.

James, G. Watson, Jr. "The Famous Cluverius-Lillian Madison Murder Case." Reprint from *Virginia Trooper.* Richmond, 1953.

———. "The Jeter Phillips Murder Case; or, The Drinker's Farm Tragedy." Richmond: 1954.

Levin, Kevin M. "'It Was a Very Sad Sight and One That Deeply Impressed Me': An Analysis of Confederate Military Executions." History Seminar Paper, University of Richmond. 2005.

Naragon, Michael D. "Ballots, Bullets, and Blood: The Political Transformation of Richmond, Virginia, 1850–1874." PhD diss., University of Pittsburgh, 1996.

Pollard, Julia C. "Life in Richmond, 1861–1865." Master's thesis, College of William and Mary, 1939.

Sheldon, Marianne P. "Richmond: The Town and Henrico County to 1820." PhD diss., University of Michigan, 1975.

Smith, Leslie W. "Richmond During Presidential Reconstruction, 1865–1867." PhD diss., University of Virginia, 1974.

Sparrow, Caroline T. "Notes Concerning the Case of the Slave Girl, Virginia, Who Was Tried Before the Hustings Court in Richmond in February and March 1843 for Setting Fire to and Burning a Dwelling Belonging to Thomas Bowles and Sterling I. Crump." Virginia Historical Society. n.d.

INDEX

Abbott, George 16
abortion 132
Abrams, Charles Z. 64
Ainsworth, — 43
Albany, N.Y. 30, 40
Alexander, Capt. George 73, 82–86, 173–76
Alexander, William 147
Alexandria, Va. 133
Alleghany County 161
Allen, John 174
Allen, Dep. Sgt. 137–40
Almshouse 60, 97, 133, 180
Amelia County 66
American Hotel 187
American Revolution 3, 15; *see also* Revolutionary War
An American Tragedy 145
Anderson, Calvin 144
Anderson, James 15
Anna (slave) 49, 51
Archer, — 183
Armstrong, William 19
army camps: Camp Lee 9, 67–68, 70, 72–78, 81–82, 85, 87, 89; Poplar Run 74–75; *see also* Chaffin's Bluff
Arnold, Gen. Benedict 7
arson 29, 31, 63, 65, 99, 119; *see also* Posey, John Price
Astor House (NYC) 176
Atkins, Thomas S. 134
Atwell, Rev. 118
August, Dep. Sgt. — 109
August, Rev. — 105
August, Thomas F. 44
Aylett, Col. W.R. 137, 178–88

Bagby, George R. 185
Baker, John 11
Baker, Dep. Marshal — 96
Baltimore 80
Baptists 147; *see also* individual clergy

Barbeito, Felix 33–36, 39
Barratta, Rev. — (Cath.) 96
Bass, Dep. Marshal — 96
Bath County 181–83
Bayman, Rev. W.A. 113
Beale Dr. — 180
Bealesville, Md. 110
Bedford County 156
Beli, Dr. — 96
Belle Isle 90
Belvidere Street 3, 9, 16, 162, 164–65
Ben (slave) 99–101
benefit of clergy 29
Bennett, Laura A. 64
Berkeley County 15
Bethea, Rainey 165
Bettman, Otto 2–3
Bicknell, Asa 34, 39
Biggs, — 182
Billups, Mary Ann 105
Billy (slave) 30
Binga, Rev. Anthony 120–21, 154
board of police commissioners 10
Bob (slave) 30
Bob, Mayor (slave) 20
Boggs, Rev. Francis J. 91–93
Bolton, Dr. James 50
Boston 34
Boswell, Rev. George H. 123, 125, 127, 129
Botetourt County 65
Bowe, Rev. Charles 106
Bowie, Dep. Sgt. — 107, 109
Bowler, John 112
Bradley, Dick 65
Bradley, Henry 65
Brady, Sgt. — 92
Brander, Michael 78
Brandt, Frederick W. 78
brick making 7
Brief Sketch of the Occurrences on Board the Brig "Crawford" ... 33
Brightman, Henry 34, 39

215

Index

Briley, Anthony 163
Briley, James 163–64
Briley, Linwood 163–64
Broad Street 8–9, 24, 28, 51, 61, 63, 97, 133, 138, 140
Broad Street Baptist Church 87
Broderick, James — 73–74
Broock, Dr. — 96
Brookfield plantation 8, 22–23
Brown, Dr. — 103
Brown, Jack 152–54
Brown, Rev. J.E. 120–21
Brown, John 57, 86
Brown, Kitty 87, 171–72
Brown, Spencer Kellogg 79, 86–89, 171
Brown, Rev. William 85
Brunswick County 118
Buchanan, Va. 65
Buckingham County 146
Bucton, Michael 98
Burfoot, Dr. W.D. 126, 130
Burlington Academy 132, 182
Burnbridge, Va. 102
Burnham, Judge — 104
burning at the stake (S.C,) 32
Burrell, Rev. 143
Burrell, S.C. 160
Burrows, Rev. J.L. 87–88, 99–100
Burton, John 16
"Butchertown" 57
Butler, Demsey 15
Butler, Otto 12
Butt, Margaret 96–98
Butt, Mrs. Mary M. 96
Byrd, Harry 158
Byrd Park 133

Cabal, Dr. — 96
Cadiz, Spain 47
Callahan, Capt. Dennis 77
Callias, Wyatt 154
Calvary Baptist Church 143
Canada 156
Candy, John 19
Caphart, John 73, 77, 85, 87–88, 169–70
capital crimes 3, 10–12, 14, 19, 29, 165; see also criminal code
Capitol Street 133
Caroline County 113
Carpenter, Rev. J.T. 87
Carrington, Dr. Charles V. 158
Carroll, Archibald 19
Carter, Dr. — 126
Cartwright, Mrs. Elizabeth 31
Cartwright, Samuel 12, 31
Cary Street 20, 37, 58, 72
Casares, Jose (Pepe) Hilario 33–34, 36–39
Caskie, John S.

Casler, John 75
Castle Godwin (prison) 70, 81
Castle Thunder (prison) 8–9, 67, 69–78, 81, 85, 87, 89, 169
Catholics 15, 37, 60–61, 147; see also execution-clergy; individual priests
Caton, John 14
Caton v. Commonwealth 14
Centreville, Va. 132
Chaffin's Bluff 9, 67, 74
chain gangs 9, 41
Chalkey, Dr. — 144
Chamberlane, Col. William 16, 18
Chamberlayne, Anne Kidley 16
Chandler, Rev. R.M. 154
Chaney, Isaac (slave), 102–4
Chapman, John 14
Charles City County 65
Charleston, S.C. 34–35
Charlottesville, Va. 150
Chase, Salmon P. 113
Cheatham, Dr. T.J. 121
Chesapeake & Ohio Railroad 153, 180
Chesterfield County 7, 10, 32, 58, 65, 145, 160; courthouse 47, 66; jail 119
Chickahominy River 81
children, murder of 3, 12, 16; see also Randolph, Lucy; Williams, Jane
Childress, Dep. Sheriff 115
Childrey, Stephen 174–75
Chimborazo Hill military hospital 3
China Street 165
Christian, George L. 113, 176–78
Christian, Virginia 161
Christian, William A. 104
City Guard 96–97
City Hall 59
City Point (Hopewell, Va.) 78
"City Spring" 49
City Watch 10
Civil War 2–3, 7, 9, 41, 66–101, 113, 145
Clara Ann (slave) 95, 150
Clarke, Sam 144
Clements, Edward 59–63
Cleveland, Ohio 161
Clozza, Albert 162
Clucker, George 81
Cluverius, Thomas J. 131–42, 145, 159; prosecution's case against 178–88
Cluverius, Willie 134, 140
Cole, Constable — 112
College Street 138
Cologne, Germany 57
Colored Burial Ground 97
Colt, John C. 186
Colt, Samuel 186
Confederate army 9, 67–78; military law 68
Continental army 14

216

Index

Coody, John 19
Cooper, William 78
counterfeiting 90, 95–96; *see also* Richardson, John
Courtney, Rev. John 20
Crane, Rev. William C. 172
Crawford (brig) 33–36
Crenshaw, John B. 105
crimes in wartime ch. 9
criminal code (Confederate states) 67; (Virginia) 11, 19, 29, 156, 165, 206n10; *see also* capital crimes
Crisp, John M. 166
Crouch, J. Royal 64
Crouch, Sheriff — 153
Croxter, Dr. — 143
Crozet, Adolphus 34
Crump, Beverley 137
Cuba 34–35
Cudlipp, William 63
Cullen, Dr. — 39
Culpeper County 95
Cunningham, Frank 136–37
Curtis, Harry 183
Custis, John Parke (Jacky) 16–17
Cuthbert, — 183

Daddy, Michael 43
Dandridge, Bartholomew 17
Daniel (slave) 41–43
Darbytown Road 112
Davis, Ernest 153–55
Davis, Pres. Jefferson 68, 70–71, 76, 78, 81, 85, 96, 101
Davis, Sam 89
Davis, Mrs. Varina 81
Davis Avenue 9
Day, William O. 98
Dean, Rev. W.H. 160
Deane, Nathaniel 34, 39
"Death Cannot Make Our Souls Afraid" (hymn) 12
death sentences commuted to transportation 12, 41, 58, 64, 98
Deaton, Capt. Spencer 76–77
debtors prison 16
Deep Run Coal Pits 19
Delaney, John 98
Del Mar College 166
Democrats 59
de Moynck, Rev. — 153
Denmark 65
desertion 67–68, 71–72, 74–78, 87, 101
Dick (slave) 16
Dickerson, Mrs. — 184
Dickerson, R. — 132
Dickinson, Rev. A.D. 77, 115
Dillard, — 183

Dillinger, John 162
Dime Museum 185
Dinwiddie County 66
Director of Public Safety 10
district courts 10–11
Dodd, John H. 64
Dodson, Edmund 34–35, 39
Doggett, Rev. D.S. 92
Dolliver, Joseph 34
Dooley, John 45
Doswell, Thomas W. 47
Dove, Dr. James 109
Dove, Rev. John 92, 99
Dover, Tennessee 64
Dowden, Mr. — 112
Downs, Richard 16
Doyle, Dr. John 97
Dreiser, Theodore 145
Drinker, George F. 112
Driscoll, Rev. Asa 154
Drummond, Constable — 118
Drummond, James 42
Dudley, City Sgt. Thomas U. 92–93, 97, 99
Dunmore, Gov. Lord 21
Dunn, A.W. 137
DuVal, Rev. John 152

Early, Sen. — 157
Eccles, John 161
Edgefield District, S.C. 32
Edmund de Langham (brig) 32
Egerton, Douglas R. 24, 27
Eighteenth Street 18, 99, 123, 149
Elam, George 95–96
electrocution 156; Va. law establishing 189–90
Ellis, Percy 161
Emporia, Va. 150
Eppes, Capt. 62, 184
espionage 67, 78, 79, 87, 90
Essex County 110
Essex (ironclad-river) 86, 172
examining courts 10, 18
Exchange Hotel 71, 183
executions: abolition (pro and con) 156, 159, 162–66; and clergy 4, 37–38, 45–46, 66, 70, 72, 82–83, 97–98, 103, 105–9, 115, 125–29, 136, 143–44, 147–48, 151, 154, 156 (*see also* individual clergymen); crowd behavior 1, 3, 12, 15, 30, 32, 37–39, 60–61, 63, 65, 70, 104, 107, 122–26, 138, 140, 149; death row church service 147, 153; en masse 4, 16, 19, 21–28, 36–40, 65–66, 74, 163; moved to Greensville Correctional Center 162; private 110, 156, 159; ritual 1, 4, 8, 12–13, 60, 75
Ezekiel, Herbert T. 104

217

Index

Farrar, J.E. 134
Fauntleroy, Samuel 99
Federal Reserve mail robbery 162
Federalist Party 26
Ferguson, Rev. Archer 143–44
Ferguson, Felix 44
Ferguson, Rev. Richard 154
Fergusson, City Sgt. Herbert 155
Fifteenth Street 97, 133
Fifth Baptist Church 106
Filmore, Pres. Millard 59
Finnegan, John 147
firing squads 3, 66, 67, 68, 70–75, 78, 90, 101
First African Church 106
First Baptist Church 37, 51–52, 54, 99
First Baptist Church (Manchester) 154
First Presbyterian Church 45
Fisher, Delila 46
Fitzgerald, Henry 126
flour milling 7
Folkes, Sen. — 157
Fourteenth Street 104
Fourth Street 37
Fox, James M'Connell 19
Franciscans 147
Frank (slave) 43
Frank A. Bliley Funeral Home, public viewing of executed persons 163
Franklin Street 113
Fredericksburg, Va. 110
Freemen's Bureau 103
Frémont, Gen. John C. 86
French and Indian War 16
Friend, Charles 117
Front Royal, Va. 72
"Funeral March" 70
Fussell, Lew L. 148–49
Futch, Hanson M. 76

Gabriel conspiracy/insurrection 4, 8, 21–28, 114
Gallahar, John 163
Gallego, Joseph 199n13
Gallego Mills 199n13
"Gallows Field" 66
gambling 9, 58
Gardner, Alexander 111
General Court 10, 14–15, 17
Gentry, John H. 99
Gerald, Mr. and Mrs. 102–3
Germans in Richmond 57
Germany 174
Gibbs, Stephen 34
Gibson, Robert 30–31
Giles (slave) 46
Gill, Sheriff — 120
Gilmore, John H. 54

Ginoulhiac, Ferdinand 34
Givins, Rev. — 118
Gladwin, Rev. A. 107, 109
Godsey, Mrs. P.O. 58
Goochland County 7, 10, 146, 153
"good old days" 2–3
Governor Street 87
Grace Street 91, 99
Granberry, Rev. J.C. 105
Grand Lodge of Virginia 91
Granger, Gen. Gordon 103
Grant, Gen. U.S. 87
Great Britain 87, 156
Green, Capt. B.W., Jr. 85
Green, Richard 117–18
Green, Thomas 17–18
Green, Winston 160–61
Greensville Correctional Center
Greensville County 118
Griffin, — 70
grog shops 58

Hailey, George T. 163
Hale, Nathan 89
Halifax County, N.C. 28
Halifax County, Va. 28
Hall, Frederick W. 92, 97, 99–100
Halyburton, J.D. 96
Hamburg, Germany 35
Hampton, Va. 35–36, 43
Hancock, Dr. — 62
hanging: experiment to revive with electricity 39–40; *see also* executions
Hangman's Day 104
Hanover County 98
Hardy, Thomas J. 64
"Hark from the Tomb" (hymn) 65
Harris, Calvert 183
Harris, Mary 99
Harris, William "Billy" (slave) 19–20
Harvard University 186
Hatcher, Jordan 52, 58–59, 64
Hatcher, Marcellus 154
Hatcher, Rev. William E. 134–39
Hauptmann, Bruno 162
Havana, Cuba 35
Hawks, D. — 126
Hayes, Rosa 154
health and disease 12, 141; small-pox epidemic 1862–63 90
Hebden, William 63
Helms, Maj. G.M. 151–53
Henrico County 3, 5, 8, 10, 15, 19, 21–22, 26, 30, 44, 152, 157; courthouse 5, 27; jail 5, 7, 23–24, 27, 59–61, 81, 119, 125–29, 142–46, 149; oyer and terminer court 28, 41
Henry (slave) 98–99

218

Index

Henry, Moses 46
Hercules (slave) 17
Hermitage Fairgrounds 9, 68
Hermitage plantation 9
Hicksford, Va. 118
Higgins, — 147
Highway 301 (film) 162
Hillyard, Rose 182
Hilton, Sidney 154
Hinchman, Dr. — 126
Hogan, Martin 70–71
Hoge, Rev. Moses D. 45, 82–83
Hoke, Rodney 161, 206n12
Holland, John 15
Hollywood Cemetery 131
Holman, Dr. — 153
Holmes, Rev. James 103, 106–7
Holmes, Mary 118
"Home of the Soul" (hymn) 136
"Home Sweet Home" 136–37
Hooker & Phillips brick-yard 142
Hopkins 142–45
Hopkins, Joshua 14
Hore, Rev. Thomas (Cath.) 37
Hore's chapel 199n13
Horsestealing 14–16, 31
"How Firm a Foundation" (hymn) 136–37
Howard, McHenry 75
Huband, Ewell M. 162
Hubbard, Henry 105–6
Hubbard, Paulina 105–6
Hughes, John H. 147
Hull, Kate 154
Hull Street 154
Hunt, Presley 16
hustings court (Richmond) 29, 58, 96, 98; as oyer and terminer court 9–10

"I Need Thee Every Hour" (hymn) 143–44
India
infanticide 12, 31, 49–53, 64, 96–97, 200n10; *see also* Randolph, Lucy
Iowa Territory 47
Iran 166
Irish in Richmond 7, 57–58, 64
Isle of Wight County 153

Jackson, Dr. Thomas 140
Jackson, William P. 58
Jackson, Mississippi 172
Jacobinism (French) 26
James, Arthur W. 206
James, G. Watson ("Cluverius-Madison Case") 135
James P. Butler & Company store 99
James River 7, 9, 24, 26, 32, 35, 46, 67, 74, 153

Jarratt, Va. 162
Jasper, Rev. John 105–107
Jefferson, Thomas 15, 25–26; *Notes on the State of Virginia* 15
Jefferson County, Tennessee 76
Jeffersonian Republicanism 26
Jeffress, Rev. H.E. 154
Jerusalem, Va. 47
"Jesus Is Calling for Thee" (hymn) 136
"Jesus Is Mine" (hymn) 143
"Jesus, Lover of My Soul" (hymn) 147
Jeter, Rev. Jeremiah 54–55, 115
Jett, William 110
Johnson, Absalom 22–23
Johnson, Pres. Andrew 102, 104
Johnson, Dep. Sgt. — 139
Johnson, George W. 64
Johnson, Gov. Joseph 58–59
Johnson, Lucinda 42
Johnson, Moses 44–45, 150
Johnson, William 94
Johnson, William Henry 117–18
Jones, Claggett 183
Jones, Thomas 78
Jordan (slave) 30
Justus, Buddy Earl 162
juvenile delinquents 8, 10

Kearns, Michael 72
Keezel, Sen. — 157
Kelleher, John 71–72
Kelly, Charles 74
Kennedy, Lewis 111
Kerr, Rev. John 37
Kesiah (slave) 12
Kessiah (slave) 31–32
Keve, Paul W. 159
Key, Col. — 81
King and Queen County 99, 132, 140, 185
King William County 18, 30, 43, 131–2, 184; courthouse 98
Knights of Liberty 80
Knox, Detective 112
Knox, Dr. J. 105, 116, 130
Knoxville, Tennessee

Lamb, James 14
Lambert, Mayor William 59
Lasseter, Elisha 16
Latrobe, Benjamin H. 19–20
law enforcement 10
Lawton, Hattie 80–82, 84
Lee, Charles Henry 122–27, 130
Lee, Gov. Fitzhugh 134
Lee, Sandy 124
Leftwich, Dr. T. 144
Legenza, Walter 162–63
Leigh, Benjamin Watkins 34

219

Index

Lemosey, Dr. 37
Letcher, Gov. John 92
Lewis, Pryce 80–81, 84
Lewis, Roy 151
Lewis, Teresa 161
Lewis, Dr. — 118
Lexington, Va. 63
Libby Prison 101–2; execution at 102–4
Liberia 54
Lincoln, Pres. Abraham 80–81
Lindbergh kidnapping case (N.J.) 162
Lipscomb, Capt. "Dinks" 120
Little Plymouth, Va. 132, 140, 185
Loch Ness Monster 33
London, Eng. 48
Loudoun County, Va. 84
Louisa County 16, 32
Louisville, Ky. 84
L'Ouverture, Toussaint 23
L.T. Christian Undertakers 140
Lucy (slave) 64
Lunenburg County 116
lynchings 3, 47, 64, 98, 110, 117, 150
Lyons, James 54, 91, 173

Macauly, Thomas 15–16
Macon, Dep. Sgt. — 137–38
Madison, Cary 182–83
Madison, Fannie Lillian 131–33, 135, 137, 180–83
Madison, Pres. James 74–75
Magruder, Dept. Sheriff — 115
Maguire, Owen 71–72
Main Street 60–61, 87, 133
Mais, Robert 162–63
Mallett, Richardson 74
Marshall, John 33, 36–37
Marshall Street 3, 33, 37, 104, 133, 138, 142
Martin (slave) 22
Martin County, N.C. 28
Martinsville Seven, execution of 4, 163
Mary (schooner) 26
Mason, Morris Odell 164
Matanzas, Cuba 34
Matthews, Dr. W.F. 144–45
Matthews County 4
Mayo, Dr. — 126
Mayo, John 9
Mayo, Joseph 54, 173–75
Mayo's Bridge 95
McCan, Dr. — 105
McClellan, Gen. George 79, 81
McCubbin, Capt. — 81
McCue, J. Samuel 150
McDonough, James 149
McGowan, Patrick 71–72
McGriffin, Thomas 117–18
McLeod, Philip 44

McMullan, Rev. A.L. 73
Means, Capt. Samuel 84–85
Medical College of Virginia 104, 138
Meekins, Duncan 163
Methodists 23, 26, 66, 160
Mexico and capital punishment 166
Meyers, Henry 96
military executions 3, 9, 67–101; ceremony 76–77; *see also* firing squads
militia units (Richmond/Henrico County): 60–61, 71, 73, 85
Miller, Barbara 123–30
Miller, Daniel 123, 126
Mills, City Sgt. — 108
Mills, James 145–46
Mills, Mrs. James 145–46
Mississippi River 86
mob action 3–4, 5, 59, 61–62, 64; *see also* executions
Mohammed, John A. 165–66
Monroe, Gov. James 21–25, 28
Monroe Street 91
Montague, Gov. Andrew Jackson 154
Montpelier, Va. 74
Monumental Church 82–83
Monumental Hotel 81
Morando, Jose (Couro) 33–39
Mount Vernon Hotel 91

Nace & Winston 49
Nanny (wife of slave Gabriel) 28
Napoleon, Louis *see* Richardson, John
Nash, Rev. Preston 152
Nashville, Tennessee 32
"Nearer My God to Thee" (hymn) 147, 154
Negro Burial Ground 8
Nelly (slave) 49–50, 54
Nelson, Rev. — 100
Nero (Bavarian boar hound) 77, 173–76
Neurehr, Constable — 126
New, W.W. 85
New Fair Grounds 68, 87
New Kent County 17–19, 65, 111
New York City 34–35, 79, 86, 134, 162
Newman, Michael 15
Newport Barracks, Ky. 86
newspaper reporting 4, 8–9
Nicholas, Philip Norbourne 145–49; relatives of 205n5
Night Watch 91
Nineteenth Street 58, 61
Ninth Street 133
Norfolk, Va. 26, 28, 35, 152
North Carolina slave insurrection 28
North Korea 166
Northampton County 17
Nottoway County 28

Index

O'Grady, Brant 150
Old Capital Prison (Washington, D.C.) 85
Old (Marshall) reservoir 131, 133
Old Point Comfort, Va. 35, 132
"On the Delaware" (poem) 182, 184
Oppenheimer, Dr. W.T. 139–40
Orange County 74
Oregon Hill 8, 57, 162–65
O'Reily, Rev. J.B. (Cath.) 153
Osawatomie, Kansas 86
Owensboro 165
Oxford, N.C. 96

Page, Hillary 119–21
Parke, John F. 72
Parker, James H. 153
Parker, John 78
Parsons 142–43
Patterson, Rev. George 75–76
Pawnee Indians 166
Payne, Joel 156
Peachy, Dr. — 92
Peatross, John N. 30
Peck, George 110
Pelticolas, Dr. — 62
penitentiary (Richmond) 3, 8–9, 11, 23, 26, 29, 39, 41, 44, 95, 104, 117, 150–53, 155, 159, 189, 196; executions at 3, 64; move all state executions to 157–59; riot 164
"Penitentiary Bottom" 9
"Penitentiary Hill" 30
Petalasharo 166
Peter (slave) 28
Petersburg, Va. 23, 66, 78, 117
Peyton, Bernard 46
Pharao, (slave) 23
Philadelphia 35, 47
Phillips, James 16
Phillips, James Jeter 105, 112–17, 131, 145; sentencing of 176–78
Phillips, Mary Emily 112–14, 177
Phillips, Peter 95
Phillis (slave) 12
Pierpont, Gov. Francis 84
Pine Street 165
Pinkerton, Allan 81–34; detective agency 79–80
pirates 33–41, 199n1, 10
Pitts, Atwell 98
Pitts, Mary Emma 112–14
Plumer, Rev. William S. 45
poisoning 19, 31, 53, 104–6
Pollard, James 43
Pollard, Joseph R. 154
Poolesville, Md. 110
Poor House Burying Ground 62
Pope, J. Robert 160
population 1, 3, 57–58

Porter, James 47
Portsmouth, Va. 159–60
Posey, Amelia 16
Posey, John 16
Posey, John Price 16–19, 159
Posey, Gen. Thomas 16
Potomac River 16
Potter, Oliver 34, 39
Potts, Capt. — 87
Powell, Mrs. Albert 160
Powell, W.A. 62
Powhatan County 7, 10
Prince George County 117
Princeton, N.J. 79
Prosser, Thomas 22
Prosser, Thomas Henry 22–23, 26
Prosser's Tavern 24, 27
prostitution 141
Providence, R.I. 34
provost marshall 68–69, 72–73, 81
Public Guard 10, 28, 37, 44
punishment other than capital 71
Putnam, Sallie Brock 90

Quakers 23
Quinn, Gov. Patrick J. 167

Raines, John 15
Randolph 18–19
Randolph, Lucy 200n10
Randolph, Rev. Peter 106
Reade, Isaac 16
Reconstruction 102
Reddy, W.F. 147
Reed, Thomas 59–63
Reid, — 43
Reid, James 65–66
Reservoir Street 133
Revolutionary War 7, 21; *see also* American Revolution
Richard (slave) 98
Richards, — 16
Richards, John R. 63
Richardson, — 137
Richardson, John (alias Louis Napoleon) 95–97
Richmond, Va.: description 7–8, 141; execution overview 3; health department report 161; industry 7; jail 5, 9, 16, 18, 23–24, 54, 133–34, 136–8 140, 142; port of 7; working conditions 141
Richmond Blues 37
Richmond, Fredericksburg and Potomac Railroad 123
Richmond Zouaves 72
Riddle, Isaac 15
Ripley, Ge. Roswell 70
Robins, — 184

221

Index

Robinson, James 14
Robinson, Norman 34
Robiou, Anthony T. 65
"Rock of Ages" (hymn) 136, 147
Rockbridge County 102
Rocketts landing 9, 174
Rockville, Md. 110
Rodgers, Charles 112
Rogers, D.W. 71–72
Ronald, Andrew 18
Rose, Lysander W. 133, 180
Rover's Delight plantation 16
Ruffin, F.G., Jr. 119
Ruffin, Col. F.G., Sr. 119
Ryan, Gov. George 166–67
Ryland, Rev. Robert 51–52

Sacred Heart Church choir 147
Saint Louis, Missouri 86
Saint Peter's Cathedral 60, 73, 147
Sampson, Rosalie 98
Santo Domingo 23, 33–34
Saunders, A.G. 153
Sawney (slave) 17
Schmidt, Gustavus 34
Schwarz, Philip 29
Scobell, John 80
Scottsville, Va. 74, 146
Scully, John 80–81, 84
Sea Serpent 33
Second African Baptist Church 97
Second Presbyterian Church 45
Second Street 20
Seeley, Rev. L.W. 97
Seventeenth Street 9, 61
Seventh Street 25
Shawnee Indians 166
Shays's Rebellion 18
Sheppard, Mosby 23
Sheridan, Gen. Philip 102
Sherman, Capt. John H. 87
Shiloh, battle of 87
Shockoe Hill 15–16, 57
Shockoe Valley 3, 8, 25, 27, 92, 138
Short, Robert G. 66
"Show Pity, Lord" (hymn) 107, 109
Simkins, — 43
Simons, W.E. 115
Simpson, Capt. James R. 85
Sitlington, Henry 161
Slater, Dr. — 111
slaves: courts 10; punishment other than execution 22; refugees of Revolutionary War 21; transportation law 31–32; urban employment 21–22; *see also* individual names
Smith, D.P. 106
Smith, E.H. 109

Smith, Henry 159–60
Smith, City Sgt. James C. 137–40
Smith, Robert 32
Smith, Sheriff — 115, 117
Smith, Thomas G. 64
Snelling, George W. 66
Solomon (slave) 22, 24
Solomon, Sheriff Simon 143, 145, 147–48
Southampton County 15, 47, 157
Southward, Sheriff — 126–27, 129
Spain and capital punishment 166
Spotsylvania County 32
Spring Street 162–64
Squires, John 70
Stafford County 110
Stanard, Robert 34
State Farm (auxiliary of penitentiary) 152–53
State Guard 45
Staunton, Va. 102
Stephen (slave) 29–30
Stewart, Mrs. — 111
Stokes, John Henry 154
Stours, James 15
Strawberry Plains, Tennessee 76
Summer Hill Plantation 119
Susan (slave) 12
Susan (Suckey), slave 31
Sussex County, Eng. 79
Sutherland, Nathaniel 64–65

Tardy, Alexander 34–36
Tardy, Frances Deane 96–97
Tardy, Samuel C. 97
Tavlor (Tyler), Albert 104–109, 115
Taylor, Joseph 16
Taylor, Richardson 26
Taylor, Samuel 66
Taylor, Rev. Stephen 38
Taylor, Warner 110
Taylor, William 110
Taylor, Dr. William H. 133–34
Tecumseh 166
Teeling, Rev. John (Cath.) 60
Tenious, Henry 161
Tenth Street 87, 133
Terry, Gen. Alfred H. 102
Third Street 20, 37
Thomas, — 126, 128
Thomas, G.W. 115
Thompson, Dr. — 65
Thorn, Catherine J. 91
Throckmorton, C.W. 157
tobacco factories 58–59
Tom (slave) 23
torture 47
T'otty, William D. 90–94
treason 14–15, 24

Tredegar Iron Works 58
Tremaine, Dr. 103
Tri-State Gang 162–63
Trower, — 42
Tucker, St. George 18
Tunstall, Mrs. Jane 132, 140, 184
Turner, George 113
Turner, Nat 47
Twelfth Street 51
Twenty-Second Street 5, 9, 37, 107
Tyler, John 16

Union army executions 78
U.S. Circuit Court 33
U.S. Commissioner of Exchange 172
U.S. Supreme Court 33, 59, 113
University of Richmond 132, 135
University of Virginia 145
Upshur, Dr. — 77

vagrancy 7, 9
Vandervaughn, Rev. Nelson T. 103
Van de Vyver, Bishop Augustin 147
Van Lew, Elizabeth 67, 89
Venable, Horace 118
Vicksburg, Mississippi 47
Victor's Old Mill 8, 92
"Virginia Cavalier" (play) 175
Virginia Central Agricultural Society 68
Virginia Central Railroad Company 98
Virginia Commonwealth University Medical School 8
Virginia Military Institute 68
Virginia Science Museum 9
Voegler, E.L. 143–144, 147–48
Voegler, John 143, 152

Waddill, — 128
Walker, — 182, 184–85
Walker, Dr. — 117
Walker, Gov. Gilbert C. 113
Walker and Harris Tobacco Company 58
Walsh, Dep. Sheriff — 115–17
Warren, Ohio 32
Washington (slave) 63
Washington, George 16, 28; and Mount Vernon 16–17
Washington County 19
Washington, D.C. 124
Watkins, Aaron 181
Watkins, Rev. — 97
Watson, George (tavern) 26
Webster, Alfonzo C. 79, 84–86

Webster, Mrs. Alice Downey 85
Webster, Daniel 59
Webster, John W. 186
Webster, Timothy 79–84
Welbers, Rev. (Cath.) 147
Wells, Gov. H.H. 113
Westham Road 112
Westmoreland County 110
Wheeler, Maurice 14
Whigs, 59
White, Maj. E.V. 85
"Whorehouse Murder" 41–43
Wicker, R.T. 50
Wickham farm 146
Wiley, — 77, 96
Wilkerson, William J. 145
William (slave) 99
Williams, Delegate 157
Williams, Emmet 182–83
Williams, Rev. F.W. 154
Williams, Jane 41, 49–53, 56, 109, 131
Williams, John 41, 49, 51, 53–56, 109, 131, 200n10
Williamsburg, Va. 7, 10
Williamsburg Road 9, 70
Williamson, Rev. George 24
Willis, Lt. — 72
Wilson, William 16
Wimbish, Henrietta 183
Winder, Gen. John W. 81–32, 84
Winston, Joseph P. 49–51
Winston, Virginia B. 49–52, 54
Wirz, Capt. Henry 11
Womble, Matthew 16
women: executed 12, 95–97, 126, 128–30, 161; murder of 46, 112, 118, 179–88; *see also* Cluverius, Thomas J.; Phillips, James Jeter; Taylor, Albert
Woodbridge, Rev. George 82–83
Woodram, William 30
Woodson, William 150–52
World's Crystal Palace Exposition (NYC) 79
Wormley, John S. 65–66
Wren, John 133, 183

Yancey, Stephen 15
"York-River train" 14
Yorktown, battle of 14
Young Guns 62
Young Men's Christian Association 143–44, 160

www.ingramcontent.com/pod-product-compliance
Ingram Content Group UK Ltd.
Pitfield, Milton Keynes, MK11 3LW, UK
UKHW041951140426
5217IPUK00015B/749